Sargent's Lady

Happy Reading!

Best Wishes

By

Judith Fabris

Judith Fabris

Sargent's Lady

By

Judith Fabris

Trade Paperback

@Copyright 2015

All Rights Reserved

Library of Congress:

Requests for information should be addressed to:

A Vegas Publisher, LLC.

284C E. Lake Mead Parkway, #262

Henderson, NV 89015

www.avegaspublisher.com

avegaspublisher@yahoo.com

First edition: 2015

Cover Design: Historical Editorial Jennifer Quinlan

Printed in the United States of America

DEDICATION

To my children,

Holly and David

and in memory of Al.

Other works by Judith Fabris:

"The Women's Financial Survival Handbook"

"The Women's Investment Handbook" NAL, Plume label, co-authored under the name of Rhoades

"Money...Cool," Archipelago Press

"The Duke of Seventh Street" Italian Americana

In Progress: "A Godly Man Meets a Stranger on Molokai" - a murder mystery

ACKNOWLEDGEMENT

A thousand thank you to my critique groups who listened to the same pages over and over again for so many years, but especially: Carol Haack, Dotti Reiss, and Mardiyah Tarantino. A special appreciation to Kathryn Jordan for her many editing suggestions. An additional thanks to Kristin Johnson for introducing me to A Vegas Publisher. My book sold two days after the publisher read it. Kristin isn't an agent, but she is my angel.

PROLOGUE

Washington D.C., Summer 1953

*P*eter Wells stood on the sidewalk, squinting at a portrait hanging on the back wall of an antique store. He cupped his hands against the sun's glare as the reflections in the storefront window blurred his view. When he could see the painting more clearly, a shiver swept through his body. That woman, those features...

He quickly stepped inside, letting his eyes adjust to the dimness of the showroom. When he walked up to the painting, his breath caught. The woman in the portrait sat sideways, her right arm comfortably draped over the back of a chair, and her shiny red hair adorned with three white feathers. Her facial expression was dreamy, and yet her green eyes looked directly at Peter. He stared at the brushstrokes, running his fingers through a thick crop of his own graying red hair. *Do I know you?*

"May I show you our collection, sir?"

A moment passed before Peter turned his attention to a spare man of medium height. White hair neatly combed with a side part, and impeccably dressed in cashmere and tweed with a white shirt and dark brown paisley tie. "As a matter of fact," Peter finally said, "I'm only interested in this portrait. Extremely interested. Do you know the woman in the painting?"

The clerk clasped his hands. "I'm told she is the renowned artist Maud Driscoll as a young woman, when she lived in London. Undoubtedly, the painting was

9

commissioned for a court presentation. Queen Victoria, I'd say looking at that unusual headdress. The Queen had some strange ideas concerning court etiquette for women. For an audience before her, she required a woman to wear those three white feathers as part of her coiffeur." The clerk pointed at the feathers.

Peter steadied his buckling knees. "I knew it. I knew it. That's her. I must have this portrait."

"I'm sorry, sir. This painting is not for sale at the moment."

Peter returned his gaze to the portrait. Maud had never said anything to him about a presentation before the Queen of England. He wondered how many other things about her life she had left unsaid: her years in Italy during World War II, the Nazis. All he knew were bits and pieces. And now, he couldn't take his eyes off the painting, her face fresh, vibrant, and beautiful. He'd never seen pictures of Maud as a young woman. He turned to the shopkeeper.

"I must have this painting. My name is Peter Wells, sir. I lived and worked in Washington D.C. during World War II. My wife and I returned to the capitol about a month ago to turn our former home into an art museum to house a large collection of Maud Driscoll paintings."

"Again, I'm sorry, Mr. Wells. I can't sell it to you. You see, I haven't been able to authenticate it yet, but it looks like it might be an early John Singer Sargent. There's no signature, but I don't want to sell it until I know it provenance."

"But, Mister...?"

"Sheridan, Mr. Wells." He straightened the lapel of his tweed jacket. "I just moved here from London, and I'm the new gallery owner."

"I don't care what it costs," Peter insisted. " I would gladly pay you as if it were an authentic Sargent." His voice rose. "I must have it. You see, Mr. Sheridan, I've met Maud Driscoll several times, in Europe as well as the states."

At Peter's statement, Mr. Sheridan's face had a look of amazement. When he recomposed himself, he said, "Mr. Wells, would you have time for a cup of tea? I'd love to know more. In London, over the years, I've sold many Driscoll paintings. Not many people can claim they've met her. I've always thought it would be wonderful to meet her."

"Maybe I shopped in your store and never knew it." Peter said. "I've combed antique stores all throughout Europe, especially in London."

"This way please," Mr. Sheridan led the way through a cluttered aisle of antique chests and *objets d'art.*

Peter followed him to a tidy back office, where tea was brewing in an iron pot.

"Have to have my afternoon cup and a scone to go with it." Mr. Sheridan said with a smile, as he removed his gold-rimmed glasses and set them down on his desk. "Milk? Sugar? And please take a savory also."

Peter made himself comfortable in the chair Mr. Sheridan indicated to him. At six feet tall and with an athletic build, the over-sized leather chair amply fit his body. "In 1918," he began, "after the war ended, I returned to L'Ecole des Beaux Arts in Paris as an architectural student..."

It took Peter close to an hour to tell his tale. And that's how, between bites of scone and sips of tea, Mr. Sheridan learned the fascinating tale of Peter's and Maud's life.

"Please let me know when you are ready to sell it. As I said, I'll pay your asking price and more. One more thing I didn't tell you Mr. Sheridan, I believe Maud Driscoll and I have more than an artist collector connection."

Mr. Sheridan's jaw dropped on hearing Peter's words. "Now I know why you are so interested in the painting. You'll be the first to know, Mr. Wells, I promise. I am so glad you stopped by and shared your story with me."

On his way out of the shop, Peter stopped one more time in front of the painting, and stared at Maud's eyes and the feathers adorning her hair. But Maud grew up in Boston. He murmured, "How in blazes did she get presented to Queen Victoria?"

CHAPTER 1

Boston, August 1889

Along the platform, keeping her hand on her dark buckram- covered hat to counter the wind gusts, a frantic Lillie Doty paced up and down the wooden slats. Her heart sank when she saw the train chugging slowly into the station, its lumbering noise deafening. The wheels screeched and clanged as the engine disgorged billows of smoke. She glanced at the passengers waiting to board carrying their suitcases towards the porters, their moods subdued and pensive. The color of their clothes against the aging red brick building made a somber tableau. She watched her mother, Esther, return from the ticket window and walk up to her husband's wheelchair.

"How are you feeling, darling?" Esther asked." We'll be in our seats shortly. Then you'll be able to rest."

He looked at her with tired, defeated eyes. "Please tell Sam to stop bouncing up and down," he said in a wheezing voice she had difficulty hearing. "My head is pounding."

"Sam!" Esther called, grabbing her five-year-old son by his jacket. "Behave!"

Lillie intervened. "I'll take care of him, Mama. You look after Papa." She turned to Sam. "Come on, brother, give me your yoyo and stand still for a minute. We're trying to get organized. Help us instead of jumping around." She turned towards the station entrance. "Where is she?" she murmured. "Please hurry. I can't leave Boston without saying goodbye."

Little did she know, at that moment, an impatient Maud Driscoll sat on the plush green leather seats of the new Stewart carriage, shouting at Caleb, the family coachman. "Hurry up, we are late!"

She had left her home on Chestnut Street, a beautiful Edwardian mansion designed by Charles Bullfinch, twenty minutes earlier, in plenty of time to arrive at the station, but the traffic impeded her progress. Her anxiety grew by the moment. She thought she heard a train whistle in the distance and shifted her body to the edge of her seat. "Caleb, what's keeping us from going faster?"

At that point, Caleb drove the carriage through the Boston Common, one of Maud's favorite places. Under a different set of circumstances she would have enjoyed a slow drive through the beautiful English gardens. But on that unusually cool summer morning she was too nervous about missing her friend before she left Boston for California. She tried to push her mass of red curls into her beige felt hat and in doing so she dislodged the pheasant feathers that decorated the top of it along with two cinnamon silk roses. "Pshaw," she grunted.

Meanwhile, Caleb had turned the carriage into Boylston Street. A smell of acrid fumes hit their nostrils. "There's a fire," Caleb shouted.

At once, Maud pulled out a white embroidered handkerchief and brought it to her nose. "This odor is horrible."

Outside the coach, Maud could see sweaty stable hands, as well as businessmen in shirt sleeves, leading horses out of a building where a blacksmith had his shop. A fire truck with horses tethered stood in the middle of the street. Two firefighters in dark blue uniforms were pulling a hose off the pump and filling worn leather buckets with water to douse the fire. The rest of the brigade moved the buckets from the truck to the burning building. Meanwhile, passersby on horseback scattered to move out of the way of the truck. A policeman tried to direct traffic. With a handkerchief still over her nose, Maud leaned out the window to see the commotion.

"That's where the traffic congestion comes from," Caleb said. "We won't be able to go through much faster than this."

He gave the horse a slight rap with his black leather crop. It wasn't going to make the carriage move any faster. The traffic stalled.

Silently, Maud drummed her fingers on her claret-colored dress. It was the latest fashion, with an elongated bodice studded with fabric buttons down the front to beyond her waist. With tense fingers, she smoothed her dress's elaborate overskirt all the way down the matching fringe.

While the Boylston Street traffic began to thin out, Lillie stood wringing her wrists and staring at the entrance with worried eyes. "She's not coming," she whispered as her expression turned to sadness. She looked at the stack of trunks the stationmaster had put

15

on the train platform. The family clothes and all the household goods they could manage were packed inside - they represented life in Boston as they knew it. She looked over at her father, a frail man, emaciated by the tuberculosis that wracked his body. She murmured, "Will we ever return?" She was afraid she already knew the answer. Her father's doctor had told them to take him to California right away, as it might be his only means of survival. What the doctor hadn't told them was that he might not survive the arduous train trip.

A stronger gust of wind whipped Lillie's face and the sides of her traveling coat. The flecks of green and gold looked like rippling grass against her slender figure. She pulled it tighter around her body, and checked to see that her father's blanket remained securely wrapped around him.

"It's late August, Papa, but I feel a chill in the air. Fall will be early, I know. California should be bright and sunny." She spoke to her father, but reassured her own thoughts.

"Time to board," the conductor called.

Esther pushed the wheelchair up to the car, and two porters lifted it into the vestibule. Sam boarded second, then Esther. The passengers were now all on board except for Lillie. She waited until the last moment as tears welled up in her eyes. The train had begun its slow departure from the station. A warning bell signaled to clear the tracks. A porter called out from the train steps.

"Hurry up, miss, the train is moving. It can't wait for you."

Lillie made one last sweeping look of the station, pulled up her skirts and made a mad dash to catch up to the last car. The porter had left open the door and the stairs for her to climb up. He put out his large, weather-beaten hand.

"Got you, miss."

He waited until Lillie safely reached the top step before he locked the bottom half of the door. Then he tightly secured the top. Lillie pressed her face against the glass pane. The platform was empty. And so was her soul. She wiped off the beads of cold sweat that had formed on her forehead, and she held onto the sides of the vestibule for balance. Had she looked out the window one more time, she would have seen Maud rushing out of the station onto the platform. She had her fancy hat in hand, and her rebellious red curls danced about her shoulders, fluffed by the wind. She stared at the tracks.

"The cars are all closed," she whispered, "and the train is picking up speed." Her stomach sank as she shook her head in disbelief. "I missed saying goodbye. Lillie will think I'm a terrible friend." She stood on the platform speechless, watching the train become a mere dot on the horizon. Five minutes later, she walked back to her carriage, plopped down in the seat and told Caleb to drive her home.

17

CHAPTER 2

*O*nseparable friends since early childhood, Maud Driscoll and Lillie Doty both graduated from high school the previous June. They had planned to attend college together, but Maud made all the preparations. Lillie knew she had to find a job to help support her family.

Lillie dabbed her eyes with her handkerchief, then walked with caution through one train car and down the aisle of the next one where she found her mother and father. Lillie took the seat next to her little brother. Sam's delicate deft hands played with his new toy, a piece of string wound tight around his fingers to play cat's cradle.

"Look, Lillie, I can make a soldier's bed."

"That's nice, Sam," Lillie mumbled. She still had tears in her eyes.

"I know you will miss Maud, Lillie, but I'll be your friend," Sam said in the most grown-up voice he could muster.

"That's so sweet, Sam," Lillie said, as she drew him close. His words made her cry all the more. Lillie whispered to herself, "I don't understand why Maud wasn't at the station. How cruel the world can be sometimes."

Lillie's depression was evident to the porter who stood in the aisle. He thought about his own daughter at home. Wanting to act kindly towards Lillie, he tapped her on the shoulder. "Miss," he said.

19

She glanced up, startled at the concern in his eyes. Thinking a glimpse of the private railcar attached to the train might lift her spirits, he asked, "Would you like to see a special railcar?"

Lillie nodded and followed him back through their coach, past several sleeping passengers, and a group of men who were playing cards. After walking through three cars, including the dining car, the porter pulled out his keys and opened the door. He ushered her inside.

Awed by the opulence, her eyes drank in the dark mauve flocked wallpaper, highly polished rosewood mahogany trim, lustrous brass lamps and comfortable overstuffed chairs of the well-appointed salon.

"This doesn't look like the inside of a train," she exclaimed, feeling grateful to the porter for the unexpected diversion.

"The bedroom part of the car holds a full-sized bed. I'm sorry I can't show it to you, but the railcar is occupied. I'm glad you liked what you saw, Miss."

"Thank you so much," she replied, as she returned to her own hard seat.

Lillie worried about her father. It would take them nine nights to cross from Boston to Los Angeles, California. She thought about the poor pioneers who had crossed the country in covered wagons or on horseback. It would be a difficult task for the Dotys, but Lillie never complained, even though her family had to change trains in Chicago in order to reach their final destination.

The kind porter found Lillie's family help to move their luggage onto the next train. The family had to walk from one part of the station to another. Since Chicago served as a hub for all railroad companies, they walked through several corridors to another part of the gigantic station. Lillie pushed her father in the cumbersome wheelchair, and her mother held Sam's hand until the porter could help them board their next train.

Lillie sighed and shrugged her shoulders. "Papa, I hope we don't have to move you another time."

She felt relieved when she saw her mother had purchased some fresh fruit, more cheese and bread to carry with them. The dining car prices were exorbitant – seventy-five cents a meal. Lillie knew every penny had to be accounted for.

At least once a day, passengers were allowed off the train while it took on more water and wood. The way stations sometimes had beef jerky or the penny candy for sale which Sam always craved.

"Don't eat so much at one time, Sam. It doesn't grow on trees," Lillie chided.

The porter had loaned her a map so she could study the terrain. Each day, she noticed the changes in scenery. Pine forests, gave way to flat plains and then red rocks, sand, and mesquite.

The day the train pulled into the Albuquerque, New Mexico station, Lillie saw a small settlement. Looking out at the activity on the station platform, she realized an Indian was staring at her through the window. He had long black stringy hair hanging loose around his shoulders and a mean scar that went from his right jaw to above his cheek. The scar startled her for a moment.

Then Lillie relaxed. She realized the window separated the two of them. Strange languages drew her attention. The station was filled with men and women with long braided hair, dressed in bright colored clothing, red, blue, black and white striped blankets, beaded soft shoes, leather-fringed leggings and jackets. They were selling woven baskets, beaded trinkets, blankets, rugs and hats called sombreros, all in vibrant hues. She thought about how much Maud would love to paint this scene.

Lillie wrote in her journal each day. She discovered it was possible to send a letter to Maud, but didn't for fear she would begin crying as she thought about all the things she had left behind.

Almost three days later, their train arrived in Los Angeles. Tired and dusty from the long journey, Lillie, her family and their belongings were carted to an area on the outskirts of town by a hired wagon. Mrs. Doty found comfortable accommodations in a rooming house filled with other new transplants.

"I'm thrilled, Lillie," her mother said. "The owner even serves meals. What a blessing. We won't have to move your father. I don't want to leave him alone."

October 3, 1889 Glendale

Dearest Maud,

    I can't believe we missed saying goodbye to each other at the train station. I just hope nothing serious happened. It was disconcerting not to be able to give you a final hug. Right now, I'm sitting at a small desk in the living room of the boarding house where Mama rented rooms for us. The window overlooks a beautiful garden filled with giant dahlias, variegated colored mums, all shades of roses, asters and little blue and yellow flowers called forget-me-nots. They make me wonder if I will ever see you again, my dearest friend. I can't believe I'm clear across the country from you. If I continue in this manner, I know I will start crying. So I won't. Every day on my journey across country, the scenery changed - from pine forests, fields of wheat to high red rocks like mountains, sand and mesquite. When we stopped in Albuquerque, New Mexico, an Indian with stringy black hair stared at me through the window. He had a mean scar across his face. I was glad a window separated us. The station was filled with people colors and artifacts you would love to paint. They sold woven baskets, beaded trinkets, blankets, rugs, and hats called sombreros. I know you would find the colors so different from Boston. On the train, our porter showed me a private rail car with a bedroom - quite luxurious. Oh Maud, I can see oranges growing on trees. The owner of the house told me, "Pick and eat anything you want." I must say the oranges taste sweet and delicious. We live on the edge of a pretty little area called Glendale. It's not even a real town, but it seems to be a hub for transplants like us. On every street, houses advertise rooms for rent. It will be a full-grown

23

town in no time with all its new residents. Papa purchased a California bungalow that will be ready for us to move into shortly after Thanksgiving. Bungalows are a popular style here. Made of clapboard wood, ours has a wonderful front porch. Mama chose dark green for the outside walls, and white trim for the windows. Large gray stones with black and white flecks comprise the foundation. Papa hired a stone mason to build a huge fireplace in the center wall of one room and Mama asked for lots of cupboards on each side of it, with doors of leaded glass. Mama was fascinated with the rugs the Indians make. I told Papa, and he let Mama buy one when the train stopped in Albuquerque. Guess that will go in front of the fireplace. The house sits on a corner property so Mama will have lots of room to grow flowers. The doctor insists Papa must stay in bed most of the day. Papa has been very weakened by the tuberculosis, but he seems to be rallying. The doctor told us Papa's symptoms were subsiding. Mama says it better be true. She doesn't want to be left a young widow with Sam and me to care for on her own. I miss you so much. You would love all the fall colors, even though the leaves don't turn as brilliant shades as those in Boston. Days are beautiful and warm with very little rain or cold weather. You could paint outside all day, every day. I know you will become a famous painter and travel the world. It's probably snowing in Boston now. I'm taking special classes in shorthand and typing at the high school. I am resigned to becoming a small town working girl. Something I never expected. As much as I dreamt about college, I can't think about it now. We need money to survive. I just pray Papa doesn't die. I love you, dear friend. To me, our friendship is like a strong tree, its branches sheltering us and providing protection.

Our friendship grew with a gentle calm, not unlike a soft breeze. I remember all the fun we had -- school, shopping, bicycling, caroling at Christmas. Those are wonderful memories I will cherish, more so because of the vast distance between us.

Lillie

Mid October, 1890

Dearest Lillie,

I was overjoyed when your letter arrived. I can't tell you how hard I tried to get to the station. There was a fire on Boylston Street, and Caleb couldn't move the carriage at more than a snail's pace. The only thing I saw when we arrived at the station was the back end of your train as it faded away in the distance. I'd much rather be adventuresome and travel to California. But the mere suggestion of it, even when I told her about the private rail car, sent mother for her smelling salts. "Daughter, you must attend a fine eastern school." Daddy never misses the chance to tell me he wants me to become a charming young lady, and he feels I will meet many eligible bachelors on our summer travels. You know Lillie, how painting is my first love, better than anything else in the world. I told mother I want to be a great artist. Her response was to pat me on the head and tell me, "Yes dear, in the privacy of our own home." Can you imagine just how angry her remarks made me? I wanted to scream and run out of the room. Do they just expect me to marry someone of their choosing and serve tea every afternoon? Why can't women be more than that? I don't want to be like my mother. I don't want babies. I want to go to Paris and paint. Lillie, I'm not maligning the fact you must work. I'm certain it will be an exciting adventure for you. I know I am unconventional and not as practical as you, but Paris and painting! It would be so wonderful. I would like that better than going to college. I miss you and our good afternoon talks. I miss our bicycle rides. Oh Lord, Lillie, why do you have to be so far away? You're the only one I can really talk to. Love to you.

Maud

CHAPTER 3

*T*he next morning Maud awakened to a dreary sky. She had been ecstatic when she received another letter from Lillie the day before. She put on her warmest bathrobe, gave her hair a quick brushing, completed her ablutions, and went downstairs for breakfast. Her mother sat at the head of the dining room table, making lists while drinking a once hot, now lukewarm cup of coffee. Maud gave her mother a wind kiss and helped herself to a cup of coffee also.

Mrs. Evangeline Driscoll, a matriarch of Boston society, wore the latest styles in clothing. Endowed with more than an ample bosom, she lived up to and looked the part. Other Boston matrons considered her taste impeccable. Maud's mother came from mainline Massachusetts, and didn't want anyone to forget it.

"Maud, your father has arranged for you to attend Wellesley College. I hope that will please you."

"Oh Mother, I never ever dreamed I would be able to attend there. I always thought it would be Lillie. She is so much smarter than I am."

"You will learn to acquit yourself, I know. I also have another surprise for you."

Maud, not certain what to expect, said, "Mother, what next?"

Her eyes lit up when she answered, "You will have a charming young lady from England as your roommate in your bedroom suite. She is the daughter of an old friend of your father's."

"How do you know she is charming?"

"Maud, don't be petulant or argumentative. It isn't becoming."

"You know I always wanted to room with Lillie."

"And you know that is absolutely impossible. Lillie is across the continent, and I daresay you two will probably not meet again."

"Mother, how can you say that? We have been best friends since we were little."

"Maud, I never did think Lillie came from the right kind of family. Her father didn't have a profession, only the common trade of a printer."

"But Lillie had the best of manners, always kind and polite. Look at the beautiful outfit she made for me as a graduation present."

"I admit she has a flair with a needle."

"Just like I want to be talented with my paint brush."

"Maud, do we need to have this tiresome conversation again? An artist is so... so bohemian. Not a proper thing for you to do. Maybe in the privacy of our home, but not in public. What do you think our friends would think of us if we allowed our daughter to become an artist?"

Not wanting to start an argument with her daughter, she changed the subject. "Darling Maud, is there anyone you would like to invite to our fall soiree?

I want to include all of Boston's eligible young men for you to meet. I'm sending out the invitations today."

"Bridget," she called to the maid, "you may clear the dining room now. I have several errands for you to accomplish."

Looking out the window, Maud watched as the overcast sky sent snow cascading. The wind whipped it downward onto the windowsill. She looked at Bridget in the kitchen and thought it was mean to send her outside on a day like this. Maud thought her mother did it just to show how important she thought she was. Maud could tell how angry her mother became with her right then, and thought she had better keep her mouth shut. *I'm glad I'm going away to college and hope my roommate will be nice.*

"Mother, I'm going upstairs and write Lillie a letter and tell her all my latest news." Under her breath she whispered, "Lillie is the only one who understands my problems."

"I'm going upstairs to paint," she said aloud.

May, 1890

Dear Lillie,

I miss you. I'm writing this to you at the boarding house and hope you will receive it and send me your new address. I've been accepted to Wellesley College. Of course, you and I both know Daddy made all the arrangements. He and Mother have even chosen a roommate for me. She is coming from England.

Life just isn't the same without your company. Mother took me shopping for my new wardrobe for college. She even hired a dressmaker, who went with us to a fabric store.

All I wanted to do was stay home and paint. I hope Wellesley will have art classes. At least school will keep me from complete boredom.

Letters aren't as good as talking with you in person, but they help.

Love,

Maud

P.S. I hope the California sun has done wonders for your father's health. Give your family my love.

June, 1890

Dearest Maud,

Wellesley College. I can just imagine how wonderful that would be. Do you remember the time we went there to visit your cousin? The three of us bicycled around the campus wearing our daring white bloomers and shirtwaist blouses. How many times did we talk about going to college together? Even if I lived in Boston, I'd be working at a bank or law firm on Milk Street. If you weren't my friend, I would never have learned how to serve a proper tea or fix my hair in such a high style. Or know I should write Shaw's of New York to get a rat for my hair. How much you taught me. I'm grateful for your friendship. Of course, I'm disappointed you can't come to California. Be pleased for me. I have a fine new position with a law firm that employed me shortly after I finished my classes. The work is interesting, and Mr. Patterson of Patterson and Sprague is paying me $14.00 a week. Can you believe that? I'm thrilled. I ranked at the very top of my stenography class. Mr. Patterson knew Miss Black, my teacher, and she recommended me. Papa told me I could attend Cumnock Finishing School in Los Angeles, but I won't even ask as it would put another burden on him. Money is very tight. I realize what different directions our lives are taking us, even more so because Glendale and Boston are so far apart. Papa opened a small print shop in Glendale, one of the first. He made Mama and me calling cards. I've enclosed one for you. The paper has a beautiful sheen to it, don't you think? Study hard, Maud. I know you will make all A's. You just have to put your mind to it, rather than dreaming about the canvases you are going to paint. But don't stop painting.

Love,

Lillie

CHAPTER 4

*M*aud and her roommate, Priscilla Wescott, were sitting on their respective beds in their living quarters at Wellesley. The two of them were examining their latest purchases from their Boston shopping trip.

"Pris, that yellow shirtwaist will look beautiful with your honey blonde hair. Do you have a suit to go with it?"

"Yes, Mummy is sending it from London. It's soft brown tweed. Maud, may I change the subject?"

"Of course, silly. Clothes aren't the only things."

"My brother Cornelius, you haven't met him."

"No, but I've seen his picture on your dresser."

"Well, Cornelius is one of those gay blade bachelors about town, and I'm worried when you come to visit us – he will sweep you off your feet and then drop you like a hot coal."

"Why Pris, what makes you say that?"

"Because that's what he does to all the young women in London. He is reported to be engaged to this one woman, because her father and mine made a pact. If they marry, my father will have almost a dynasty under him and can easily stand for parliament which he would like to do."

"Why would someone marry just to have a dynasty?" said Maud.

"It would mean a lot of monetary support and backing for my father."

"I can't imagine a father who would do that." Maud shook her head.

"You don't know my father." Priscilla sighed.

"That's very sad. Well, I will try not to become enamored with Cornelius. I think the only reason Mother and Father gave me permission to go to Europe is they want me to meet all the eligible bachelors. I believe she thinks her self-importance in society will make me," Maud stood up, and made a wide swath into the air with her hand, "a very good catch."

Priscilla rolled back on her bed laughing. "Well, from what I have seen, your mother and mine will make a marvelous pair."

Maud laughed too.

"Let's go down to the little tea shop and have some tea, Maud. We have a lot to talk about. It's the only place I've been able to find a good scone too." Grabbing Maud's arm, they left their room, arm in arm, happy about their latest conspiratorial conversation.

May 17, 1891

Dear Lillie,

    I love Wellesley. I love school. I can't believe the spring semester is almost over. Best of all, Mama and Daddy have agreed to let me go to Europe this summer. Of course, Mama will be my chaperone. We will stay with Priscilla Wescott and her family. They live just outside of London. We are meeting in Paris because our ship debarks in France, and we are going to tour there first. Priscilla is my roommate at Wellesley. You would love her. Maybe one of these years it will happen. Wouldn't that be wonderful? Priscilla is blonde with blue eyes, petite and has this wonderful accent. When one meets her, her demeanor seems prim and proper. That's misleading. She is full of life and loves to laugh and have fun, like we did. Oh Lillie, her friendship means a great deal to me. It's nice to have someone to talk with again. I miss you terribly. You know where your life is going. I don't have the slightest idea - yet. Except I want to paint, paint, paint.

In haste,

Love,

Maud

Christmas 1891

Dearest Maud,

Christmas isn't white here. We had to make our own delivery for the Christmas tree we purchased from a tree lot on Brand. That's the main street to Third Street where we live. Mama saw a couple of strapping young lads, and they took pity on us. They carried the tree most of the way. One of them built us a tree stand so it would fit in our living room. Then Mama gave them cocoa and Christmas cookies plus a dime each for all their work. I think she could have given them no money at all, and they would have been happy. You remember how good her Christmas cookies taste!

I'm going Christmas caroling with some of the neighbors. This will be a new experience not having to trudge through snow and freeze for a couple of hours. Afterwards, there will be a small reception. I will meet Mama, Papa, and Sam then.

Mama has taught me so much about cooking. I enjoy accompanying her to the butcher shop. Can you believe our garden is now growing what is called winter vegetables, squash, beans, and a pumpkin for Sam? I've learned a lot of different ways to cook squash. Our neighbors are Italian, and I'm going to learn how to make spaghetti. Mrs. Orsini brought over a pot of tomato sauce as a Christmas present. Maud, if you could paint like this sauce tastes, I know you would be instantly famous.

I hope you like your present. I designed it myself.

41

We have a library close to our home. I've been attending a book club there. Right now, we're reading Herman Melville. I think the moderator chose the book because Melville died this year. Do you enjoy reading him? I'd rather read Pearl Buck. She's wonderful. A recipe in our daily newspaper was attributed to her. I wonder if she knew how to prepare it, although it was entitled 'Oriental Ribs.' I sound more like a housewife than a working girl, but Maud, cooking is wonderful. I just want to remain trim and be able to wear those new straight skirts without feeling my body protruding from every angle.

Papa is not well, Maud. I'm so worried about him. Mama keeps a smile on her face, but I'm afraid if he dies, I don't know how we will keep the house? What will Mama do for money? I would be the only one earning money, and it's not much.

I wish we could be together for the holidays. I miss our Christmas tea, but not as much as I miss you. Merry Christmas to you and your family. I love you. Enjoy the holidays.

Lillie

March, 1892

Dearest Lillie,

Lillie, your papa will get better. It just takes time. Did he have a relapse from the tuberculosis? Maybe he's working too hard. If you had any idea the number of times I've worn my painting smock you would be so pleased. Dove gray is so pretty. You have wonderful taste in fabric, Lillie. I even had mother's dressmaker copy it and make me several more. I don't want the one you designed for me worn down to threads. It's wonderful!! Priscilla wanted one too. She doesn't even paint, or do anything in the arts. She just thinks it's such a clever design because it has pockets and is attractive. I gave her one of the ones I had made, a burgundy-checked gingham. She actually wears it over her dress when we attend classes. She thinks you must be so smart. I wish you two could meet. You'd like each other. I know it. I just don't want you to be unhappy because I made another friend. I'm certain you will find someone close to you also. You have so many other things to think about right now. I want to go back to Europe this summer. I think mother and father will let me, but I have to wait and see. Priscilla's family has asked me to be their houseguest again. Of course, I'd rather visit you, but Daddy won't let me go across country without a chaperone, and mother refuses to go. Mother told me American trains are a barbaric way of traveling. Can you imagine? I hope I never become a snob. Sometimes I wonder if that's what she is trying to make me. I promise you Lillie, I won't ever become one. Take care of yourself. I talk about you all the time. Your ears should be burning. I send you lots of love. Maud

43

April 10, 1892

Dear Maud,

I'm so glad you liked the smock. That was very kind of you to give one to Priscilla. I can't promise it will keep paint off your nose though!

What I haven't told you about, Maud, is what is not civilized here in Glendale. The streets do not have cobblestones to pave the roads where horses and carriages travel. The trolleys we have are pulled by horses. They are open, and when it rains we have no windows to protect us from the elements. The dirt and mud can be miserable. I am ever so grateful the rain doesn't fall that often, and when it does, it's late at night or very early in the morning. Of course, this is April, and the showers are more than usual. I'm told it has been an unusual spring. It takes forever to wash clothes in a tub, let them dry, and then use the damnable heavy iron to remove the wrinkles. I think this is one of the hardest chores in captivity. Forgive my unladylike outburst, but it is the only way I can describe it. Your friend is becoming not so meek and mild. You are so fortunate to have a maid like Bridget to do all that for you. Am I complaining? I suppose so. But who would I complain to if you weren't my confidante? I would never tell Mama any of this, because I try to relieve her of all the washing and ironing chores. She has more than enough to do with Daddy and watching Sam. We actually have a grammar school in Glendale, and it is built of brick. It has three classrooms. A lot different from Boston, (sigh).

I truly believe when Glendale becomes a real town, it will be lovely and modern with sidewalks. Our streets now, as primitive as they might be, are lined with beautiful magnolia, elm, and a type of poplar tree. We also have maples - not the brilliant leaf turning kind as Boston.

I don't want to complain, but the dirt in Glendale doesn't look as bad as the mud we encountered upon arrival in Los Angeles. The stench was horrible. I think Mother and I wanted to shout for joy when we were able to engage the services of a wagon right away. Cobblestone streets will one day be part of where I live. Electric street lamps too. I can't wait for progress to catch up with us.

We really are pioneers in the true sense - except we don't have to worry about marauding Indians setting fire to covered wagons, and we have indoor plumbing. What we don't have are men my age that I can meet, and be courted. How about you? Have you met any charming bachelors? Someone your mother hasn't 'found' for you?

What do I do for fun? We play cards, go on picnics, and Mother and I love to go to the general store and look at all the beautiful fabrics. Designing clothes for me must be what you feel about painting. There is a new fabric called dotted Swiss. It makes the most delightful summer dresses. Someday dresses will be shorter, they are too cumbersome. I took out all the undergarments that are supposed to be worn with today's skirt, and made a suit with a much straighter line. It's soft gray tweed, and I have a yellow shirtwaist blouse to go with it. My hair is so long I feel like my chignon, see I am learning French words also - giggle, giggle, is top heavy. What would you think if I cut it all off, and had a short bob? Certainly easier to take care of.

You are probably saying to yourself, Lillie, stop all this nonsense. I promise, Maud, I won't be so oppressive in my next letter. I love you a lot. Happy Spring and Easter.

Lillie

September 10, 1893

Dearest Lillie,

I am so very sorry about your Papa. I just returned from England with Priscilla when I received your letter. It seems all I write about is one happy journey after another. You must think me so insensitive of the pain you must be suffering. And your Mama? How is she doing? How is Sam? It must be so difficult for him at his young age to lose his father. Will you give them both hugs for me?

School starts in another week. I love you.

Maud.

Postscript. I think I would like to live in Europe - Paris especially, but I haven't said anything to anyone except you. I'd like to spread my wings like a beautiful butterfly, only the wings are my palette, and the brush strokes my journey.

May 19, 1894

Dearest Maud,

Oh my glory! You've graduated from Wellesley! And you are going to England for the summer. It sounds so wonderful. Please send me a letter from wherever you are. I go to the library and read all the books about the beautiful and exciting cities like London and Paris. What are the women wearing? I love the beautiful clothes. Someday, I'll design for other ladies, not just Mama and me.

Thank you again for your words of sympathy when Papa died. I know how much you loved him too. I'm thinking of this again because today would have been Papa's fifty-third birthday. Mama seems to be all right. As you can imagine, living on my salary alone had been difficult. I couldn't pay all the bills. After serious discussion, Mama moved into the back bedroom and we rented out hers and Papa's room to a Mrs. Kate Hasting. With a small raise Mr. Patterson gave me and our new boarder, Mama and I are able to keep the house running smoothly. Mrs. Hasting and Mama are about the same age and act more like friends than boarder and landlady. Sam has a good friend in the neighbor's boy, and they ride their tricycles till they have worn themselves out, or they play a new game, "Cowboys and Indians."

One of the stenographers in my office told me that Mr. Patterson would like to pursue a courtship with me. He is a nice man, Maud. I have to admit, I haven't met anyone else. There are so few single men around my age or even just a few years older. Mr.

51

Patterson is fourteen years older than I am. He asked me out to dinner. Mama and Mrs. Hasting discussed it and decided it would be proper for me to accept. So, I am going. What do you think about that? If Papa were here, I am not certain he would permit it without a chaperone, especially if we were still living in Boston. But the world is changing, and Mama and I are modernizing with it. I haven't met anyone except Mr. Patterson with whom I would want to spend an evening.

It's been lonely with no women my age to confide in. All the more why I treasure your letters.

I love you,

Lillie

June 11, 1894

Dearest Maud,

For once I have some exciting news from me to you. I have opened a tiny alterations and tailoring shop on Brand Boulevard. Mama will do alterations during the day, and I will keep my day position at the law firm. Anyway, I will put a frock I designed and made in the window, and it will be for sale as is, or I will custom make it to fit whatever body type. I met someone I thought was a very nice gentleman by the name of Austin Bailey. I actually rented the store from him. We, Mama and I, decided to call the store Lillie's Designs with a small sign in the window, advertising alterations. Austin helped me paint the store and then Mama invited him to dinner. I found out he loved to dance so every Saturday night, Austin took Mama and me to the pavilion in the park where we danced until almost midnight. I thought I fell in love with him. I missed him when he was not around, and joyous each time I saw him. Mama liked him too. We found out he was married, and the next day he skipped town without paying any of his bills. Unknown to us, his wife even became a customer in my shop. Why oh why do such cads exist - especially when I'd like to meet a nice man? I think I had better return to sewing my latest creation, or I will never get it done by Saturday to put in my shop window. I love you, dear friend.

Lillie

CHAPTER 5

Boston, Spring, 1895

*T*he Driscoll mansion resembled a beehive. Following Mr. Driscoll's orders, the workmen were installing a huge new electric chandelier in the ballroom. A large flower wagon arrived and directed to the kitchen delivery entrance. The aroma of the lilacs wafted throughout the house. Mrs. Driscoll orchestrated the bevy of maids and butlers engaged for the evening event. White damask tablecloths covered the tables of ten which were being set for the guests. Round, low crystal bowls filled with white and lavender freesias decorated each table. Gleaming silver candelabras graced the ornate buffet tables.

Upstairs in her room, Maud busied herself watching the finishing touches being added to her ball gown. The seamstress had spent hours upon hours beading Maud's dress so it sparkled like the finest of diamonds. Designed by Olive, the newest, most fashionable Victorian ball gown designer in America, her gown spoke volumes.

The finest pale green silk taffeta fabric exposed provocative décolletage. The bell-shaped skirt billowed in simple folds. Yellow silk roses cascaded from five tiny *Alencon* pockets. Maud was excited about her new dancing slippers imported from Italy, made from the softest, palest doeskin with four side buttons and a low but narrower heel. She took them out of the box, put them on and began dancing around her bedroom until her mother walked in.

"Maud, Maud. Whatever am I to do with you? Your conduct is so unbecoming. It's your debutante ball tonight, and here you are dancing like a giddy goose."

"Mother, why did you have to insist on adding the lace insert in the bosom of my beautiful dress? It makes me feel like a prim schoolteacher." She babbled on. "I'm glad you invited the Wescotts and that they were able to book return passage from London to Boston."

"I do wish Cornelius wasn't coming. I find him rather insufferable."

"Why do you say that? Hasn't he been most gentlemanly in his conduct? Besides Mother, according to Priscilla, he's practically engaged."

"I'm sorry Maud. I just don't believe that. Up to now, I suppose his conduct towards you has been above reproach. Every time I saw him, he was always on his way out of the house with his male friends, going to his club to play cricket. I do have to agree with you though. He is a debonair young man. However, I'm certain he is known as a rogue when it comes to the young women of London. The Wescott's upstairs maid told me he has gained a reputation as a man about town. I know she would have lost her position if I breathed that information back to Mrs. Wescott."

"Mother, Cornelius, or Neil as he likes to be called, hasn't even given me more than a glance for the last two years when we were entertained by the Wescotts."

"Look at yourself in the mirror, my darling. You are no longer a young excitable teenager. You have become a beautiful young woman. I'm afraid your father and I will have to guard you from over attentiveness by all your suitors."

"Mother, all I know is that Neil has been nothing but charming to me. Priscilla has been a wonderful friend, and her family has been so kind to us. I'm truly looking forward to this summer in London. And if Neil takes a liking to me, it will certainly make the summer more interesting."

"Maud. Please be careful. I think Neil, as you call him, is not a very nice man. He is what your father and I would call a rake. I believe he goes after every beautiful young woman he meets. You would become another of his conquests."

"I've always thought he was so handsome in his white flannels, going off to his club. Tall and blond with gray eyes. Oh Mother, he really is something."

"Well, guard against being swept away by his charms, my precious pet. This will be a special evening for you to remember. Before we all go downstairs to receive our guests, your father would like to see you. May I call him to come in now?"

"Just let me complete dressing first." Maud looked into the mirror to touch up her coiffure, a mass of beautiful dark-red hair, artfully piled on the top of her head. In front of each ear were wisps of curly tendrils, softening the features of her face. She was a striking young woman, slender figure, creamy skin and glowing green eyes. Maud added a diamond pin to her hair, and attached her diamond stud earrings.

"Do I look like a debutante?" She asked her mother, as she made an exaggerated curtsy toward her.

"Just perfect my darling. Here comes your father."

"Daddy," Maud gave him a large hug. "You look so very handsome in your evening clothes."

"Close your eyes darling, and put your back towards me." Her father placed a beautiful strand of matching pearls around her neck. He then faced her towards her mirror. "Now open."

"Oh, they're stunning." Maud gently fingered the necklace. She kept looking at herself in the mirror. "Thank you. Thank you. I will love wearing them." She hugged him again. "They will be my favorite piece of jewelry."

Standing in the foyer, Maud, her mother and father warmly greeted each guest. The moment Maud and Neil made eye contact in the receiving line, the air was charged with anticipation.

In evening dress, Maud thought Neil looked like a Greek god. She felt as if she were intoxicated with champagne.

Feelings never aroused in her before made her body tingle, a new sensation she couldn't describe. Neil touched her hand. She felt a current sweep between them. She knew she wanted to explore these emotions. The caress by his hand caused a different kind of restlessness inside her.

I wish Mother liked Neil better. She told me to be wary of someone like him. She even called him a rake and told me to be careful. Mother thinks he would sully my reputation. I don't believe it. Neil likes me too much to ever hurt me. All these thoughts buzzed in Maud's head as she waited for the musicians to begin playing.

Maud could hear the sound of the violins. After Mr. Driscoll claimed the first dance with his daughter, Neil approached Maud.

"May I have the honor of the first waltz, Miss Driscoll?"

"It would be my pleasure, Mr. Wescott."

The music of the orchestra filled the air. Neil and Maud joined the other couples on the dance floor. Neil spoke non-stop in his animated conversation.

"We will have a wonderful time in London this summer, Maud. I'll take you dancing at some of the posh clubs. You can come and watch me play cricket at the Boughton. I'm the team captain this year."

"How exciting. I know nothing about cricket. Will you teach me?"

"Of course."

"You dance beautifully, Miss Driscoll. I can't wait until you allow me to have another waltz with you. Then I can hold you in my arms again."

Maud blushed.

"And I thank you, kind sir. But I would be amiss if I didn't dance with several of the other young men my Mother must have pressured into attending." Her contagious laughter filled the room.

"No one would have to be persuaded to dance with you, beautiful lady. Did anyone ever tell you your eyes are the most incredible green?"

"You're turning my head, kind sir. Now since the music has ended, would you escort me to the vacant chair next to Priscilla?"

"I'll get us both a cup of punch. I've been told food will not be served until midnight." Neil said.

The next morning, Maud sat at the dressing table in her sunny bedroom. The adrenaline inside her body pumped twofold. What with all the excitement of the previous evening, she had found it difficult to have a good night's sleep. She brushed her hair with swift and purposeful strokes. Maud looked at the smiling reflection in the gilt edged mirror in front of her. A soft peach, silk kimono hung loosely wrapped around her waist. The pale pink blossoms in the fabric danced, gently accompanying her motions as she methodically moved her arm up and down. She stopped brushing her hair, deftly pulling the combed results into a fashionable upsweep, securing it with large hairpins keeping it off the nape of her neck.

She sighed dreamily, giving herself a warm hug.

She couldn't stop talking to herself. "Oh, he's so wonderful. I can't believe I'm going to London with the

Wescotts tomorrow. It's like a dream come true. Neil is so charming and gentlemanly, I just know he likes me".

Maud's thoughts continued to return to the last evening. Even though she hadn't wanted a debutante ball, she closed her eyes and smiled as she relived the entire scenario.

"I could have danced forever. Sometimes I believe my mother has strange ideas about a young woman's behavior. I wish she hadn't insisted on that lace insert. I love the dress anyway, and when I arrive in London, I'm going to have it removed. It's too old fashioned. With my beautiful shoes, I could dance from London to Paris." Maud spoke the words to herself.

Maud re-lived being introduced to all the invited guests. She smiled. From the moment she clasped her white-gloved hand on her father's arm to the last note of the evening, she felt she had been waltzing through a fairy tale dream.

She smiled to herself. "My gown looked even more spectacular under the new electric chandelier. And my beautiful new strand of pearls – oh they were luminescent. Even Daddy's usually staid demeanor softened. I know he liked all the attention too. Oh yes, I must get ready for London."

CHAPTER 6

Maud's parents and the Wescotts made a formidable entourage when they arrived at the harbor pier. It took two porters several trips to secure the luggage into the proper stateroom for everyone.

Maud's quarters were next to her friend's parents, then Priscilla, then Neil. Maud thought her room luxurious even for ship travel. Mr. Wescott had seen to all the details. Maud thought he acted like a colonel of a regiment and not the father of her friend: precise and exacting. Not at all like Neil, who acted reserved and overpowered by his father's demeanor and actions.

Overjoyed to be traveling on the same ship with Neil, Maud's conversation about Neil with her mother still echoed in the back of her head.

"Maud, dear girl. Please be careful. I don't want to see you hurt. And my child, I don't want to see your reputation sullied."

"Nothing is going to spoil this summer in spite of my mother's protestations. She'll change her mind. She'll see." Maud told herself.

A few days out of Boston, the seas were calm, the sky a bright azure blue. Wisps of white clouds floated high above. Maud looked at the polished wood and brass trimmed railings as she walked about the deck. To impress Neil, she had on her newest Gibson Girl outfit – a frilly white blouse, and navy faille skirt, accompanied by a straw navy and white hat. Walking down the passageway to join Priscilla and Neil she overheard her name in their conversation. Being curious she stood in a shadowed recess of the passageway and listened.

"Neil, just look at what has happened."

Priscilla's voice raised an octave, Maud knew how upset she sounded. She would stay and listen and not walk away.

"Your actions have been deplorable. You should never have come to Boston with us. Maud may have captivated your heart, Neil, but you are supposed to marry Margaret, even though your engagement hasn't been formally announced. I know Maud turned your head with just one smile. She is as sweet as a honeybee. I don't want you hurting her."

Maud heard Neil chuckle.

"All the more reason I should see her again."

"Neil Wescott, you are infuriating. I hate to even think about what could happen while Maud is our houseguest this summer. You're my brother, and I love you. And I love Maud like a sister. It would be so unfair to Maud if she has feelings for you."

Maud felt her chest taking in a deep breath. She knew whatever feelings she had for Neil were more than a passing excitement. Remaining hidden in a recess in the passageway, she continued to eavesdrop on Priscilla's and Neil's conversation.

"That is why you must help me."

"This is so upsetting. What about Margaret? What about her feelings?"

"My lord," thought Maud. He has another woman in the wings." Maud began to perspire, and felt dizzy. She stayed however, to listen to their conversation.

"Pris, I know already Maud is the only woman in the world for me. She touched me as no one ever has before. I confess I didn't pay much attention to her last summer. I played the role of the elusive bachelor so to speak. But now you must help me. Please. I implore you. I must convince Father. I don't love Margaret - barely even like her. She really is insufferable. Can't think beyond clothes and balls. Who is going, where and when? She reads nothing but the society page. She can't even hold an interesting conversation."

Silence followed. Maud remained in her hiding place when Neil started speaking again.

"Maud is just the opposite. She may love clothes, but she is interested in the world, and art and music and good times. She and I have so much in common, I'd rather remain a bachelor the rest of my life than be forced to marry Margaret."

"I really feel so sad for you and Maud." For a moment Priscilla held her breath. "Father thinks Maud is a delightful young woman and my friend. But you know him. Once he is set on something, he will never change. I know he won't even entertain the thought of you two marrying."

"There must be a way out. I'm so in love with Maud. I feel I'm being treated like father's lackey, not his son. What difference can it make as to whom I choose to marry? Maud comes from a wonderful family."

Maud couldn't listen to anymore of the conversation. Feeling lightheaded from what she heard, made her way back to her cabin, soaked a hanky, and dabbed her face before she returned to the outer deck.

Maud realized she would have to act like nothing had happened. She worried how she could do it now since she knew what Neil's intentions were. She had to continue to be carefree and not find herself alone with him. She thought the weather beautiful and intended to enjoy the crossing and dance with Neil every evening.

CHAPTER 7

As the summer wore on, Maud, Priscilla and Neil were spending more and more time exploring London and Essex. Neil's mind forgot all about Margaret. Not so with Priscilla. Despite the excitement of a court debut by a commoner, high in her priorities stood the concern over the relationship between Maud and Neil. Even though they were never alone, Priscilla could sense a palpable magnetism growing between them. She worried the electric tension would develop into a full-blown love affair. Maud's heart would be shattered if Neil were forced by their father to marry Margaret. Right now Priscilla felt inept because she knew nothing short of a kidnapping or murdering Margaret would make it possible to stop their mutual feelings for each other. Even worse, she had to keep all these thoughts to herself. Even sadder, Neil and Maud, no matter what they felt would be separated right after their court presentation, Neil to a formal engagement with Margaret, and Maud a return alone to Boston.

If any free time between existed fittings and shopping, Priscilla and Maud could be found in the stands at the Boughton Cricket Club, cheering on the team. Of course, the fact Neil captained the team made the sport all the more exciting. Maud watched the ball being hit back and forth. It really made no sense to her until Priscilla and Neil began to explain.

"Cricket is played with a bat and ball," he told her. "The captain makes most of the important decisions regarding play. That includes setting the fielding positions, alternating the bowlers, and taking the toss."

Neil briefly explained some rudimentary facts about cricket, then left the two young women and took his place on the field.

"Watch Neil now Maud, he is going to call the coin toss. Whoever wins the toss will bat first. Oh look, Neil won the toss," Priscilla said excitedly.

After watching the game for a while, Priscilla turned to Maud.

"See the young man with the black hair?"

"Yes, I do. He has the bat in his hand."

"Well, he can hit, but he was hurt last week, so he can't run. So Neil will put someone in who has already been up to bat, as his runner. See, he is all suited up just like the batter. Otherwise it wouldn't be fair."

"What happens if the player can't play at all?"

"Neil would find a substitute for him. If the injured player can return to the game, then the substitute must leave. There are so many rules and nuances to cricket, I know I can't tell you all in one day. If we keep coming to the matches, I know you will assimilate it."

Maud became very familiar with London. The Wescott's city home was situated in an area called Mayfair. Their mansion, Maud described in a letter to her parents, was huge. "It's in Belgrave Square and even larger than our home in Boston. Part of the time we stay in Essex at the Wescott's country home. Mother, it's even larger than the house in London. The Wescotts bought another estate the year after you were here with me."

Maud liked London best because she and Priscilla could spend time shopping on Bond Street. They could visit all the art galleries where Maud would select her favorites, wishing her paintings were good enough to hang on the same walls. She was confident enough to believe that one day she would take her place among the exhibiting artists. *How exciting that would be,* she mused.

Maud thought the new Tower Bridge spanning the Thames River, a wonder to behold. She even persuaded Priscilla to come with her one day while she sketched it.

The majority of Maud's days were spent in the company of Priscilla and her mother. Mrs. Wescott busily groomed them for their court presentation to Queen Victoria. Maud never realized how the act of a curtsy could play such an important part in a young English woman's life, but she practiced right along with Priscilla. It took several months of grueling preparation for this presentation ceremony to the Queen at St. James Court. They were measured and re-measured for their presentation gowns. Each young woman had to wear three large white feathers, a particular kind of headdress, mandated by the Queen. In an odd way, Maud thought the feathers an elegant statement. And then there was the required train. She was relieved to learn someone would be watching each young woman so she wouldn't trip or fall on her gown. All the dresses were white, but of different materials. Maud's was of Chinese shantung silk, narrow skirt and low cut bodice with off the shoulder neckline. The neckline itself decorated with beautiful seed pearls and translucent sequins creating a stunning effect. Priscilla's dress made from softly flowing white satin taffeta had very simple lines. Diamond-shaped appliqués of white brocade hand sewn on the skirt, with each diamond containing a border of seed pearls. Both young women wore the traditional sixteen-button white kid gloves. Maud and Priscilla complemented each other in coloring; Priscilla with her flaxen hair and violet blue eyes, next to Maud's cat green eyes and creamy complexion, not like most redheads that suffered with freckles. Mr. and Mrs. Wescott arranged for a portrait sitting for both girls done by a fine young artist in London.

When not practicing the fine art of being presented to London society, Priscilla, Maud, and Neil became a known and inseparable triumvirate around London. They received numerous invitations for parties and galas. Neil escorted them to the National Gallery, the museums, the theatre, and the symphony.

One afternoon, Priscilla came hurriedly into the Wescott library to find Maud happily perusing one of the books she found on the shelves.

"Maud, oh Maud, look what arrived in the afternoon mail." She held up a large cream-colored envelope, with a crest on it.

"What is it, Pris?" Maud could see the excitement in her friend's eyes.

"This is the ball I have been talking about. I have been waiting for years to receive an invitation."

"Years?"

"Well, maybe not that long but this is the most exciting ball of the season. Listen to this." Priscilla pulled the card from the envelope and began to read. "Lord Malcolm and Lady Muriel Trent Malcolm request the honour of your presence for dinner and dancing on Saturday, October ten. Receiving line begins at 9:00 p.m." Priscilla looked up. "We must send our acceptance including you by the next post."

"Who are they?" questioned Maud.

"They're known for their magnificent balls and their home is the showplace of all Essex. Oh, Maud, this evening will almost be as exciting as meeting the Queen. We must find Mother so we can go to Harrods to buy new gowns. We just can't wear anything we currently have in our wardrobes. Our evening frocks must be special."

Neil, Maud, and Priscilla were standing in the receiving line at the Malcolms. *Maud looks like a dream walking*, Neil thought. He knew he was falling deeper in love with her. He escorted his sister and Maud through the receiving line. Maud's gown, the latest from Paris, had a multi-layered skirt of burgundy mousseline. The bodice in matching burgundy velvet, with sweeping décolletage, and sleeves the same shade as the skirt. Thin burgundy satin ribbons encircled her miniscule waist to complete the outfit. She wore heirloom diamond earrings.

71

"That burgundy shouldn't be for redheads, but on Maud," he inhaled, "it's magnificent." *Oh Maud,* he thought silently, *I'm so in love with you. You're everything I've ever wanted and could not hope to find.*

Maud smiled graciously as she curtsied to Lord and Lady Malcolm.

Priscilla told him Margaret's parents were also guests of the Malcolms for the evening.

"I'm apprehensive. I know Margaret will be in attendance. I've got to avoid her at all costs," he murmured. "Help me, help me, Pris," he whispered. "The more I see of Margaret, the sourer my stomach feels."

"Neil, my heart aches for you. I understand how you are feeling, but father is not going to release you from your engagement."

"It's so unfair. He's turned me into his duty, honor and country. For God and for England and the Wescott name. I can't stand it. I feel like a pawn in a chess game." His manner quickly changed. "Good evening Lord and Lady Malcolm. My sister, Priscilla, and our houseguest from America, Miss Maud Driscoll."

"Thank you, Cornelius. It is good to see you this evening."

When Neil heard the musicians beginning to tune their instruments, he escorted the ladies to chairs inside the ballroom.

"Not a butler in sight. I'm going to find some refreshments for us."

A friend of Priscilla's asked her for the dance, so when Neil returned with the glasses of champagne, he set them on a table and took Maud's hand, leading her to the dance floor.

"Neil, what an exquisite room, with all the mirrors in gilt frames and the murals, it reminds me of Versailles."

"It should. It's supposed to be a replica."

"No wonder Pris was so excited over the invitation."

"Maud, you look beautiful this evening."

"Thank you, kind sir."

When dinner was announced, Maud found herself on the arm of Mr. Wescott. They seated her between him and Mr. Church. *What a way to meet him, but I guess it could be worse. I feel so uncomfortable.* Maud could hear the voices inside her head telling her it would be just fine. *Maud, concentrate on your food and speak only when spoken to. I don't have to be a scintillating conversationalist.*

"Maud, I'm surprised Neil hasn't brought you over to have tea with my daughter, Margaret."

I'm not, Maud thought to herself, nodding at Mr. Church.

"I haven't seen much of him," she lied. "I know he has been working on a project for his father."

"Well, the next time you young people go out on the town, Margaret should go with you."

Well I never, she thought. *The gall of that man. I don't like him. It's no wonder Neil wants nothing to do with Margaret.*

She had seen Neil disappear into another room. She knew he would have to sit with Margaret at the dinner table.

"What do you think of this evening, Maud dear?" asked Mr. Wescott.

"I'm overwhelmed. Lord Malcolm's home, the dinner repast, the opulence. I've been entertained in some of the most exquisite homes on the eastern seaboard of the United States, and I have never seen anything like this. It's amazing."

"Priscilla thought you would be impressed."

"Maybe one day my paintings will grace the walls of a home such as this. Oh, don't be a dreamer," she silently mused. *"As if I could paint that well? Maybe not now, but I will."*

"May I have the honor of this dance, Miss Driscoll?"

Maud was afraid to say no. Mr. Church couldn't talk about anything more than the upcoming marriage of his daughter to Neil. I'm afraid to answer more than a simple yes or no. She knew the Church and Wescott families were very close, but with all the confidences she and Priscilla shared with Neil, Maud found it difficult to believe Neil planned to marry Margaret.

Will I have an opportunity to talk to Priscilla or Neil about this? Why is my body shaking underneath this beautiful ball gown? Maybe I am coming down

74

with something. No I'm fine, but I think I'm falling in love with Neil, and this is certainly going to present a problem, for me anyway. Maud smiled, relieved to see Neil reenter with Priscilla.

"I don't think I can stand another minute of Margaret or her father. I've actually been avoiding them all evening, except at dinner. I know how much you wanted to be at this party, but would you and Maud mind terribly if we left early?"

"I can't allow you to suffer all evening. I think Maud would agree to leave early."

On a rainy night a few weeks later, the three of them had tickets to see La Boheme at Covent Garden. Priscilla, suffering with a dreadful cold was remaining in bed. Neil and Maud decided not to forego the performance since it was such a new opera. Mrs. Wescott allowed Neil to escort Maud without a chaperone. As Leopold wept at the death of Mimi, Neil took Maud's hand instinctively. Not a word passed between them, nor had any sign of affection, but Maud knew she had passed the point of no return. *Neil is my destiny.*

As they settled in the hansom after the performance, Neil sat beside Maud rather than across from her. He had removed his heavy overcoat and laid it on the opposite seat so he could be nearer to her. Neil gently placed his two hands on Maud's shoulders and turned her towards him.

She saw the tenderness in his soft gray eyes. They spoke volumes. For the first time in Neil's life, he experienced a sincere honest feeling of love welling up inside of him, and it overwhelmed him. This reality eclipsed all the casual relationships of his past. His passion for Maud made him set aside thoughts of his pending responsibilities.

"Maud, you must know I adore you, and want nothing more than for you to be my wife."

"Neil, my darling, I love you too. But, you haven't finished school." *What about Margaret Church, the woman you have never mentioned to me, but I have heard about from Priscilla, and Mr. Church?* All these thoughts were tumbling about in her mind.

Neil wrapped his arms around her, pressed her close, and kissed her with the passion he had felt since her first met her. Maud reciprocated. *I've never felt kisses like this; my body is turning to jelly. I can't resist his advances. Am I letting myself in for heartbreak? I do want to marry Neil, but what about Margaret? He's never talked about her.*

"Darling, are you willing to wait until I complete school? Just one more year, then I will be in the firm with my father. He wants me to open a Paris office. We could live there, and you could have your painting studio."

"I am so happy. I can't wait to tell my family. Of course, you will have to ask permission of my parents, but I already know they would approve."

"You can't tell your parents yet. You can't even tell Priscilla."

"Why not?" Maud looked at him.

"Do you remember meeting Margaret Church the first time you came to dinner?"

"Yes, she wore the most beautiful dress." Maud was just about to say something regarding her conversation with Mr. Church at the Malcolm's dinner table.

Now maybe I will find out what's between the Churches and the Wescotts.

But Neil continued. "Well, that's all she has, just what you see, but..." Neil hesitated, then plunged forward, "Margaret's parents and my parents have assumed all our lives we would be married. They are best friends, and no matter what I say, they will not let me marry, unless I marry her."

Maud's body recoiled. "How then can you propose to me? Her father told me you were engaged to her. But I couldn't believe it. What about Margaret? Doesn't she have anything to say in this?" Her eyes flashed in hurt and anger.

Neil placed his hands on hers, and brought them close to his mouth. He kissed them several times and continued speaking. "Yesterday, Margaret told me she had been busy embroidering for her trousseau. Then she told me 'W's were not the easiest letters to embroider. I couldn't wait to get away from her. Maudie, I so want to marry you, but I don't know what Father will do if I tell him. I don't love Margaret. I'm not even sure I like her. I think Father will probably disown me. I couldn't live on just a solicitor's salary. I have no intention of being poor, when my family has so much money."

"Neil, I have my own money. We would never be poor."

Neil sat back and nervously touched his blonde mustache. "I know, my love, but my father and Mr. Church have betrothed the two of us without my consent. Mr. Church even went so far as to prepare the engagement announcement to be read in church. Father told him he would have to hold off because I had another year of studies to complete. I don't think Mr. Church was very happy about it. Father wants to stand for parliament."

"Why does he need Mr. Church's influence to carry the district?" Maud asked.

Neil's comments underscored his unhappiness.

"Can't you talk with your father? Can't you tell Margaret you're in love with me? I know you have been put in a difficult situation, but you should speak with Margaret. You must tell her how you feel about me. It's not right to let her think you are going to marry her. Can't you speak with your father while I am still here?"

"Now is certainly not a good time. I don't even know when it would be a proper time. Mother and father just consider you a friend of Priscilla, and a charming houseguest. I don't think they ever thought of you as someone I would fall in love with. Margaret they've known since the day she was born. You're supposed to be sailing for Boston in a few weeks, and now I know I don't want to lose you. I will talk with father soon, I promise, my love."

Maud thought a minute. "I wonder if I could study art in Paris, then you could come and visit me. I've been told there are several women studying at the Academie Julien. I know I can persuade my parents to let me enroll in classes there. If I stayed in London, our feelings would become too obvious. I don't think it would be difficult to find someone in Paris to be my chaperone, or at least someone my parents would feel comfortable with, so I will look and act like a proper young lady student. Neil," she said, looking into his eyes, "even if you had to marry Margaret, I would still be in Paris for you." *What am I getting myself into? I can't help it. I love him too much to let him go. I may have to settle for less than a wedding ring.*

"Oh Maudie, would you do that for me? I would visit you as often as I could. Oh, you wonderful, dear girl. I love you so much." Neil hugged her tightly again.

Maud's heart should have been singing but immediately, her head filled with dark, unhappy scenarios. She kept hearing her mother's admonitions. *Maybe I should be having those same doubts. Neil doesn't seem to have the emotional strength needed to object to his father's wishes. More like his demands. I might be making a bad decision.*

Maud was talking to herself but to Neil she said, "I love you too. I know you will find a way to surmount your father's objections. I have great faith in you." She hugged him again.

September 1, 1895

Dear, dear Lillie,

I can't believe I am living in Europe. Well, actually Paris is where I have an apartment, but Priscilla and I have been touring Italy with her mother. She was my roommate during the entire time we were at Wellesley. I wrote you about her. Well, she and her family invited me to live in London with them for a few months. Can you believe I was presented at court! The only thing I remember is that it was freezing cold, and court protocol didn't allow us to wear a coat, or shawl or any garment that would help keep us warm. We had to be presented one by one. Everyone's dress had to have a train. Thank goodness someone was designated to carry it, or I would probably have fallen flat on my face. Priscilla's mother was also my sponsor. As a gift to me and Priscilla, she had our portraits painted by a young but talented artist. John Sargent, I think that's his name. He never put his signature on mine. I guess the whole occasion has been indelibly etched in my mind. But you know me; I would rather be in day clothes and an apron, painting. I persuaded Mother and Daddy to let me study art and live in Paris. Mother wasn't too keen about the idea, but since I had graduated from college, I think she and Daddy decided I must be mature enough. Madame Ebert who owns the building where I live agreed to be my chaperone. I literally had to beg my parents, but once Mother came to Paris and spoke with Madame Ebert personally, she was satisfied I had found someone competent to watch over me. Mother is also paying her a small stipend to ensure that.

81

Right now, I'm writing this while sitting next to the Ponte Vecchio Bridge in Florence. This city is filled with the most beautiful art and sculpture everywhere I look. I love the city of Venice best. Everywhere one goes, one must ride in a gondola - romantic, but impractical. I am afraid I might fall in. The Venetians use flat barges to transport everything else.

I love painting in Italy. The colors are so vibrant and alive. What a horrible experience with Mr. Bailey. I'm so sorry he turned out to be such a cad. Tell me, are you seeing Mr. Patterson socially? He might be someone you should consider. Is he as handsome as you are pretty? I have met someone, but I can't talk about it. It's too complicated to write in a letter. Just know I'm very happy, and I hope you are too.

Love from your dearest friend,

Maud

November 1, 1897

Dearest Maudie,

Oh Maudie, you remembered my birthday. The Venetian glass beads are just beautiful. I can picture myself being serenaded in one of those gondolas. Mr. Patterson (George) took Mama and me out for dinner at the Hotel Croyden - our newest and most opulent hotel. It's in Los Angeles, and we took the electric motor trolley to the hotel. It's quite modern and certainly enables one to reach a destination much faster. When the doorman ushered us into the hotel lobby, we entered a wonderland. The hotel decorator must have spent a lot of time in Europe. The lobby looks like pictures I've seen in Godey's and the Pictorial Review. Huge chandeliers dripping with crystal prisms give an aura of being in a French palace. Beautiful red silk wallpaper with muted vertical stripes in the same red tones covers the walls. The furniture is extremely ornate, all gilded, overstuffed chairs and sofas in rich ecru satin brocades. All I can say is it was the most elegantly decorated room I have ever seen, except in magazines. And the food was pure ambrosia. One of the latest dishes the hotel serves is creamed peas in this most marvelous of puff pastry shells. I had that with lamb chops. I'm only glad I didn't request potatoes as a side dish. Or you would have a friend who looks like a house! I shouldn't be going on so about the food and the hotel, but it was such a special evening.

George gave me a book of poems, Sonnets of the Portuguese by Elizabeth Barrett Browning. He must have overheard me say how much I loved her poems. He hasn't formally declared his intentions but the poetry seems to say

83

so. I told you he is fourteen years older than I am. What do you think?

I loved reading about all your latest adventures. My life is mundane and orderly compared to yours, but I am not complaining. Just knowing I will probably spend the rest of my life with George fills me with happiness. I like his kisses too.

Love, love and a million thank yous.

Lillie

CHAPTER 8

Early summer, 1898

*M*aud was amazed the year had passed so quickly. She adored living in Paris, painting, studying, and walking around the neighborhood. Neil would make the journey once a month to spend a few days with her. At first, he stayed in a nearby hotel, but he and Maud were so in love, they couldn't stay away from each other. Maud did not espouse the hedonistic lifestyle, *la vie moderne*, currently sweeping over Europe. But she still had a continued wish for freedom of expression in her art. Madame Ebert had gone to Nantes to care for her daughter and new grandchild, leaving Maud without a chaperone. Maud realized her willpower to be circumspect with Neil had reached the level of non-existence.

Then, unexpectedly, Neil arrived to spend the Easter holidays with her. Maud opened the door of her apartment to find Neil standing there with a huge bouquet of spring flowers. She ushered him inside where the flowers were all but forgotten as they embraced each other.

"Oh my darling, I couldn't wait to see you. Let's elope, I can't stand being away from you any longer."

"Neil, what about your father?"

"I don't care. I just want you for my own."

"I want you too." Maud could feel her heart pounding. Her resolve melted away in his arms.

Neil picked her up and carried her into the bedroom, then carefully unbuttoned her dress.

"Neil, I'm nervous." Maud shivered as he kissed and caressed her nipples.

"Don't be afraid my darling, I will be as gentle as I can." He tenderly lifted her onto her bed.

"But this is my first time. I don't know what to do."

"I will guide you." He kissed her mouth again. After he removed all Maud's undergarments, he quickly removed his clothing, and lay on the bed beside her.

His tongue began to trace the lines of her body; he lightly kissed her neck, and then traced and explored her body very slowly.

Maud quivered as his tongue found her most hidden spot and entered it.

"Oh my God, Neil. Oh, oh, oh." Her cries were uncontrollable. Her body felt at fever pitch.

"What do I do now?"

"Touch me, darling, feel me with your tongue."

Maud tentatively touched his engorged penis.

"Kiss me sweetheart." Maud turned on her side to face Neil.

"Maud, let me put you on your back." Neil kissed her nipples and sucked one and then the other. Then he pushed her legs apart and swiftly entered.

"Oh darling, I hope I didn't hurt you."

"It was a pain of pleasure," she whispered.

The two bodies rocked together until the wave crested, and came roaring down over them.

"Oh my God, my god. Maud. Maud. I love you so much. I will love you forever, my darling."

Maud remained in a stage of euphoria while they spent the rest of the weekend in Maud's bed, the white counterpane drenched in perspiration.

"Neil, I can't get enough of you. Lovemaking is so wonderful. I'm so glad we discovered each other."

"Me too, sweetheart."

She and Neil discussed marriage. He again suggested eloping, but in the end, they both decided it would be better to have a formal wedding and not disappoint Maud's parents. When Neil left to return to London, Maud felt lost without him. Even without a marriage ceremony, she felt like she had been on a honeymoon. Her eyes teared up when they realized Neil had to return to England.

June arrived on one of those incredible, balmy, late spring days. Even though the summer wasn't quite in full bloom, many artists had their easels open, engrossed in mixing paint on their palettes. Then after numerous, seemingly effortless sweeps from their brushes, beautiful figures and objects began to form on the canvasses, as if by magic.

Maud had made several friends among them, and her work they considered excellent. She had even sold a few canvasses while she sat on the banks of the Seine painting. She had become a regular fixture sitting on her child-sized stool, her feet entangled in its legs. Intent on making just the right strokes, to enhance the water she brushed the blues onto her canvas. Her teachers at the Academie had been quite pleased with her work. Maud loved the plein air style, so graceful and freeing. Claude, a friend she had met while painting at the beach in Argenteuil, had introduced her to the style. His finished product captivated her and she wanted to paint in the same manner.

Since their idyllic weekend, Maud hadn't seen or heard from Neil. Almost two months passed, and she didn't know what to think. Was Neil hurt or ill? She worried. Then things worsened. She thought maybe she had the flu, or food poisoning. She needed to see a doctor.

"Young lady, you're pregnant."

His news both surprised and dismayed her. The stigma of being pregnant and unmarried weighed heavily on her. Grateful she hadn't started showing, her morning sickness had been minimal, but just enough to send her to the doctor.

"I'm so glad Priscilla is coming to visit me next weekend. I'm thrilled I can see her without a chaperone."

Since Madame had left, the two young women would visit without a chaperone. Mrs. Wescott having met Madame on two or three occasions felt Priscilla would be well protected. *When I tell Priscilla my news, I won't have to worry about anyone else hearing my innermost secrets. I will have to talk to someone about my predicament, and Priscilla seems my wisest choice, since she is my closest friend in Europe and Neil's sister.*

Maud picked up her painting equipment, packed it away, and with her stool and easel in hand walked towards a narrow side street. The window boxes on the half-timbered houses were overflowing with brightly colored geraniums. The flower vendor on the corner was selling beautiful mixed bouquets of lilies and roses. Maud bought one in yellow, then disappeared into her doorway. Before she walked up the two flights to her sunny apartment where she could throw open the windows and look at the Seine, she collected her mail. When she saw an envelope in Neil's handwriting, she ran up the stairs, set her painting equipment down in the doorway, and sat down to read his letter. She tore it open and scanned the contents.

Undated

Dearest darling joy of my heart,

No matter what happens, just know that I have loved you with all my heart and soul and being. You are the only person in the world for me. However, my father told me if I don't do as he bids, he will disown me and remove my name from anything connected with the Wescott family. Therefore, I have agreed to marry Margaret within the fortnight. Oh my darling, please

89

*forgive me. I will never forget you. I don't have the
strength to relinquish my family inheritance. Forgive me
for being such a coward.*

*Only our families will be present. It will probably
be the most talked about wedding of the season, or so it
seems like it to the Churches. Margaret's father is
sending us to Greece for our honeymoon, then I may go
to Paris as Father wants me to open an office there.
Margaret insists on going to Paris with me. Margaret
told her parents she was pregnant. You and I both know
Margaret was lying. We have hardly seen anything of
each other since I met you. I told father she was lying. I
had never been near her. I told him I wanted to marry
you. But I tell you, Maud, Father was adamant. I know
something else must be brewing between him and Mr.
Church because he wouldn't listen to me. He agreed you
were a lovely woman, but he was very persistent I marry
Margaret and the sooner the better. He didn't want any
scandal in the house of Wescott. How can there be a
scandal if she's not pregnant?*

*Priscilla has always known I am in love with you,
but I guess I am too weak to stand up to my parents. In
fact, Maud, I know Priscilla always hoped you and I
would be married. It's what I wanted because you would
be the most marvelous of wives. But father will not
listen to me, nor will Mother. Maudie, I love you with all
my heart. But maybe it would be better if you just forgot
about me. I am my father's son, and I must continue the
house of Wescott.*

Neil

"No, No," she screamed. "He can't have done that. He loved me. Why? Why?"

She let the letter drop to the floor. Maud pounded her fists into her bed pillow, then the bed, then pounded the wall. Uncontrollable tears streamed down her cheeks. She wiped them away with a part of the painting smock she was wearing. Oh God, I let myself be carried away with Neil just once and that happened over three months ago. All he had to do was profess his undying love for me, and I capitulated. How could I have been so stupid? Now Neil is going to be married, and our child will be a bastard. My parents will die of apoplexy. I know. How could Mother have been so right? Priscilla will have some ideas. All these thoughts swirled around in Maud's head. I'm so glad she's coming to visit soon.

Maud knew something was wrong when she opened the door to welcome Priscilla. Priscilla, usually bubbly and happy was as white as a sheet.

"Pris, darling. I know all about Neil's getting married. I'm so upset. But you – you look like a ghost."

"Maud, let's go inside." Priscilla collapsed on her couch. "Please come sit with me, Maud. I have to talk to you."

Maud seated herself next to Priscilla and gave her a warm hug. Priscilla took Maud's hands, looked into her eyes and began to cry.

"Priscilla, what is wrong?" Maud mirrored Priscilla's concerned looks.

Priscilla looked stricken. Gasping for breath, and gulping in air, she tried to tell Maud what was wrong. "It's Neil," she managed to get the words out.

"What about Neil?"

"Oh Maudie, he's, he's, he's dead."

"My god, Priscilla, how, when?" Maud's own body was wracked by her sobs when she heard the news.

"Two and a half months ago."

That's right after he left me.

Priscilla desperately tried to compose herself, but she couldn't stop crying. "He told Father he wanted to marry you. This was the night before the wedding." Priscilla sobbed. Maud brought out several clean handkerchiefs from her bureau drawer. Priscilla wiped her eyes only to have them tear up again. "I heard him tell Father he would never wed Margaret, and that he would rather be dead. Father became apoplectic. Neil stormed out of the house, slamming the front door. He ran to the stables and saddled his horse." Priscilla paused, took another clean handkerchief and brushed away more tears. "He stopped at a pub in the neighboring village, evidently a place filled with unsavory patrons. Witnesses said the same. One of the men at the bar began to badger him and Neil was ready for a fight. So was the other man. He drew a knife and stabbed Neil several times. The pub keeper told us poor Neil didn't have a chance. Oh Maud, I'm so devastated. You poor darling. I feel so guilty because I never went to Mother with Neil's dilemma. Oh Maud, he loved you so much."

Maud looked at Priscilla, and said, "Priscilla, it's worse than that. I'm going to have Neil's baby in about seven months. Now I can't return to Boston. I can't keep it. I don't know what to do." Maud began to cry again. "Neil told me in a letter his father forced him to marry.

Priscilla blanched. "Oh my dear, dear Maud. I will help you all I can. Do you know someone who could adopt your baby? Do your parents know? Do you have a doctor?" Priscilla peppered Maud with questions. The two of them sat talking for hours, trying to reach some workable conclusions. They cried, they held each other, they talked.

"Maybe you could pretend you were widowed and take the baby back to Boston with you," suggested Priscilla.

"Mother would have an apoplectic fit. No, Pris. Not a good solution."

"Let a friend keep the baby."

"That would be too hard on me."

Other possible scenarios were discussed, but adoption appeared to be the most logical solution to Maud's pregnancy.

"No, Neil didn't know it yet, and no, my parents don't know either. We talked about eloping the last time he was here, but decided we both were too honorable to do that. I know I am an unconventional woman, but I certainly can't go back to Boston unmarried and with a baby. I would love to keep him, but I don't see how. I just want to make sure he will have a good home."

"How do you know it's a boy, Maud?"

"I just know Pris."

"What if it's a girl?"

"Pris, you ninny. If this weren't such a serious subject I would be laughing at that question. It's just a feeling I have. I don't care whether it's a boy or girl. I can't keep the baby. Oh dear God, what am I going to do?" Maud hugged her body and rocked an imaginary baby in her arms.

"We must be pragmatic about this," Priscilla said, composing herself. "Tomorrow, we will go have a long conversation with your doctor. How far along do you think you are? Has the doctor done any kinds of tests?"

Priscilla became the all-knowing expert. "Maud, we will have to trust him to help you. I'm certain he can find someone to adopt it when the time comes. If he doesn't know anyone, I'm confident a little extra money might encourage him to find someone for you. I'd love to keep the baby too as it is a part of you and Neil, but I believe the world and the Wescott family are not ready to withstand your dilemma, let alone understand it. We'll work it out, Maud. Together. I know that is what Neil would want."

She put her arms around Maud, and they both began to cry again.

"Is there any way you could stay and be with me through all of this? I don't think I can handle it alone."

"I think so. You must come and recuperate in Essex before you return to Boston, or whatever you decide to do."

"I'd like that very much, Priscilla. Do you think your parents will let me in your house? Maybe they blame me for Neil's death."

"Oh Maudie, how can they do that? You were in another country."

"But their last conversation according to you, was about me."

"My dearest friend, don't even think those thoughts. I have more faith in my father than that. He is probably blaming himself he didn't listen to Neil. You will be more of a comfort than a thorn. Besides, you even left the country so that Neil could straighten out the entire wedding plans regarding Margaret with our father. He told Father he would never wed, nor bed Margaret. He deeply loved you. I know father must be feeling a lot of guilt, because Neil had to find a way out of the predicament Father put him in."

"Oh Priscilla, darling, I'm feeling at my wit's end. I never imagined in my life I would ever be in a situation like this. I feel so stupid. I shouldn't have allowed Neil to make love to me until a ring was on my finger, and a marriage license on the bureau. I am no better than a common prostitute. I don't want to think about this for a little bit. Please let's have a cup of tea and try to think about some pleasant things."

"Good suggestion," said Priscilla. "This has all been too much for me to digest."

Maud stood and put her arms around Priscilla again. "Thank you my dear, dear friend, for being here. I'm so grateful to you and for you. You are the only one who knows of my dilemma. I would be so ostracized from society if anyone else knew."

"Maud, this is a terrible time to tell you my happy news. Kenneth Colchester whom I met several years ago, asked me to marry him, and I accepted. When you come and stay with my family, we'll have the wedding so you can be part of it – my maid of honor that is if you want to."

"Oh Pris, I'd be honored. I'm glad someone has happy news."

Maud stayed in the maternity hospital for several days after the birth of her little boy, following a short labor and easy delivery.

Look at all his red hair, it's like mine. Of course, his eyes are blue. But I wonder if they will be gray like Neil's were. He has Neil's jaw. Dear God, I hate to give him up. He's so beautiful. The couple who is going to adopt him look prosperous. The doctor said they were very kind people.

As the couple gently carried the baby away in the clothes they had brought for him, Maud had difficulty watching. She turned her head towards her pillow and cried as though her heart would break. Losing her baby and his father all at once…"Oh Neil!"

October 6, 1898

Lillie dear,

I'm so sorry I've been so lax in writing you since I returned to Boston, but putting a pen to paper has been difficult. After Neil died, I had to tell my parents. Papa decided it was best to let me stay in Paris to have the baby. If I returned to Boston, I would be an embarrassment to them. They were enraged I could behave the way I did. However, Papa consented to let Priscilla stay with me. Priscilla would have done it anyway. She sailed from London to meet me and kept me company during my confinement. I stayed in Paris for a month after the baby was born. I wanted so badly to keep him. It was a boy. He was so beautiful. I saw the adoptive couple for a brief moment, when they came to collect my baby. They looked well dressed and prosperous. I'm sure the baby will have a good home. How I wish I could have given him a name. How I wish I could tell him never to forget me. He won't even grow up speaking English. Oh Lillie, I was so devastated to give him up. But I had no choice.

Before I returned to Boston, I went to stay with the Wescotts. They welcomed me with open arms. They never knew about the baby. Priscilla was married while I was there, and I was her maid of honor. Would you believe she is now a duchess? I will never become accustomed to all these titles. Duchess of Colchester. She will be living in Essex, which is outside of London. You can even find a little town called Colchester on a map. Kenneth is a delightful man, and I am so happy for her. He came to call on her during my last few months of confinement, and was so helpful. I wish you could meet my English friends. They would love you as much as I do.

Kenneth bought a perfectly gorgeous brick home for them. It's huge. Outbuildings, stables, formal gardens, I'm certain you have seen pictures of estates in magazines. It is two stories with many dormers in the attic. Their home, called Bodicea Hall, is situated in such a beautiful place, it made me feel like I was in the middle of a park. It's very different because so many of the large estate homes don't have this much wildlife all around. Deer feed each morning and evening at the pond. Really it's as big as a lake. I will paint it someday. Kenneth could just take one of his horses and go deer hunting on their property. I don't think he likes hunting however. I loathe hunting as a sport. I don't see how I can be writing about things so mundane when I long for those I loved. Oh, Lillie my heart aches. I miss Neil. I miss our baby. I didn't even get to hold him more than a few times. He had red fuzzy hair on his dear little head. Life doesn't seem fair. I'm not sure I'll ever get married. Maybe I should have kept to my original resolve not to fall in love, but just to paint. I want you and George to get married soon. I at least want to be a godparent. Priscilla and Kenneth will hold my secret forever. You know I'm now what they call "soiled." What is so special about virginity?

Please, please destroy this letter. It will be our secret forever.

Love,

Maud.

November 1, 1898

Dearest Maudie,

Of course I promise to keep your secret. My heart aches for you. I wish I could do something to assuage your grief, not only for Neil, but for your baby boy too.

Try to keep busy; grief may always be with you, but time will lessen the pain.

I'm glad you have had Priscilla with you. I wish you would come and visit me.

I love you,

Lillie

February 8, 1901

Dearest Maudie,

I'm writing this, my first correspondence as Mrs. George Patterson. I'm married to a wonderful, lovely man. Doesn't he look handsome in the photograph? I wish you could see how he looks at me with his dark gray eyes and brown hair. But he does look distinguished wearing his hat, don't you think? Can you see my Venetian beads? I wore them with a pale blue wool suit. Mama hand-embroidered a white chiffon blouse for me, with the neckline to especially show the beads. The hat I'm wearing is also pale blue felt with a light blue satin trim and veiling. I looked ever so smart. I thought about you and all the beautiful clothes you told me you had bought in Paris. Someday, I'll get there. George has promised.

We had a very small ceremony at the home of a judge. I wish you could have been my maid of honor. Only Mama, my brother Sam, and George's parents were there. Sam, bless his heart, gave me away. He looked so adult for all his twelve years.

For our honeymoon, we took a train and went south to San Diego, California. It's a small beach town. From there, we took a ferry across the bay and stayed in this beautiful resort hotel, the Hotel Del Coronado. We could actually have taken a train almost to the front door of the hotel, but George thought I would enjoy the ferry ride. The hotel is huge. It was built by two Midwestern businessmen who moved there a few years ago. It's supposed to be like a European castle, except it has red roofed turrets, and is built of wood. George tells me that in summer, there is an actual tent city on the beach where

101

people who can't afford the hotel come to spend the summer. Although Coronado is referred to as an island, it is a narrow isthmus. People refer to the area as The Silver Strand. It is truly beautiful. President Roosevelt stayed here. The hotel is the grandest place I've ever stayed in my life. High carved wood ceilings. Beautiful furniture, trimmed with carved wood, huge crystal chandeliers, festooned with more hanging crystal drops. There's a bathroom for every guest room, and hot and cold water one can regulate from the faucets. I think it's called pressurized. The waiters wear white gloves, and tea is served every afternoon. A string quartet plays at every meal. Oh Maud, it was such a wonderful honeymoon. We walked on the beach and had breakfast in bed. It was like a dream. I'm reading A Compendium of Household Advice. I'm so glad Mother taught me how to cook. I can hopefully run a smooth home for George. He has told me I can engage a woman to help in the house, but I'd rather be alone with him when we both are at home. I like the togetherness. We're both working so hard. My shop is expanding. I've hired two more seamstresses. George asked me if I wouldn't like to give up my secretarial duties for wifely duties and enjoy my designing more. I think I will. Oh Maud, it's such fun to work with beautiful fabrics. The special thing about my dresses is Mama's handiwork. They look so elegant if I do say so myself!! I pray your life is now filled with happy times, and you are busy painting. I don't know what I would do without your letters. Our friendship is so special to me. Will we ever get to see each other again?

Love,

Lillie

December 30, 1908

Dearest Lillie,

Well, it has taken ten years but your dear friend has changed her mind again. I am going to get married. I met a perfectly charming gentleman during my last trip to Paris. Mother is so pleased I won't be a spinster. She has turned all her attention to preparing for the 'wedding of the century' in Boston. Ted, my intended, turns out to be a relative of the Boston McKeowns. I know you have met someone in his family at one of my mother's teas. His full name is Theodore Hartson McKeown. He spends most of his time in London. He is very handsome, loves art, and we seem to have so much in common. Believe it or not, I was introduced to Ted through a London gallery owner. I am not certain whether we will live in Boston or London. But can you come and be my matron of honor? Priscilla will be in my wedding party also. I so want you to meet her. The wedding is scheduled for the last part of June. Of course, you know Mr. Patterson is invited too. The Driscoll home has plenty of room for you to stay with us. Happy New Year to you both.

Love,

Maud

July 20, 1909

Dearest Maud,

    The baby dress arrived for your godchild and namesake, only we will call her Evie. Maud Evelyn Patterson is the name on her birth certificate. I know you were the most beautiful bride ever. I looked like a house at the time you were getting married. Of course, George wouldn't even let me do anything or go anywhere during my confinement. The only thing he permitted was designing clothes for the shop to sew and sell. Of course, I'm no longer in George's office. I'm glad clothes are getting shorter and looser, all those undergarments I didn't have to wear. I think I will keep them off for good. Do you think I'm being daring? I felt so badly I couldn't be in Boston for you. I was glad Priscilla was coming from London. Someday I will meet her. Right now England is far away.   Mama's doing just fine. She's going to get married!!!!! Remember me telling you about our boarder, Kate Hasting. Well, she has a brother Frank. He's been courting Mama since the Christmas before last. They are going to be married this Christmas. He bought Mama a lovely house, and she's getting ready to move. Kate bought Mama's house, so everything is turning out perfectly. Mama is so happy. She looks like a young bride. Hard to believe she was only forty when Papa died. I have to admit Frank is a real catch. He too, was a young widower. Never had children, so Sam, my brother and he have been having a fine time. I have enclosed a picture of George, me, and little Evie. I have to brag she is so cute with light brown hair and gray eyes like George. Be certain to send us a picture of you and Ted. Write and tell me all your news. Love, Lillie

November 11, 1912

Italy

Dearest Lillie,

I don't even know where to begin. I am surprised you haven't read about me in the Los Angeles papers. I have never been so mortified, or sad, or hurt and any number of other adjectives I might use to describe how I feel. My marriage has been the biggest sham of the century. I thought Ted had become a little distant towards me, but I assumed it was just from the heavy work pressures he was under. Ted and I settled into family life. He worked very hard. Mother kept asking me when she and Father would have grandchildren. I couldn't tell her Ted had been sleeping in our guestroom because he had been coming home so late from work, and didn't want to wake me. I know now it was his excuse.

Mother and I had been out shopping all day. When we returned to Beacon Hill, I wanted to show her the latest dresses I had made by the dressmaker. We were in my dressing room, when I heard noises coming from our bedroom. When I walked into the bedroom, I saw movement coming from under the spread. Being more curious than cautious, I walked over to the bed. Ted's head suddenly appeared. Then another male head appeared. It was his clerk from the brokerage house.

All I remember doing was screaming and running down the stairs, sobbing all the way to my parent's home.

107

When my mother arrived home, she found me in my old bedroom. I told Mother, "I don't ever want to walk inside that house again, not even to retrieve my belongings." I asked Mother and Daddy to help me. I wanted an annulment and money to return to Europe and live there. My parents didn't even blink when I told them this. All I can say is everything reminding me of Ted was gone. There was no longer any trace of him. It was like he never existed. The worst thing I can think of, though, is Ted never even said he was sorry.

Mother told me there were all kinds of rumors but Daddy quashed them before they got out of hand. I'm sure the old dowagers had a good time. Gave them something to talk about when they had tea. Don't be so catty, Maud!

When I was able to adjust to the situation, and leave the confines of my bedroom, Daddy made an appointment for me with one of his lawyer friends. The lawyer even came to the house to save me any embarrassment. I was told I would receive a very nice settlement, plus the proceeds from the sale of our house, and that Mr. McKeown, had left for Australia. If that is true, I will probably never find out.

All I knew was I didn't want to see him again. I wanted to believe he had ruined my life. But since I survived after Neil's death and giving up my child, I knew I could survive whatever Ted had done to me. The lawyer and my father will sell the house, and cable the proceeds to my bank in Florence, Italy.

Of course I fled to Europe, to Italy this time, because all I want to do is paint, paint, paint!

108

I hope to find a little cottage with a garden where I can grow flowers to paint and have a   spacious studio to put my soul on canvas. I'm not ready to face the world yet and so far my choice in men has failed me. You're so lucky to have someone as steady as George.

Love,

Maud

Christmas, 1912

Dearest Maud,

I had to write you as soon as I received your letter. I am crying for you. I am so distraught for you about everything, your marriage, your home. I just want you to be as happy as I am. I can understand why you wanted to leave Boston, but to decide to move back to Europe? I know Europe must be closer than California, but George and I would love to have you visit us. Since you were the victim, the scandal that surrounds Ted shouldn't spill over to you.

Where does the time go? Can you believe we're both thirty years old? Little Evie is over two, and now I'm expecting again. The picture makes Evie look a lot more angelic than she is. Of course, she doesn't have your red hair!! Mama and Frank are wonderful. Sam is nineteen-years-old this year and doing extremely well in school. He wants to be a doctor. That's all he can talk about. His grades in school are top notch, and Frank said he would pay for his college and medical school, as long as Sam continues on this course. Mama couldn't be more proud of him. Papa would be happy too, because Frank is taking good care of Mama and Sam

I hope your Christmas can be a merry one for you.

Love,

Lillie

April 16, 1914

Dearest Lillie,

      I've been attending special painting classes three
times a week, and then go and paint out in the vineyards,
or under the olive trees, or out in my lovely patio filled
with flowers. My small villa sits on what I would call a
knoll. I found the most precious spot I was hoping for.
I live in an area called Tuscany. If you look on a
map, find Lucca. That's the closest actual town.

      My house is dwarfed by the surrounding landscape.
Serpentine rows of vineyards wind up and down and around
the hills. It is absolutely breathtaking when the leaves are
in full foliage. In late spring, it's like a sea of green
waves that billow and roll in the breeze. At certain times of
the day, my olive trees look like they have been silvered
with a paintbrush. I only have a few trees, but everyone
refers to them as a grove. My little garden isn't much but
it's filled with joyful colors of red, pinks, oranges, and
yellows. I have two tomato plants, and I think ubiquitous
zucchini. I hope soon to be able to show you what I
mean.

I'm not certain how much longer I will be able to
paint and travel at leisure. I bought my cottage, and
I intend to keep it, even if there is a war. I'd love
to stay here without thinking about a war encroaching
on Italy. Life is changing in Tuscany, as well as
other parts of Europe. The war really scares me, and
it seems to be coming closer and closer. I'll stay as
long as it is safe for me to be here, then go to Essex
to visit Priscilla and Kenneth Colchester and their

children. From there I will book passage for
Boston. I don't want to be in Europe and caught up
in a war. That is all anyone talks about these days.
It makes for very depressing dinner conversation.
Kenneth has been given a commission in the British
Expeditionary Forces, and he is waiting for his
orders. Right now he's stationed very close to home. I
haven't seen them for almost a year. They had twin
girls last year, Emma and Sophie. Priscilla had
barely recovered from the birth of Thomas when she
became pregnant again. I know I can help her even
if she has a retinue of household help. I can even
cook now. Italian, of course. Quite an
accomplishment for me. Knowing how patriotic the
Colchesters are, it wouldn't surprise me one bit, if all
the help left to serve their country in some form or
another. Priscilla is like you in that way, practical
and full of ingenuity.

     There's a package from me coming to you. Love
to you and kiss Evie for me and tell her it's from her
godmother and aunt. My Italian is improving daily, thank
goodness.

Love,

Maud.

June 10, 1914

Dearest Maudie,

Your exquisite painting arrived yesterday. I'm sending this letter to Priscilla, as I know it will get into your hands eventually. Maudie, you are wonderful. It's no wonder you wanted to return to Europe to study. I'm glad you have set down some roots. Now I know where you're going to be. We'd love to have you visit us. Your life is so exciting. I think mine is too, but it's different. I am a married businesswoman. I design clothes. I cook dinner. George and I bicycle ride. I can actually walk to my shop. It now has a sign, 'Lillie's'. Only a small sign in the window says alterations. It's busy. You would be very proud of me, I think, because I have become a voracious reader, and am now active in several discussion groups. I sometimes wonder what my life would have been like if I had been able to go to college.

I may never have met George, and then I would feel so empty. He is a wonderful husband and companion; generous, kind, and loving.

Thank you, thank you again for the painting. It's a wonderful reminder of you. It will go over our fireplace. George and I love the colors. Are the sunflowers really that large?

How far apart we are in miles, but you are never far from my heart, dear friend.

Love,

Lillie

Maud and Priscilla both knelt on the grass at the cemetery. They placed bouquets of calla lilies and white roses in front of Neil's headstone.

"Oh Pris, you cannot imagine how much I loved him. I fell in love with him the moment I saw him at my debutante ball."

"I know, Maudie. He loved you too. I only wish Father had relented. Neil would still be here, and you would be my sister. Maybe one of these days, someone like Kenneth will come walking into your life."

"Sometimes I'm afraid to accept an invitation for dinner with a man for fear I'll taint his life or mine."

"Don't be so hard on yourself. You've been single for a while now. It will happen, Maud. I know it will."

"Pragmatic Pris, you sound like someone with rose-colored glasses. But I love you for it." Maud gave Priscilla a sisterly hug.

"There's a lovely tea shoppe nearby. I'm famished. How about you? You have a long train ride into London yet, then another long one to arrive in Liverpool to board your ship. I wish we could take you into London so you wouldn't have to change trains."

"It's not a problem. I'm accustomed to travel, and I will find a porter to take all my luggage and the trunk. Good lord, I can't believe all the things I have accumulated in the last couple of years. I wish I could have taken some of the furniture though. I know we are on the brink of a war. Just thinking about it sends cold shivers down my spine."

The elusive sun was now in full view, warming the damp air.

"I'm glad I wore a full-brimmed hat. The sun seems to want to play tricks on us. Give me the bouquets, Pris, and I'll make one large arrangement." Maud deftly mixed the lilies and roses, handing the large arrangement to Pris.

"Pris dear, you place them on Neil's grave." Maud gave a small sigh.

"It won't be long before you will be back in Italy again. I know."

"I hope and pray you are right."

Maud and Priscilla walked down the path to the main road of the cemetery, and stopped to look at the dignified, old stone church that stood inside the cemetery entrance. Then they went out the front gate. They rode in Kenneth's Rolls Royce a short distance through a leafy grove of shade trees to a small village. The chauffeur drove them down a cobblestoned street while Maud looked at the quaint buildings. They were almost through the entire town when Priscilla asked her chauffeur to stop in front of a picturesque cottage.

Maud didn't know where to look first. The little town reminded her of illustrations in English storybooks, small brick fronted buildings with painted wooden signs hanging above the doorways: a drapers, bicycle shop, bakery, and apothecary. Little cobblestone mews filled with interesting looking houses. Her artist's eye drank in all the color and architecture.

"Pris, may we stop at the apothecary before we return to Bodicea? Wouldn't this street be wonderful to paint? Look at all its interesting nooks and crannies."

"Of course, Maud, you haven't even looked at the cottage yet. This is where we'll have a spot of tea."

"Oh Pris. What a wonderful place. No wonder you wanted to stop here. I can't leave here until I've sketched and begun painting this cottage. That purple wisteria vine hanging over the eaves is just too beautiful for words, and this yellow cottage itself. Who would have ever thought to paint an orange door, even though it's faded now? You can't drag me away."

They sat at a table in the garden. Maud put up her easel, sketched and then brought out her paints, brushes and a small palette. She worked quickly with deft strokes. The cottage came alive as she painted and the flowers grew right in front of her.

They stayed long past the time they should have left for Maud to catch her train, but as they were finishing their tea, a young man came running through the garden.

"They sunk the Lusitania! They sunk the Lusitania! Damn Germans. They sunk the Lusitania!"

Maud paled and looked at Priscilla. "The Lusitania – that's my ship! I think you might be having me as a houseguest longer than you expected."

"At least you weren't a passenger on board."

They hurriedly rose and picked up their purses. Maud scooped up her brushes and palette. They hustled to the street to find Priscilla's chauffeur to take them back to Bodicea. In the chilling excitement of the news, Maud left her painting. Returning within the half hour, the painting had disappeared.

When the proprietress was questioned, she knew nothing. "I didn't see anyone take off with a paintin'. Sorry."

"I feel so badly because I wanted you and Kenneth to have it." *The Yellow Cottage will always be one of my favorite paintings. I wonder what will become of it.* She thought remorsefully...

Mr. Wescott and Kenneth had been frantic when they thought Maud might be in Liverpool and alone. They were overjoyed when Priscilla returned to the house with Maud in tow. Mr. Wescott, through his connections was able to book passage for Maud on another ship filled to capacity with refugees just like Maud. *Thank you Mr. Wescott, for booking a private stateroom for me. I'm grateful for the privacy.*

Maud thought wistfully. *Mr. Wescott must have had to pay a pretty penny to get me these accommodations. I just want to be back on American soil. For the first time in my life, I can say I'm frightened.*

May 19, 1915

Dearest Lillie,

Sometimes I think my life consists only of crisis and danger. I think I might trade for your 'mundane' life. Since the Germans sunk the Lusitania, I had no transportation home. Neil's father, who is now in the British Parliament was able to book passage for me on another ship going to the United States. He reminds me so much of Neil, except an older version. I miss Neil so much. Oh Lillie, I wonder where my darling son is and if he is safe. Priscilla and I had been sending monthly drafts through her solicitor here in London. He had been forwarding them to the parents for my baby's welfare and to help raise him. We heard just before I left for Boston it no longer was possible to deliver any more money because the Germans had taken over the entire French banking system. And whomever my doctor was using was no longer around. But with the war on, it is impossible to learn anything. I just hope he is safe.

I had left my painting at that little yellow cottage in West Brompton. We returned to retrieve it less than a half an hour later, but it was gone. It makes me sad because I had signed it. It would have made a wonderful memory of a special afternoon.

Now I know I was meant to be a survivor because I arrived back in Boston without incident. The crossing was tolerable, and the food edible. I don't think anyone cared. All the passengers just wanted to be home on American soil.

Father bought another automobile. It seems to have the latest features. I'm learning to drive it. It will be a wonderful way for me to get around Boston, and if I dare, down to the Cape or up to Newport. It certainly keeps us warmer than the open air one he had before. It was a cold winter - and I would love to be somewhere nice and warm. I know California must be warmer than here. I am a loyal American, but my heart is in Europe.

War is the most horrific thing. Lillie, I just hope the United States doesn't become involved. I'm going to see if I can volunteer my services to the Red Cross or some other organization. Glad you are safe in California.

Love,

Maud

August 10, 1917

Dearest Maud,

The war going on overseas is causing all kinds of speculation here. Sam told me if the United States becomes involved, he will enlist right after he graduates. That's so frightening to me.

I worry about it constantly. I have been volunteering for the Red Cross. Whatever we can do, we do - from bandage rolling to running errands. No matter where we go, or what we do, war is on the minds of everyone.

The family is all fine, but what of you? I hope this letter reaches you.

Love,

Lillie

December 3, 1917

Dearest Lillie,

So wonderful to hear from you. In spite of the cold and snow here, you and I seem to be doing the same things for the Red Cross. Our minds seem to be working in like purposes. I'm glad. Somehow it makes me feel closer to you, even though we are clear across the continent from each other.

I had a short letter from Priscilla. She's driving an ambulance, and they turned a wing of their home into a military hospital. Kenneth is now part of the British Secret Service. Very hush-hush. Even Priscilla can't know where he is or what he does.

She said the devastation and destruction is terrible. Death and dying all around. Oh, Lillie, I pray every day for my son's safety. It's been seventeen years, and sometimes I think the emptiness is unbearable. I wish I had been braver and kept my baby. He was a part of Neil I would always have. So many 'should haves,' - 'would haves.' Don't pay any attention to my ranting. It's just I detest how this war has brought so much unhappiness and sorrow in Europe.

I love you,

Maud

CHAPTER 10

Washington D.C. 1953

Peter couldn't wait to tell Evie about the painting he
had found in the antique store.

"Is he going to sell you the painting?"

"I think so, but he says he wants to authenticate
it first."

"Well, keep on him. You don't want to lose it.
It would be a great coup for the museum, and Maud
would be thrilled beyond words."

"How well I know. I plan to return to see him
next week."

True to his word, Peter arrived at the store mid-
morning to find Mr. Sheridan busy dusting and cleaning.

"Mr. Wells, good morning. You are a good
reason for me to stop and have a cup of tea. Besides I
want to hear more of your story. If you were born in
France, what made you decide to come to America?"

"Ever since I knew I wanted to build tall
buildings, America and its new architecture were calling
to me. Then when my school closed and boarded up
awaiting the onslaught of Germans to occupy Paris, I
knew I had to go home. I had no transportation. The
trains weren't running for Parisians anymore, only the
German soldiers." Peter sat back in the comfortable
chair and his thoughts took him back to architectural
school and Paris... his classroom.

Paris, 1917

A stoop-shouldered professor stood in front of his class.
He removed a pair of spectacles, set them down on the
podium, and looked out at his students. He took a
handkerchief from his breast pocket, wiped the tears
filling his eyes. "Gentlemen, quiet please."

A class of eleven young men, including Pieter
Weiler, sat in silence waiting for their professor to
speak.

"Within the hour L'Ecole des Beaux Arts will
have finished boarding up its doors and windows in an
effort to protect our treasured school. I know we all
pray our country will defeat the enemy. In the
meantime, long live France."

Everyone in the room put his right arm fist up in
solidarity. Then the professor collected his books and
glasses, left the podium and walked out.

A low buzz could be heard among the young
architects-to-be.

Gilbert asked, "What should we do?"

"I have to find a way to get back home to
Cieux," Pieter told him. "I loved my first year here at
L'Ecole. I hope its doors won't be closed forever. Good
luck you guys, and stay alive. I want to see all of you
again. *Bonne chance.*"

His friends, Jean Yves and Gilbert patted him on
the back. *"Bonne chance, Pieter."*

Pieter's carefree teenage life no longer existed.
Everything depended on survival. He had his knapsack
and a canteen. With the few coins he had in his pocket,
he purchased some cheese and bread.

Pieter traveled in daylight as the road was
unfamiliar to him. He hid himself in every clump of

bushes he saw, whether he needed to or not. Afraid he might see a German at every turn, he took no chances. He considered himself lucky not to encounter any. On the way, he met one French family willing to feed and house him for a night as he made his trek home.

Tired but still alert, Pieter came to a small forest. Men and women were tramping through the woods with dazed looks on their faces and sometimes walking in circles. To a gregarious seventeen-year-old, the aimlessness meant nothing. All he saw were people traveling or walking around without purpose. Pieter would learn much about this condition called shellshock before he would reach his home.

After several days of circuitous travel, where Pieter hid in the bushes every few hundred feet, he looked up and froze in his tracks. Not more than thirty paces away, he saw enemy soldiers. He spied a small clump of bushes and crouched down in the shrubbery foliage, hoping the thickness concealed him from their line of vision. The soldiers had established a makeshift campsite. Pieter watched as the soldiers ate their meal. Ravenous, he clutched his empty stomach before it made a noisy growl.

Cold sweat made his shirt wet and clammy. *Merde. Those damn Germans look mean. I don't want to confront any of them. They're scary. If I'm caught, I could like and tell them I'm attached to another unit. But I don't have a uniform. Maybe I can tell them I ran away from home so I could join the German army. I can't tell them they overlooked me while conscripting my friends. I know the Germans grabbed everyone in sight. If anyone refused to go, they were shot. With a name like Weiler who would believe my Swiss heritage? Not the Germans. So help me God, I won't get caught.*

129

Pieter remained hidden in the bushes until the enemy left. He took a deep breath and smelled remnants of burning gunpowder.

Pieter eyed a discarded bicycle at the side of the road and pedaled it until it would no longer hold together. The area so familiar to him with its green fields filled with hay, farm vegetables and dairy cows in the pastures, had disappeared into oblivion. The land lay fallow now, strafed by German bullets, filled with man-made trenches and bomb holes scorched black from impact. Thousands upon thousands of German soldier's footprints had been stamped upon the fields. Any cows that managed to survive the onslaught weren't allowed to venture beyond the barn pens.

He thought about all the happy times he had had helping his friends at harvest time, and the delicious ice cream his mother made in the hot weather. Nothing existed now. He wondered if this farmland would ever return to normal. The gunpowder smelled liked charred wood, metal, and rotten eggs stung his nostrils. His happy days were gone. All kinds of thoughts occupied Pieter's mind. There were no physical reminders of those warm sun filled days, only what memories he kept in his heart.

Pieter cautiously made his way down a worn dirt path, semi-hidden from passersby. He could see the main road. A group of German soldiers sat around a small fire on the opposite side of the path, away from where he was walking. Pieter again took refuge in a small clump of bushes, hoping the shrubbery was thick enough to conceal him.

A tired and wary Pieter arrived at the outskirts of Cieux and discovered the roads had all been destroyed. He could have thrown a rock across the town square and a reverberating echo would be the only sound he heard. Businesses were boarded up. The small village yielded no clue to the whereabouts of its occupants. He shook his head back and forth. *"Non, non.* How can this be?"

When he arrived at where his home should have been, a pile of rubble greeted him. He stared in disbelief. *"Mon dieu.* What has happened? Are my parents inside?"

His boyhood home looked so forlorn. He carefully made his way towards the charred remains, remnants, barely standing. Parts of the roof were missing, and the shingles had made gaping holes where they fell into the living room and bedrooms, the floors covered in a sea of broken glass.

He searched for his parents, first in the damaged outbuildings, and then through the ruins of his home. Pieter searched each room for pictures or mementos he might salvage. He found a few family photos, charred books, and his father's journal, the only things the Germans hadn't taken or destroyed. He studied the photos. Pleased to find one of his parents when they had been on holiday, he momentarily pressed it close to his heart. Inside the journal's broken spine, Pieter found a few francs. The once handcrafted leather cover had been ripped and shredded.

Pieter visualized his father sitting at his desk reading out of his journal, and his mother playing Brahms or Mozart on the piano. He then looked closer at the journal cover and found some papers with Paris markings on them. These might be important, he thought.

Knowing time was precious, and he had to leave, he stuffed the papers, along with the journal and

131

pictures he found into his empty knapsack and the money inside his pocket. "I'll give the papers to my father as soon as I find him."

The Germans had ransacked everything else inside the house including tearing keys from his mother's piano. A heartsick Pieter went outside to see if he could find some answers as to why his parents were nowhere to be seen.

Pieter made his way across the field to a neighboring farm. He found the farmer and his family living in the barn with a cow. No vestiges of their house remained.

"Have you seen my parents?" Pieter asked. He looked around at the destruction. "Good lord, you're lucky you're still alive. It looks like you were bombed out."

"We were, Pieter," the man called. "Come sit with us."

The couple looked at each other, their eyes making contact while trying to decide what to do. The husband nodded to the woman and she walked over to Pieter and put her arms around him. She looked into his eyes. "Darling boy, you don't know?" she said.

"What?"

"I'm so sorry to be the one to tell you this," said the woman. "Your parents," she paused and took a deep breath, "are both dead."

"How? When? Where?" Pieter clenched his fists. He couldn't respond with more than monosyllabic words. He tried to be stoic, and broke away from her embrace. He paced back and forth from one end of the barn to the other. He didn't want to cry, but tears burned his cheeks. He took his sleeve to rub them away. He walked back to the farmer and his wife.

"Pieter, we only know from what another farmer told us," the man began. He stopped for a moment, and his wife urged him to continue. "The Germans marched into the town, rounded up many men including your father. The soldiers paraded all the men to the city hall, forced them against the wall facing the town square. Shot them. The mayor tried to stop it, and they shot him too."

"And what they did to your poor mother." The wife continued. "Such a brave soul. She told me she had bad stomach pains. She even went to see the head German to beg him for permission to be seen by a doctor. He refused, and had a soldier escort her back to the house. She collapsed on the way."

"The filthy bastard," added the husband with disgust.

"Did she suffer?"

"Pieter, I don't know what illness she had. I'm so sorry, but yes she was in a great deal of pain," the wife said.

The farmer and his wife were bereft for Pieter. They tried to comfort him, but Pieter wanted to bear his sorrow like he thought a man should. He held back his tears, but cried in silence. "Where are they buried?" he asked in a whisper.

"Near the church, Pieter. I snuck into town, and put markers on their graves," said the farmer. "They were good friends of ours too, and we grieve with you."

"I'm very grateful." Pieter's green eyes were bloodshot. The woman gave him a damp towel to wipe his face. Dirt and grime came off exposing a multitude of freckles. "Now I must go see them before I leave the area. There's nothing left for me here."

"Where will you go, Pieter?"

133

"Right now, I don't know. Join up with the Americans if I could. The French resistance if I could find someone. I just know I have to leave this place."

"We understand, Pieter, and wish you Godspeed," the man and woman both told him.

The young man grabbed Pieter's arm. "Please don't attempt to go back to Cieux. The place is crawling with Germans."

"I must. I'll be careful," he told the farmer.

"Then let me give you a cap to hide your hair. We don't want you a moving target for those damn Krauts," the man said.

The wife brought over some cheese and a partial loaf of bread to Pieter, along with a sausage. A starved Pieter gobbled down the sausage, and ate a small chunk of cheese. The rest of the food, he put in his knapsack.

"I wish we had more to give you, but what we have we're happy to share," the wife said.

"Thank you, thank you. I'm grateful. I haven't eaten in two days."

Pieter then left the kind neighbors who helped him. He inched his way towards the little farming village, all the time seeing the horrors of his parents' death. Like a slow motion movie the death scene appeared in his mind's eye, over and over again and he felt powerless. Even at his young age, Pieter knew he had to find his parent's graves and say goodbye. He realized the dangers, but it didn't matter anymore. His eyes witnessed how much destruction the Germans had caused.

In 1914, the Germans invaded France with a vengeance. Now 1917, they were still wreaking havoc

134

over the land with their tanks, guns, and overall cruelty to the French people.

Pieter found where his mother and father were buried near the Catholic Church. As Pieter looked up to see the church, he nearly tripped on the steeple that had toppled to the ground. Where once a beautiful cross had been mounted were now splintered remains. It looked like someone had melted away the cross where it had fallen.

Pieter stood over his parent's graves and vowed he would return to give them a proper burial. Then he checked his cap, making certain none of his hair showed. He realized the truth in the farmer's words. Red hair did make a great moving target, something he did not want to become. The town square looked deserted. The shops were closed. Most of the windows had been broken, and some of the buildings had collapsed from fires. So much of the cobblestone road destroyed, it was impassable to anything but German tanks. His eyes took in how much destruction the Germans had caused, the town square in ruins from their tanks and artillery.

His parents had been murdered and his family home, gone. His eyes misted. He knew then nothing would keep him from leaving France. He had wanted to immigrate to America, and knew someday he would do it. Right now survival rose to the top of his list.....

Somewhere in France, 1918

Sam Doty told Pieter he had joined the army on his twenty-fourth birthday, right after his college graduation. A serious minded young man, his grades

135

were excellent and he graduated at the top of his class. Patriotic to his country, he enlisted in the army after discussing it with Frank and his mother. He received a commission of Lieutenant, and then promoted to Captain after a battle in which he showed amazing courage. He was a handsome young man, 'the spitting image of your father,' his mother told him. Sam couldn't remember him too well, as he had died when Sam was very young. He and his stepfather, Frank, had a wonderful relationship. He had taught Sam self-reliance from climbing a tree, to learning how to change a flat tire.

Sam couldn't wait for the war to end so he could get out of uniform and begin medical school. He couldn't believe his good fortune when he received his acceptance letter to the new medical school in Los Angeles. "Of course, the school will wait for your tour of duty to be over." He loved getting the letters from his Mother and his sister Lillie even though they were few and far between.

Barely recovered from his wounds, Sam had bivouacked his men in Arras and knew the next day would be strenuous. He and the young red-headed Frenchman had struck up an unlikely friendship in spite of all the hardships. In exchange for Pieter teaching him more French, Sam reciprocated with English lessons.

"Quesque c'est cette chose en Anglais?"

"It is a tent, Pieter."

"La meme chose en Francais tente."

"Ou est votre tente, Sam?"

"My tent is here, Pieter." Pieter repeated it slowly.

These conversations went on between the two of them, both Pieter and Sam's vocabulary increasing daily.

Pieter had been a great help. He hoped they would become friends after the war. Pieter gave him opportunities to laugh, especially when he tried to grow a mustache with only baby-fine hair above his lip. Hard to believe there was only a gap of seven years between them. He wanted Pieter to go with him to America. He had already written Lillie and his mother about it. He even mailed a picture to Lillie.

It was a tough walk from camp that morning. Pieter and Sam, and with a company of soldiers darted from bush to tree to bush, taking cover as best they could as so many of the trees had been felled by the constant barrage of machine gun fire. Inside the perimeter where fighting was concentrated, allies and enemies alike had trampled entire wheat and oat fields. Now the German soldiers, occupying the hills around them for the last year, kept shelling them.

Once this would have been a beautiful place for a picnic. I miss the family picnics. It was a thought to momentarily relieve Sam's mind from the war. It didn't last long. Now all he could smell was gunpowder residue, dirt, old blood, and scorched earth.

Sam had issued carbines with bayonets to each of his men, as well as Pieter. Machine guns and gas masks were also part of the issue.

All carried grenades, including Pieter. As an officer, Sam was equipped with a sidearm. When the Germans failed to break through, a counter offensive was planned. The day began. Bombs burst, guns blazed. The smoke of battle, the groans of the wounded, the smell of human blood. The Germans were keeping up a continual barrage of machine gun fire.

Sam ordered his sergeant to take the platoon across the field to the riverbank where they could cross in relative safety. The battle took place over the course of two days.

Sam collapsed as he looked up towards a blue, blue, sky. Then everything went black. Pieter could see Sam had been hit in the last barrage. Pieter had to move carefully so his actions wouldn't draw the attention of the Germans still in the area. The rest of Sam's company had moved on ahead, leaving Sam where he lay. Pieter crawled at a snail's pace, his right cheek hugging the ground, his helmet pushed to the left. The dust from the dirt clogged his nostrils. The shelling was so furious, Pieter could not reach Sam to attend to him. Sam wasn't moving. Pieter thought he was dead. At the first cessation of the barrage, he crawled over to where Sam lay. Pieter picked up his friend's body and carried him to the nearest dressing station where the wounded were receiving medical aid or dying. Sam was still breathing.

When they entered the tent, a doctor yelled, "Put him on the cot next to you." He then hastened to Sam's bedside, checked his vitals and gave him something for the pain. Pieter realized there was nothing more he could do for Sam except to find the major, and tell him Sam had been badly wounded.

138

"Who brought the captain into the dressing station?" inquired the doctor.

"The boy," answered the sergeant.

"This young man saved his life. I can't do anything more for him here. Captain Doty needs hospital care. I would get him to Rouen as soon as feasible."

"Do you speak any French, doctor? The boy speaks no English."

"Not well, but I will try. Young man what is your name?" He asked in French.

"Pieter, *monsieur,*" Pieter answered. "Sir, where will you take Sam?" Pieter asked the doctor.

"To a hospital in Rouen. So far we've kept the Germans out of there. Captain Doty needs rest." He gave Pieter a fatherly pat on the back. "Would you like to go with the orderly and accompany Sam as his attendant?"

"Yes, monsieur, I'd very much like to do that if it is permissible."

"Of course Pieter, I know he thinks a great deal of you. I hope life will treat you well after this terrible war is over. If we do not meet again, I can only wish you the best of luck. How do you say it, *bonne chance?* *Bonne chance*, Pieter."

Pieter knew Rouen would be a step closer to Paris. He remembered the lovely village where Joan of Arc had her life sacrificed. He didn't want the same fate.

Once they arrived at the hospital and Sam secured in a comfortable bed, Sam gave Pieter a piece of paper with his name and address in Glendale, California. Through an interpreter, he told him to write and let him know where he was and how he was doing. "Make certain you do it in English," Sam laughed with the interpreter, and when Pieter heard the interpreter's translation, he laughed too.

Other than thinking about his parents, nothing more important occupied Pieter's mind. He remained with Sam until the orderlies came to take him to the train. Pieter and Sam said their goodbyes. Sam would be sent back to the United States and Pieter would continue his journey to Paris.

Meanwhile the colonel realized Pieter's information had saved many lives that battle day. He wanted to do something to help the young French lad.

"How would you like to stay at the hospital and work for Doctor Goodhue? I know you want to go to Paris. This will be a way to help you get there. And, maybe he can teach you some English while you teach him French."

Pieter worked long hours for Dr. Goodhue, following his orders and those of other medical personnel; running for bandages they needed, restocking supplies for the surgery. He talked to the wounded and lit cigarettes for them if they asked for one. He relayed messages. He helped set up another advanced dressing station where wounded could be moved quickly to the railway or other transportation.

Pieter, amazed to see soldiers on horses, spent some of his free time feeding and watering the animals. Seeing Pieter's gentleness with their horses, some of the cavalry soldiers allowed him to curry and otherwise care for their mounts.

The hospital in Rouen was a busy place. Each week ambulances would arrive with supplies from the Red Cross, and take soldiers to other locations.

"Pieter, come and talk with me." The doctor motioned him to a chair in his office. "Tomorrow, a contingent of soldiers will be walking along with the ambulances taking them back to a location near Paris," Dr. Goodhue told him. "You can go with them if you would like. I'd love to have you stay, but I know how much you want to return to Paris. I'm grateful for all your good work."

"Thank you. Thank you," a smiling Pieter replied.

The next day, Pieter started his long trek toward Paris. He joined a group of soldiers marching in single file on each side of the road at about an eight pace interval. All along the way he saw dressing-station doctors caring for the wounded. Ambulances were filled beyond capacity. They carried injured soldiers, while other soldiers walked beside the slow moving vehicles. The procession was continual and snail-paced. Soldiers sloshed along in the cold rain that would soon turn to snow. The road was a series of freezing mud holes. They took every step carefully because the water made the ground barely discernible, even though indented with bomb craters, rocks and other debris.

The journey seemed endless. Pieter didn't know what was worse – the rain or the freezing cold. By the time they arrived, at the clearing station, he was exhausted. They were somewhere on the outskirts of Paris, after having traveled almost two days with only water, and less than minimal food. At last, the ambulances stopped in front of a badly bombed-out church. Pieter thought he recognized it. He had been here once before with his mother and father. He knew he had been in this part of France before, but war had changed the landscape. The cathedral was only a shell of its former magnificence. The terrible damage made the night scene eerie. The walls appeared to be yellow from the light of the lanterns, and candles gray with age. Carpet, blankets or canvas covered window openings that once glistened with stained glass. The heavy oak doors were gone. Pews had been pushed to one side where soldiers could sit and talk or smoke.

Tired as he was, Pieter introduced himself in his fractured English.

"What can I do to help?" Pieter asked the man in charge. He told him what he had been doing for Sam and the captain. "I speak French and German also."

The doctor in charge was happy to have his offer of help. He sent Pieter on errands, checking conditions of the wounded and supplying cigarettes when he could find them. The Red Cross came from Paris in limousines supplying much needed medicines. When this contingent of limousines returned to Paris, Pieter was allowed to leave with them. His brief time with the United States Army was over. It was November 11, 1918...

CHAPTER 11

Washington D.C. 1953

"Oh yes, Mr. Sheridan, I must have been lost. My memories of those days poured through my mind."

"No problem. But your story was most interesting, and I'll be waiting for the next installment."

Peter laughed. "Well, if I'm going to be buying a painting at Sargent's prices, I guess I'll just have to come back and tell you the rest."

As Peter walked the few blocks toward his home, his thoughts turned to Sam Doty who turned out to be Evie's uncle. His daydream of Sam left him unsettled.

Paris 1918

Located next to the apartment house where Pieter found lodging, he saw a sign in a bistro window saying waiter wanted. Pieter cleaned himself up, combed his unruly red hair and applied for the job. Waiting tables at the bistro gave him a small salary and tips. Meals were included if he ate on the premises. After he became familiar with the routine, Pieter asked the owner for some paper and to borrow a pen. He wrote a letter to Sam telling him all about the latest happenings, where he lived and worked. Once he posted the letter, it was an anxious wait for a reply.

Weeks passed, and no answer. He walked over to L'Ecole and the building still remained boarded up tight. No one seemed to be on the premises. He looked for Jean Yves or Gilbert with no success.

Well, maybe it will open in a few weeks, the war hasn't been over that long, he thought.

As Pieter sat in his bedroom that night, he opened the knapsack he carried all the way from Cieux. He had forgotten about the papers inside. Pulling them out, he sat down to read them by lamplight. Pieter's mouth went agape as he read the words appearing on the pages. Baby boy born April 26, 1898 to American mother and English father, deceased.

The name of the mother was blackened out, leaving an empty line where the mother would be named. The adopting parents, Henri and Claudette Weiler took possession of a baby boy. Dated Paris, April 30, 1898.

"Those are my parents." Pieter exclaimed out loud. "I'm adopted," he gasped. "I'm part American and part English. I wonder who my real mother is. Why didn't my parents ever tell me? Maybe they were planning to and then that damnable war." Pieter's mind traveled a mile a minute as he digested everything he read. "I'll never know. Does my real mother have red hair? Neither my mother nor father did. Are my eyes the same color?" Pieter tossed and turned most of the night in strange searching dreams. Faceless images of women with red hair appeared to him. "When I get to America, I will look for her. Maybe Sam can help me."

Pieter's employer at the bistro, pleased with Pieter's job performance, promoted him to head waiter, and then as maître d'. Wanting to save as much money as he could, Pieter ate the majority of his meals at the bistro.

One afternoon, the postman came with a letter for Pieter. It was the letter he wrote to Sam. Stamped across the front of it in red was Party unknown. Return to sender. A crushed Pieter took the letter upstairs to his room. He set it down on his table, and pounded his fist. He picked up his desk lamp, and it was only his better judgment keeping him from throwing it across the room. He sat down in his chair and put his arms on his desk.

"Sam, where are you?" Pieter sent his words out into an empty room. He realized it would be up to him alone to secure enough money for passage.

A few weeks later, he discovered L'Ecole would be reopening. He signed up for some classes and told his professor he would be happy to tutor for extra money. "I can tutor in math or drafting," he eagerly told the man. He wanted sufficient money for a ticket to go study in the United States.

Several weeks after his initial contact with L'Ecole, he found Gilbert in one of his classes.

"Have you seen Jean Yves?" Pieter asked, leaning over to talk with his friend.

"I heard he may have gone to England. I haven't seen him since the day we all parted company."

145

"I want to go to America." Pieter blurted out. He then told Gilbert all that had happened to him since he left school on the day it closed.

It took Pieter almost two years before he scraped up enough money for passage, but he did it. And the bistro owner gave him some extra money as severance pay.

"*Bonne chance*, Pieter." He kissed Pieter on both cheeks. "Remember me, and send me a letter sometime. The bistro will miss you."

December 8, 1918 Glendale

Dearest Maudie,

I'm so glad to hear from you. Sam, thank the good Lord, came home in one piece. He had been wounded twice in France, but he told us about this young Frenchman who saved his life. He'll be starting medical school soon. Sam wanted to bring him to California but somehow they lost touch.

Evie and Steve are doing just fine and growing like weeds. I am so glad this horrible conflict has ended. Too many good young men are gone. I'm still rolling bandages for the Red Cross. You are so right. War is horrible. I hope and pray we will never see another one. Are you going back to Italy? I wish you would come and visit George and me.

I've been trying my hand at designing more sophisticated clothing, and I love it. My clientele seems to be flourishing. I would love to be able to make you a beautiful outfit. We may not be New York or Boston, but the opera draws all society around Southern California, and the clothes are beautiful. George and I attended one of the large galas, and I'll be catty and say I had the prettiest dress there. Of course it was long, but it had a full skirt with alternating panels of robin's egg blue and navy satin. The bodice was dark navy, off the shoulder neckline, trimmed in iridescent sequins. A long sash descended from the waist, navy on one side and light blue on the other. It had a pretty navy fringe. I made myself a long navy blue satin coat to wear with it. I also wore the Venetian beads a very dear friend sent me many years ago. When I came out of the bedroom George clapped his hands, and wanted to know what dress designer had spent his fortune on my dress. He thought I looked so elegant. So did I. It's fun to be writing happy things again. Much love,

Lillie

CHAPTER 12

1920 – New York City and Boston

Pieter kept pinching his arm to make certain everything was real. A steerage ticket was all he could afford, but now he stood on the deck of the ship, passing the Statue of Liberty in New York harbor. The pinching didn't stop until he was standing in line at Ellis Island, waiting to be processed to enter the United States. Almost 6'1" tall, he combed his neatly-trimmed red hair, and wore his best clothes, inexpensive but neat and clean.

"Open your mouth, please." They checked his teeth, his eyes, and went over his skin and hair with a fine toothcomb.

"Can't read your name, son."

"It's Weiler, sir." Pieter answered.

"Yeah, well you just had your name changed," said the man processing Pieter's papers. "Your last name is now Wells. It was too hard to decipher what you wrote."

Pieter Wells. Sounds like a good American name to me, he thought.

"Thank you, sir."

"Pieter Wells." When he was called to the other side of the gate, overcome with excitement, he took a deep breath. For a moment, Pieter thought he might cry.

Where do I go, where shall I live? All these thoughts went through his head. With the help of Sam and the rest of the soldiers, his English had steadily improved. He was so grateful. As the hawkers and the grifters looked for their easy marks, Pieter knew he was safe because he looked American and spoke English.

He found a cab and asked to be taken to a nice but inexpensive hotel, so he could get his bearings. He kept pointing to places, asking his driver to tell him what is was, where they were. It looked so different than France. The buildings were plainer. Many of them were wood. It looked like there were houses right next door to shops. Everything was clustered together. Not at all like Cieux. *Where were the fields and the trees?* Pieter hoped there would be time to explore. Once settled in his room, he checked to see his money was still safely sewn inside his pockets. He would have to find out where he could get American money. Pieter took out some of the French notes, but left the rest in hiding. New York was a big place, and the cab driver had told him it was not the best idea for a young man to be on his own.

The first place he visited was the library. Having been a student, he knew someone there who could tell him names of architectural schools.

The New York Library was a cavernous building with books on shelves everywhere. Pieter walked over to a woman standing behind a desk. She smiled at him. Pieter smiled back and told her what he was looking for.

"Do you have a library card?" asked the librarian.

"No, Madame. I just emigrated here from France. I have only been here one day. I'm looking for a university where I can study architecture." Pieter explained.

She opened a file cabinet and took out a small catalog entitled Massachusetts Institute of Technology. Pieter had heard about the Institute, but didn't know if he was qualified to attend this prestigious American university. Records from his schooling were destroyed during the war, and his schooling in Paris after the war had been sporadic to nil.

"Well, I can't let you have this because you don't have a card."

He recalled how waiting tables at the small Parisian bistro gave him the opportunity to use his English. Pieter decided if he were going to attend this institution, he would have to speak to the people in person.

"Where is this Massachusetts Institute of Technology?" asked Pieter.

"Just outside Boston. It's in another state, young man. You will need to take the train. I'm certain someone at your hotel can direct you."

"How much does it cost in American money?"

"About three dollars, I think. If you go to the bank, they will exchange your money to American dollars." Pieter had never thought about travel money. After Pieter learned all he needed from the librarian, she directed him to the closest bank.

151

"Just go out the front door, to your left. It's only two blocks, across the street."

"Thank you for your help."

"Good luck, young man."

The next morning, Pieter packed his shirts and pants in his suitcase, and asked the desk clerk how he could get to the train station. He was pleased to find it only a few blocks away. He found the ticket window and paid his fare. A six-hour train ride with no food left Pieter famished. He had loved sitting by the train window, watching all the new landscape of his adopted country. He asked directions to the university, and was pointed in the right direction. Pieter toted his suitcase for what seemed like miles, looking for a place to stay, when he saw a house sign that read *Rooms for Rent*. A tired Pieter brushed his clothes to remove some of the dust, shook his cap, and tried to straighten his thick red hair without a comb. With the cap back on, he was able to hide most of it. An elderly woman came to the door, and Pieter removed his cap.

"Madame, I am looking for a room to rent." The French accent was obvious. The little woman's blue eyes sparkled, and she answered him in French.

"It has been so long since I spoke my beautiful French. Welcome young man. Where are you from?"

It turned out they were from different parts of France, but it didn't matter, because Pieter knew he had found a nice place to live. What was even better, he discovered it was close to the architectural school where he wanted to study. He had walked all the way to the outskirts of Boston, trudging with his suitcase until he was literally inside the township of Cambridge. The Massachusetts Institute of Technology was located on the Charles River, close to where Madame Paget, his landlady lived. He hadn't even noticed the river he had been so intent on walking.

Madame Paget fed Pieter until he told her to stop.

"My stomach is so full I can't move." Pieter was ready to collapse on the bed for a good rest, his feet screaming tired from the long walk. The next morning, after a hearty breakfast Madam Paget had prepared for him, she gave him directions to the university. Pieter walked along the path adjacent to the Charles River until he came to the campus. The trees were leafy green, and reminded him of happier days in France with his family. "I can't think about that now, I have more pressing matters to contemplate."

"You want to attend our School of Architecture?"

"Yes sir," he replied in the best English he could muster.

"Well, how do I know you have the qualifications?"

"I was studying at L'Ecole des Beaux Arts, before the Great War began, sir. My father was killed in the war. My mother is also dead. I worked for the American army until the war ended. I can speak and read German, as well as French. My captain friend in the army taught me what English I know. I can read it slowly. I speak it better."

153

"You seem to be doing admirably, Mr. Wells."

"I know all my records from school have been destroyed, but I would be willing to take tests to show I am qualified." Pieter made a forceful reply to the Dean's questions. "I also need a job to help me get through school." Before the Dean could reply, Pieter added, "I can tutor in math, some science, German or French, sir. I know how to wait table and scrub floors. I will do anything to study architecture here."

Dean MacLaurin scratched his bearded chin, "Young man, you are just the type of ambitious person we want attending our university. You will, however, have to take some tests to qualify. If you pass, we can find work for you."

The results of Pieter's tests impressed the Dean. "Pieter welcome to M.I.T."

Pieter loved his classes. His English steadily improved with the papers he had to write. He applied much of the art history he learned from his years in France. Now he was able to understand the concepts of architectural design in the old buildings he remembered.

Someday, I'll travel there again, and really appreciate them.

He supported himself, tutoring math to other students. The School of Architecture at MIT, the abbreviated form he quickly learned, was based on the same principles as L'Ecole. Pieter knew his education couldn't be any better.

During his free time, Pieter wandered around Boston, went to museums, and looked at every new building site. He discovered a baseball team, the Boston Red Sox, and many weekends he could be found in the stands watching intently as the players batted the little white ball with a wooden bat, and ran around the diamond-shaped field. He was introduced to ice-skating, something he never did as a boy, and the wonderful game of hockey. Pieter, a natural athlete, had fellow students always asking him to come and scrimmage on the ice. With his tutoring, and other projects the Dean gave him, he was able to provide himself a decent living while studying and living at Madam Paget's.

Many times, he wanted to pinch himself. To think, eight years ago, he was foraging around the countryside of France with the American Army, dodging German soldiers, and saving the life of his newly found friend Sam Doty. Pieter's life as well as his English improved daily. He loved to sketch and often would sit on the grass at the Institute and sketch the buildings, dreaming of what he would build in the future.

All too soon these wonderful halcyon days of school were over and he was graduating. It seemed like yesterday he had made his first visit to MIT. Pieter almost danced across the campus in cap and gown. Madam Paget was the only one to see him graduate, but he didn't care. He had worked hard.

Now he was an architect, and he would receive a diploma from the 'Massachusetts Institute of Technology'. He would be licensed and gainfully employed in the field of his choice. After Pieter entered the senior architectural contest, he received inquiries from several firms. He debated about going to New York or to Chicago where so much innovative work was being built. Wooed by the New York City firm of McKim, Mead and White, he joined the premier architectural firm in the eastern United States.

I hope I didn't make a mistake going with McKim. They're not modern enough for my taste. I want to do more exciting projects. After two years at the McKim firm, Pieter joined a fellow MIT graduate, Raymond Mathewson Hood.

When Pieter first came to New York, he settled in a flat of a brownstone in Gramercy Park. He loved the sycamore trees planted around the perimeter. Although he didn't know their names, the cacophony of colors brought vibrancy in contrast to the brownstones that lined the street. Pieter loved the light airiness of his apartment, especially in spring. Every time he went outside, he breathed the fragrant air filled with the aroma of lilac blossoms. He watched the squirrels cavorting on the lawn, and the residents walking their dogs. It reminded him of the Place de Vosges in Paris, homes surrounding a small park.

As Pieter's bank account grew, he was able to enjoy the cultural aspects of the city he now called home. He enjoyed dining out, becoming a regular at Delmonico's. The pursuits of Wall Street intrigued him, and he became a serious investor. He devoured the business sections of the paper, looking for interesting stocks to purchase. Peter's place in society was also changing. No longer the war immigrant, he was making a name for himself in the architectural world. He had become a man about town even though no female had yet caught his fancy.

Pieter's financial acumen accompanied the growing size of his bank account. He was doing so well that when the owner of Pieter's building stopped to speak with him, Pieter asked him about buying the property.

"Mr. Wells, I decided to sell all my holdings and go west. My daughter lives in San Francisco, and since my wife died, I have no family in New York."

"I'd be thrilled to buy the brownstone." Pieter did, and converted the entire building into his home. Pieter felt all the buildings and the new skyscrapers should be built with windows everywhere, so views of the city would be even more wondrous.

Hood and Wells, from a simple beginning, became an auspicious architectural firm that would eventually cover both the United States and Europe. Matt Hood had won the competition for the Chicago Tribune Building in 1922, and Dean MacLaurin told him about Pieter Wells. Hood's first major commission was the McGraw Hill Building in 1931, and he and Pieter were the driving forces in the design of Rockefeller Center.

Pieter was called to consult on many new skyscrapers. Whether New York City, or Chicago, he made himself available. Matt sent Pieter to London to consult with English architects on building a large cathedral. His fortunes as well as his name were growing.

Thrilled to be in London, Pieter enjoyed walking down Maiden Lane, wandering through antique shops, browsing the bookstalls, staying at Claridge's and taking high tea in the afternoon.

On one of his visits to an antique store, he came across a damaged painting of a yellow cottage, surrounded by a garden filled with wisteria. In spite of its age and the smudging's on the lower right hand corner, the colors were so real. The yellow of the cottage, the faded orange door, and the splashes of pale purple from the blossoms seemed to jump off the canvas.

"Do you know the painter?"

"I haven't been able to decipher the signature, it's so smudged."

"The colors are magnificent."

"That they are, young man. It's my feeling Maud Driscoll is the artist. You know, she painted in Europe for many years."

"I want to buy it. Can you wrap it well so I can travel with it back to New York?"

"My pleasure, sir."

Pieter paid for his purchase and the shopkeeper handed him his wrapped package.

New York

Pieter and Matt had been working feverishly on architectural plans for the New York Telephone Company when a commission was received to begin drawings for the Chrysler building.

Pieter was overjoyed when Matt asked him to go to Paris to look at that city's newest buildings. Paris was building its first skyscraper. Peter felt the flying buttresses he saw on the Notre Dame Cathedral would be absolutely magnificent if they could be done in glass or with a great deal of glass and steel to support the weight.

The two of them usually would travel together, but two months earlier, Peter had been best man at Matt's wedding in Saint Patrick's Cathedral. Matt had no wish to leave Jessamyn, so the two of them would have their own cabin shipboard, and planned to roam Paris on a delayed honeymoon.

Paris

Pieter hadn't met anyone he wanted a serious relationship with and school and work kept him so occupied, he hadn't even tried to pursue it. Oh yes, he had a few dates after he started working in New York, but none of the women piqued his interest.

During the past few years, Pieter had become more interested in acquiring Maud Driscoll paintings. He felt drawn to the plein air style and boldness of her colors. So different from the straight lines and exactness of architecture. Certainly they were not as expensive as the Corot or Sisley that he already owned. Of course, they had been dead many years. Driscoll was still alive.

Pieter brought painting equipment because he was determined to do some painting along the Seine. Pieter knew Driscoll was from Boston, but spent most of her time as an expatriate somewhere in France or Italy.

159

He wondered if they both could have been in Boston at the same time. It could have been while he attended school and poor as the proverbial church mouse, not the rising young architectural mogul he had become.

Once Pieter had seen enough of the flying buttresses around Paris, and ready for another adventure - painting where Maud Driscoll had painted, he couldn't wait.

Pieter walked up and down the pathway next to the River Seine, studied the various angles and building structures, and then realized he stood at the place he had searched for, very near L'Odeon. He unpacked his brushes and paints, put up his easel and went to work. He deftly drew the background and then painstakingly attempted to paint the flower seller on the corner with the girl in the red hair and white apron buying yellow roses. That had been his latest Maud Driscoll purchase. Peter wanted to see if he could copy her style.

He watched couples strolling along, and smiling at each other while enjoying their walk. I wish I had someone I could share my life with. I remodeled my brownstone with all the latest furniture. I've added windows to make a wonderful sunroom, but I sit there each morning - alone. Pieter, stop being so maudlin. You're not even thirty. Go to those parties Matt and his wife are inviting you to.

Talking to himself always brought out his best resolve.

CHAPTER 13

*M*aud walked leisurely down the path that paralleled the Seine. She breathed in the aroma from the apple blossoms on the trees. She thought about her first visit to Paris with Priscilla and Neil; her apartment in L'Odeon. How long ago.

How old would my son be? Was he still alive? She thought about all the adventures that led her from continent to continent and back again. But she always returned to visit Paris.

Maud stopped to observe some of the painters. One of them was painting in her style. His colors were bold, the background muted. It captivated and also amazed her there were people who thought she was worthy of copying.

She watched the red-haired young man with the bushy mustache who seriously worked on his canvas. He stopped and looked up.

"Good morning." His accent had almost disappeared. *Why had he said good morning in English?* Pieter wondered.

"Good morning to you, young man. Where are you from?" Maud was enjoying the conversation.

"I live in New York City. And you?"

"I'm from Boston, but I spend most of my time in Italy and France."

"My name is Pieter Wells." When he stood up, he towered over Maud. He took off his hat.

"I'm Maud Driscoll."

"Oh, good Lord. Oh, Miss Driscoll, I'm so sorry. You are **the** Maud Driscoll! The painter I am trying so hard to emulate. My apologies, Miss Driscoll." He stumbled over his words. "I love your work. I wanted to see if I could paint in your style." He emphasized the 'if'. Pieter became silent for a few moments. "I walked up and down until I thought I found the right angle. Miss Driscoll, would you join me in a cup of coffee? I'd love to talk with you more."

"I'm quite honored, young man. If you ask me, I think you are showing some promising talent."

At a small café not too far from where Pieter had been painting, they ordered coffee.

"Would you like to paint all the time?"

"Yes, but it is not a very lucrative occupation. I'm an architect. I studied at MIT. Miss Driscoll, I own several of your paintings. I began collecting those years ago. My favorite is hanging over the fireplace in my living room. I just love it. I believe it speaks to me. Do you know what I mean?"

"Yes, Pieter, I do. Which one is your favorite?" Maud was most interested.

"It's a picture along the Seine, but there is a flower seller, and she is selling a bouquet of yellow flowers to a red-haired young woman."

Maud stared at him. *What is he telling me? That was the picture I was painting the day I received Neil's letter telling me he was going to marry Margaret Church.* She regained her composure, but the memories continued to well up inside of her. *I left that painting in Italy. I never imagined it would ever be hanging on a wall in New York, in this man's home. I can't believe it.*

All these thoughts were circulating inside Maud's head.

"I can't believe it. Do you think you might sell it back to me? It's a picture I had to leave behind when I fled Italy before the war. That flower vendor stood right outside the window of my apartment. The young woman in the picture is me. I painted it when I studied art in Paris. It was always one of my favorites, and I would love to own it again. That picture holds a great deal of sentimental value for me."

"Let me think about it." Then he looked at his watch. "I'm sorry, I promised my friend Matt and his wife I would meet them back at our hotel at 6:00 pm. We have theater tickets this evening. Otherwise, I would invite you for dinner."

"Perhaps the three of you would like to attend my art opening at the Duveen Gallerie. I have almost sixty paintings in the show, and they all are up for sale."

"We are staying at the George Cinq."

"Oh, what a coincidence. So am I."

"I'm just about ready to call it a day since the sunlight is changing. Are you going back to the hotel now?"

"No, I think I will continue my walk a little longer."

"I will look forward to seeing you again at your opening."

"Wonderful."

Pieter paid the bill, collected his art equipment, and accompanied Maud to the corner, where he hailed a taxi. So excited, he could hardly contain himself. "Maud Driscoll, Maud Driscoll. I can't believe it. Matt won't believe it either."

Pieter dialed Matt's room as soon as he returned to the hotel. "Matt, you just won't believe this."

"Pieter, you must have had some day. Are you drunk? Oh my god, your voice. You sound like a raving lunatic." He laughed. "What is going on?"

"I met her, I met her."

"Who's her? Calm down Pieter and tell me. I don't think I've ever seen you so excited, not even when we won the bid for the cathedral in London."

"Maud Driscoll. We had coffee together. She is staying in this hotel. She invited us to her art opening at Duveen Gallerie. I said yes, without even asking you. Hope it's okay."

"Why that sounds marvelous. We'd love to meet her."

"She wants to buy one of my paintings."

"Why?"

"Well I guess she can tell you. But evidently it is a painting that is very special to her. She lost it when she had to leave Italy before the war. It's the painting of the flower seller. She painted it in Paris while she attended art school."

"I'm Matt Hood, Miss Driscoll, and this is my wife, Jessamyn. Thank you so much for inviting us to your opening. I can't tell you what a fan you have in Pieter. He's a wonderful, creative business partner. I'd hate to lose him to the art world."

"Oh, you're an architect too. I think I can understand how you feel. When I was young, my parents didn't want me to paint. But my friends encouraged me. In fact, the year I spent at Academie Julien studying art, my English friends and one dear friend who moved to California from Boston thought if I didn't continue to paint, my life would be over. They were so right."

Maud wasn't sure why she wanted to bare her life to these virtual strangers, but for some reason they seemed more like family coming to visit. It could have been her living room, not an art gallery.

"Oh, tell us how you came to work in Paris?" Pieter was eager to know. He studied her intently, watching her movements.

"I could never tell my story by the end of the evening, but we will talk another time. I traveled from Italy to do this exhibition. Duveen is a friend of my agent. Once you have reviewed the entire show, then I will tell you about myself in detail. How much longer will you be here?"

"Only a few more days. Matt is teaching an architectural seminar at L'Ecole de Beaux Arts. Jessamyn is having a wonderful time shopping. I'm on my way to see Giverny. As you can guess, I'm also a Monet fan. Then I'm off to Normandy so I can see where my parents are buried."

"Then you weren't born in the United States?" Maud asked.

"No, I'm not certain exactly where I was born. I was adopted. I grew up in Arbon, Switzerland and then in France. When Cieux was overrun by the Germans, I decided to strike out for Paris, hoping an American would meet me before a German soldier captured me. My uncle owned a dairy there. During the war, I met an American soldier who befriended me after one of the last battles before the war ended. I was going to California with him. But I wound up in Boston when I finally immigrated to the United States. I went to MIT for my architectural degree. After graduation, I worked in New York for a large firm, and then Matt asked me if I would like to go into partnership with him. And that's my story."

"So, you're the Hood and Wells who changed the skyline of so many cities."

"That's us," they answered laughing.

"I'm more than impressed. But Wells, that's neither Swiss nor French." Maud said questioningly.

"No, at first it was Weiler, Kurtis Pieter Weiler. Kurt with a 'K'. I dropped the Kurt and Ellis Island changed the Weiler to Wells. And that was that."

"You have had quite a journey. Where are your parents?"

"They were both killed by the Germans during the war. I escaped. I never returned to my hometown, or any of the relatives I knew. I packed a bag, took what money I could find and set out to find my way. Now I want to go back there, and see if there is anyone left and to find my parents graves to put gravestones on them. I wasn't even sixteen then. I wanted to revisit how I grew up."

Maud knew she had to pry. She caught her breath and asked, "Do you know anything about your real parents?"

"Not much, other than they weren't married. That's what the adoption papers indicated. My father was English, and my mother American. But my adoptive parents were wonderful – I don't know anyone who could have been so blessed."

Maud couldn't go on. She was counting backwards. *I want to ask him his birth date but I'm afraid. Maybe after time has passed, I will. It will be difficult for me to unbury the past.*

The gallery began to fill with art patrons and genuine well-wishers. The art show, an impressive gathering of the art world and devoted entirely to Driscoll paintings. A main gallery where the larger

167

canvasses hung on the walls, plus two adjacent smaller rooms for the more modest canvasses. Large jardinières held fresh flowers, complimenting Maud's florals even more. The paintings themselves seemed to tell much of Maud's life - her time in Paris - living in her cottage in Tuscany. Artists from everywhere, as well as known personalities from every field had gathered to pay homage to Maud and her accomplishments, yet Pieter had a chance to speak to her. One of the things Pieter told her was he was leaving for Giverny in the morning, then he would travel to the south of France before returning to the United States.

How long will it be before I can talk to him again?

"I'm sorry but I need to go mingle with some of my other guests."

Matt looked at his pocket watch. "We need to be leaving anyway. Our dinner reservation is in half an hour. Jess, Pieter. Miss Driscoll, thank you."

"Thank you so much for the lovely evening, Miss Driscoll. I'll be back to the gallery. I saw another painting of yours I particularly liked."

"Would you please call me Maud? For some reason, I feel very connected, and I do not know why." Maud's heart raced, but afraid to venture further. There would still be time to ask Pieter for his birth date.

Pieter gave her his card.

"We never had a chance to discuss my painting you own. I truly would like to have it again. Think about it, Pieter. I would be happy to exchange it for any of my paintings at the show."

"I will, Maud."

When Pieter arrived in his beloved town of Cieux, he stayed at a small bed and breakfast owned by a dairy farmer and his wife. She was a wonderful cook, and the cakes and sweet breads with homemade jam and butter each morning were a real treat.

Pieter asked the farmer many questions, but he was a newcomer to the area. He suggested Pieter go talk to the village priest. So Pieter set out on foot to the local Catholic Church. He found an elderly priest in the churchyard weeding, raking, and doing chores Pieter would have hired a young gardener to do. The priest didn't speak English, so Pieter spoke with him in French.

"Yes, I have heard of the Weilers. I replaced the priest who was killed in 1918. Yes, there is another graveyard, not connected with the church, and not connected with any of the military cemeteries. Would you like me to take you there?"

"That would be wonderful, Father." Pieter was filled with remembrances of those terrible days when he was a teenager. There were bittersweet memories when he found his parent's graves. His grief, long held in check, overflowed. He cried for several minutes, then he went with the priest to the local stone cutter and made arrangements for headstones to honor his parents.

After accomplishing this, the pall lifted from him. True, his parents had been dead for many years, but he had wonderful memories and now he had honored them.

When he had completed all he could do for them posthumously, Pieter spent two more days in Cieux, and even took time to climb the 318 steps to the top of Mont San Michele.

When Pieter returned to New York, he asked Matt to sponsor him for citizenship, a proud day when the two of them left the courthouse. Pieter had legally changed his name to disconnect him from his sad past. He knew it would be many years before he ever went back to his hometown again. That chapter in his life closed forever.

Now Peter Wells, he had the world at his feet, good friends, and a wonderful career.

CHAPTER 14

$\mathcal{A}$ year later, Peter again found himself in Paris. It was July 14, Bastille Day, and Paris was celebrating on this warm summer day. He was enjoying his lunch at a sidewalk café, reminiscing how similar it was to the one where he had his first job. The pâté was excellent, and he savored the last bit of it spread on the remains of a baguette. He polished off the last cornichon, and squeezed the lemon rind into his expresso when a young woman stopped at his table.

"Excuse me sir, but may I sit down, there doesn't seem to be another table available? I've been walking on the Champs Elysees for hours now, and I need to rest my feet."

He looked at the young woman and admired the clothes she wore. Peter laughed. She was obviously an American. "Of course, but how did you know I am American?"

"I didn't. You just looked like the nicest man sitting here." As she flirted with him, Peter loved it, an unexpected pleasure for him. She was different from any woman he had previously met.

"Aha, well just to burst your bubble, I happen to have grown up in France. I am now an American citizen in Paris on a business trip. I live in New York."

"How wonderful, I live in New York too. I design clothes. Well, not really. I'm just starting. I'm an apprentice, but my boss thinks I'm a natural with

171

copying, so she brought me to Paris with her. I copy from memory all the designs she likes from the shows we see, and then we go back to New York, and she decides which ones would make the best sellers."

"Sounds like that would be very challenging."

"I suppose it is, but I do enjoy wearing all the beautiful clothes. I have a passion for beautiful fabrics and design. The more I learn, the more I want to be a recognized designer like my boss. Well, someday." The young woman's green eyes flashed excitement underneath her large lavender straw picture hat. Peter was intrigued. He liked the way her eyes looked directly at his. He didn't know much about clothing design, but he knew enough to realize this young woman dressed elegantly.

"What do you do in New York?"

"I'm an architect. My firm has built many of the new skyscrapers along Fifth Avenue. By the way, my name is Peter Wells. Yours?" He asked. "May I buy you an expresso?"

"I'm Sybil Meecham, and I would love a cup of coffee."

"Happy to meet you, Sybil. How long are you staying in Paris?"

"Unfortunately, we are sailing the day after tomorrow."

"Oh that's too bad," he lamented.

172

Peter and Sybil spent the next half hour asking questions about each other. "I live in a flat in the east sixties. What about you?"

"Gramercy Park."

"I love it there. All the trees and flowers."

"Do you like music?"

"Yes, especially the kind I can dance to."

"I'm not a good dancer."

"I could teach you."

"Sybil, may I call upon you in New York? May we have dinner together when I return?"

"I would like that, Peter. Here is my address, and I do have a phone." She added some numbers to the piece of paper.

"Here is my card, and I will look forward to seeing you again. Right now I have to be rude. I have an appointment in twenty minutes, and I must be on time. It was a pleasure to meet you. Enjoy the espresso."

CHAPTER 15

New York

Sybil introduced Peter to the kind of New York life he had never experienced before.

Familiar with all the trendiest night spots, Sybil went dancing with Peter at least twice a week. It didn't matter to Peter he lavished his money on Sybil. So full of life, she brought excitement and pleasure, and he loved being with her.

One afternoon, they were walking on Fifth Avenue, when Peter stopped in front of Tiffany's. The jewelry displayed in the window dazzled the two of them. "Do you see anything you like?"

"Peter love, what a silly question. It's all magnificent. I love it all." She gushed over the window display.

Peter saw a diamond ring he especially liked. He thought it would look beautiful on the fourth finger of Sybil's left hand.

"Let's go inside, darling." He escorted her to the establishment's front door and opened it.

They were greeted by a clerk who asked them to sit down at one of the counters.

"Sir, you have a ring in the left hand corner of your window. Could we see that please?"

"My pleasure."

The clerk returned with the ring. He laid out a piece of black velvet on the glass counter and placed the ring on it. Peter nodded approvingly and picked it up. He took Sybil's left hand and placed the ring on her finger.

"Not very romantic, but I love you, Sybil. Will you marry me?"

The clerk beamed. Sybil's eyes opened wide.

"Oh, Peter. It's beautiful. I don't know what to say. Of course the answer is yes."

Because neither of them had any family, they decided to be married by a Justice of the Peace at City Hall. Peter thought Sybil looked smashing in her silk taffeta wedding suit.

She explained to Peter, "The fabric is called peau de soie." A short skirt with a jacket that had a high-boat neckline, decorated with seed pearls. She made a cloche of the same material with a swath of fabric circling the base, pleated in tiny folds. Sybil's shoes were white and she wore long white gloves. Peter gave her a bouquet of stephanotis and bouvardia arranged with soft white netting and small green ivy leaves.

After the ceremony, a chauffeured limousine drove them to Tavern on the Green where the Hoods greeted them and had ordered a champagne lunch. Neither Sybil nor Peter could remember anything about the sumptuous food the Hoods ordered. They were anxious to start their honeymoon.

176

Peter had made arrangements with several hotels on the way to Niagara Falls, a splendid two weeks of wining, dining, and dancing, not to mention the moonlit walks Peter especially loved. Sybil preferred the dancing.

When they returned to New York City, Peter and Sybil settled in his brownstone in Gramercy Park. Peter gave Sybil carte blanche to refurnish the brownstone however she desired, and although Peter didn't particularly like her choices of furniture, he wanted to do everything he could to please her.

For Peter, a wonderful first year of marriage followed, but after the second, he began to feel like he was a coat rack whenever her friends came for cocktails. Sybil seemed to prefer being out in the evenings instead of staying home. The latest seasonal fashions filled her closets, but she never seemed satisfied. Sybil changed, almost imperceptibly at first, but Peter sensed her discontent. She never wanted to talk about her feelings. He could never get her to communicate with him about their relationship. She seemed happy only when Peter took her out to some smart new restaurant, or trendy nightclub. Then she would smile at Peter, and be very agreeable. Peter wanted her to stop working because he earned very good income and could support the two of them in a comfortable style. Because Sybil put up such a fuss, and refused to speak to him for days, a distressed Peter relented.

One day at her work, Eunice, the factory supervisor was in the washroom, modeling a dress she had made.

"Oh Euni, you really do look fantastic. Where did you get the fabric?"

"Out of the scraps our boss is no longer using."

"Didn't you ask her if you could have the fabric?"

"Sybil honey, it was in the disposal bin. I saw no need to ask her. You should take a look. There's some stuff I think you would really like."

Sybil felt Peter never took her anywhere where she could wear glamorous clothes, but the fabric striking her fancy looked perfect for twirling around a dance floor. A luscious shade of dark red with a sheen making the material sparkle under the lights.

"I've got to make a dress out of this. I've missed dancing so much." Her heart raced. Thoughts of going dancing with someone tall, dark, and distinguished filled her mind.

"Euni, I want to go dancing. I know Peter would never take me. Where can we go?"

"Just leave it to me, Sybil. There are a couple of salesmen from out of town who are here every month. They're always asking for a pretty girl who likes to go dancing. They really are a couple of swells. I think you will especially like Tony."

Peter thought Sybil acted distracted but said nothing. Until the evening she and Eunice had been planning arrived, Sybil thought of nothing else except Tony and his dashing manners. A sharp dresser, he looked like an experienced ladies' man. Typical Italian, Tony was the exact opposite of Peter. Black hair, swarthy in color, his piercing brown eyes danced in the light. Tony wore a heavy gold chain around his neck. He had an expensive watch, to match the expensive clothes he wore. Sybil figured his shirt alone must have set him back at least $50, even if he had bought it wholesale. Sybil realized the wifely routine didn't appeal to her. Peter was kind and charming, but a serious minded person. *I need to party, not be a housewife. I like nightlife. Peter is just too introverted for me. Tony seems more my style. Besides, he just loves to dance with me. And he likes to take me to nice places.*

"Sybil honey, where have you been all my life? You are one crazy lady. Just the kind I like. I'm going to Hollywood. I want to be an actor. Maybe you should come along."

"Oh Tony," Sybil laughed, and shook all her platinum blonde marcelled waves as she tipped her head back in rhythm to the music. *You're so rugged and handsome,* she thought to herself. She batted her eyelashes, outrageously flirting at him. "I can't imagine the studios wouldn't scoop you right up to be a leading man." Sybil basked in the excitement and fun Tony brought into her life. She wondered where it would lead. Tony had asked her to spend the night with him. She was debating how she could sneak away from Peter when the perfect opportunity arose. She wouldn't have to lie after all.

It was Peter who provided the alibi. He told Sybil he needed to go to Boston overnight for his firm.

179

"Will you be all right while I'm gone?"

"Of course, Peter, I will probably just go out with the girls." Sybil didn't even have to lie to him. But it was the beginning of the end. She brought Tony home with her that night. She realized she didn't care anymore. *Peter be damned,* she thought to herself.

Sybil wanted excitement, and Peter wanted his home. He loved to sit by the fire, reading and listening to good music. And he adored Sybil's company. For Sybil, being home was a chore. Whatever Peter did was never enough for her.

Peter had begun to make stock purchases in some of the companies whose buildings he designed. The stock market seemed to be expanding exponentially, and Peter's net worth increased at the same rate. Peter bought, bought and bought as he thought about venturing into real estate, and purchasing land where he and Matt could build office buildings.

One evening in early October 1929, while Peter read some business reports, he had an uneasy premonition something dire was going to happen to the securities market – and soon. With speculation at an all-time high, an unprecedented number of people borrowed money to buy stock at horribly inflated prices. They were buying anything. Peter knew he was predicting something disastrous, but the feeling didn't leave him. He had planned to buy a corner of Madison and Fifth Avenue, but the premonition was so prevailing, he gave up the idea. The next day he called his customer's man at Lee Higginson, and asked him to sell everything in his portfolio.

"Are you sure you want to do that, Peter? Everything is going up." The man was astonished, but did as Peter asked.

"Is there some way I can sell a stock, and buy it back, hopefully at lesser price?"

"Yes, it's what we call shorting. It's not done often, I would have to check and see if I could get the stock you wanted to short first. Is there any particular company you want to short?"

"Yes," Peter answered, "Sell about 1000 shares each of the ten largest industrials," Peter instructed him.

"Did I hear you right, Peter? That's an extremely dangerous thing to do. Stocks are going up, not down. That's all the money you had in the market and then some. I know what an uncanny mind you have for stocks. I won't dissuade you. Of course, it will give me a wonderful commission." They both laughed.

Peter's intuition proved to be true, and by the thirtieth of October, Peter was a millionaire many times over, while Wall Street brokers and investors who had lost their entire fortunes, had been jumping out of Wall Street building windows and committing suicide.

When Peter tried to tell Sybil of his great financial coup because of the market crash, she had little interest, except to learn Peter had a lot more money she could spend.

It was 1930, and four years into their marriage when Sybil discovered her pregnancy, furious, especially since she had been using a birth control device the doctor gave her. Peter wanted a child. She didn't. In fact, she wanted to leave Peter. She had been planning on telling him that she wanted to move to Hollywood with Eunice because the manufacturing firm where she had been designing dresses had been sold, and her boss was retiring. Hardly any communication of significance passed between Sybil and Peter.

"As good an excuse as any," Sybil thought. She had applied to all of the Hollywood studios to be a dress designer. She had applied for and accepted a position as an assistant designer for Consolidated Film Studios, without even telling Peter what she planned to do. Sybil thought the idea of Hollywood certainly more exciting than anything surrounding the life of a baby, even though she could have a nanny. She didn't want to be the lady of the house.

"I'm not going to let a sniveling brat keep me from what I want to do." She thought about all the fun she had been having with Tony, and seeing him again in Hollywood would be great. "He doesn't have to know that I've had a baby in between."

"I want no part of it." She emphatically told herself. "Babies, mewling fussy babies. Not when I can be doing something exciting in Hollywood."

"Peter, I don't want this baby," she told him matter-of-factly. "I would have had an abortion except I am too far along to do it safely."

Peter looked at her, aghast. "Sybil, how can you say that? I'm sure you don't mean it. I know we will have a boy, darling. You will feel much better as time goes along. You just have all the symptoms of early pregnancy. You know how much I love you. And we will both love our child."

"Peter, that's absolute rubbish. I am not the mothering type. In fact, I've been using birth control so I wouldn't get pregnant. I will have the baby, but you can keep it, and you can take care of it. Once more, you can also move out of this bedroom. I'm only going to stay until after the baby is born, and then I'm going to Hollywood. I accepted a new job with Consolidated Films, and Eunice and I have decided to strike out together. I want a divorce."

Sybil's words stung Peter, as he thought the two of them led a happy life. He took her to the finest restaurants; she had a closet full of beautiful clothes. He had even purchased an expensive emerald ring for her, something she had seen in a jeweler's shop window.

"Why didn't you tell me you were unhappy?" He hadn't cried in many years, but his eyes were watery, and tears shone on his cheeks. "Sybil, I love you. You have all the money you could want, a beautiful home, beautiful clothes. What have I done to make you so unhappy?"

"Not really anything, Peter. It's just that I like single life better. You make my decision seem like this is

183

the world's worst tragedy. I hear about people getting divorced all the time. I don't hate you. I just don't love you anymore, and I want to do something exciting with my life. You and a baby aren't part of it. I'm sorry Peter. I'm going out now. Don't wait up for me."

She picked up her satin clutch that matched her navy faille dress and the cloche she so smartly wore. She hurriedly walked across the room, left their bedroom, went down the stairs and out the front door with military precision. She never once looked back or stopped to give her words or Peter a second thought.

Peter couldn't believe the cruelty of her words. The pain he felt seared to the core of his being. His shoulders sagged. His gait mirrored an old man's as he walked down the stairs to his study, and slumped in his brown leather chair. Unable to comprehend why Sybil's unhappiness and request for a divorce had completely bewildered him. Peter knew he had to survive and survive well because of the baby.

When he regained his composure, Peter planned to retain a lawyer. He thought about all his adoptive parents had done to keep him alive. Who was my birth mother? Am I really half American anyway? I wish I knew where Sam's family lived. He hadn't thought about Sam since he arrived at Ellis Island, more than ten years ago. I'm going to be a father, and my child's mother doesn't even want him. Is history repeating itself? I want my child, and I want it to have a happy childhood.

During the months of Sybil's pregnancy, she hardly said a civil word to him except for yes and no. Peter worked long hours on a large project for the Irving Trust Company. In fact, he even had a bed installed in a

184

back closet of his office, so he could sleep there all night instead of returning to Gramercy Park.

Sybil's behavior belied the fact of her pregnancy. She didn't want to stay confined while pregnant, and spent her days shopping, at lunch, at matinees, and her evenings in the company of people Peter described to himself as "Hollywood" types. Sybil kept her body bound so the baby wouldn't show. She would not let the baby interfere with her social routine.

"Sybil, please. If you must go out, please think about the baby." Peter asked her. "Please be more careful."

"The hell with you, and with the baby. I'm not the baby's keeper. Now don't bother me, I'll be late for my dinner date." She slammed the door behind her before he could even reply.

At the very last of her pregnancy, Sybil became housebound because she was so large, and the binding made her even more uncomfortable. She wheedled and whined until Peter found someone to cater to her needs and to look after her. Peter made arrangements with the hospital where Sybil was to give birth. The hospital found a lady to come home with the baby.

Through Matt, Peter found himself a good attorney, who drew up papers Sybil would need to sign giving Peter custody of the baby, along with the divorce. An angry Peter gave her a lump sum settlement. He didn't want anyone saying he hadn't been generous to Sybil.

Sybil stayed at the Gramercy Park house until the day she went to the hospital. When she took a cab

185

to the hospital to give birth, Peter had everything she owned and any reminder of her packed into trunks and taken to a local hotel. He hadn't told her he was going to do this, but Sybil would not be allowed to enter the doors of his home again.

When Peter came to the hospital with the lawyer accompanying him, so Sybil would sign all the necessary papers, Peter told her what he had done.

"That's just fine with me. I already have my train tickets to go west. And I can't wait to get away from you, the baby and New York. Give me those papers to sign."

A screaming Michael Wells greeted the world with a full shock of red hair. Anxious to leave the confines of her room, Sybil didn't even want to see the baby. Peter never saw her again. He focused all his attention in non-working hours on his son.

A kindly Scots lady, Molly Harcus, a widow and nanny who had no children except the ones she cared for, saw to every one of Michael's needs. She adored her employer and her young charge, and began to prepare meals for the three of them. Little Michael loved to draw. And Molly forever watched his small hands given to drawing on the beautiful mahogany paneled walls of his Daddy's office. When Michael turned three, Peter invited Molly to live with them. He had a small apartment built inside his brownstone, so she would also have her privacy.

"Peter, I can't tell you how nice this is. Thank you so much for all your kindness. The apartment is wonderful, even the furniture."

"Michael and I have been lucky to have you come into our lives." Peter knew he had made a good decision. *Molly will always be part of this family*, he thought.

CHAPTER 16

1916-1930 – Maud

*W*ar years made travel impossible, so not by choice, Maud spent those years in Boston. She felt stifled by the stuffiness of Boston society, and longed to return to Europe. She too volunteered for the Red Cross making bandages during the War, but she didn't feel fulfilled with the assignments her mother managed to find for her. She would have preferred driving an ambulance, or something just as unconventional. Her painting suffered because she herself suffered. She worried about Priscilla and her husband Ken, as they lived in England. She worried about the little boy she never knew.

She and Lillie wrote continuously about what they were doing to help the war effort. Making bandages was just part of it. Maud felt satisfied knowing she was helping the cause. If only she were a nurse, she felt she could have been more useful. Priscilla managed to take a nursing course and worked as a volunteer at the hospital in her home in Essex. Kenneth, now a barrister, spent much time in trial. He applauded Priscilla's contribution to the war effort.

Maud knew when she could return to Europe, it would be to Italy. Then maybe the memories she created for herself would be alive and not buried in a cold grave in West Brompton.

In 1920, she sailed from New York, arriving in Rome shortly before summer began. The warm Italian sun welcomed her and Maud felt as if she had been reborn. She had come home. The fields were being tilled again. She could see the beginnings of grape rootstock planted in the vineyards. She smelled the clean earth, and saw groves and groves of olive trees. Hungry to have a place of her own, Maud, more European in her thinking than American, chattered in Italian like a native. Drawn again to Tuscany, it became her first consideration, with its red soil, the green of olive trees, the yellow and brown of sunflowers, all vibrant wonderful colors to put on canvas. She constantly painted in her mind, and the rich colors lay in wait for her to mix them on her palette.

Happy she had learned to drive a car, she purchased a little Horch 855, and set out from Rome. Just outside of Lucca, she spied a small 'for sale' sign. She drove tentatively up the olive tree lined drive to the crest and a breathtaking view greeted her. Maud could see the village below, the duomo sat in the center of the town square. She saw the red clay tiled roofs, like a patchwork quilt of reds and browns and clean whites hop-scotching over the terrain. She studied the house at the end of the dirt road. Old, but charming: with an area for a garden, she could make it beautiful again. This would be her new home. When she went to see the property she had purchased before the war, the house had fallen into disarray, the garden foraged by farm animals, the roof looked as if it would collapse at any moment. She didn't want to work that hard to rebuild it.

Just then, she saw an older Italian gentleman walking towards her from the adjoining farmhouse.

"Are you interested in the property?"

"Oh, yes."

"I'm Roberto Lunardi, and I'm the owner. Would you like to see the inside of the house?" He said in English. "You're American."

"Yes, I am, but I've spent so much time in Italy, I feel more at home here. Where did you learn to speak such good English?"

"I lived and worked in New York City for a few years and engaged a private tutor."

"The house also comes with seven acres. The land is not farmed now, but it is good for growing grapes. As you can see, you will have an olive grove."

Maud laughed. "Ten trees are still considered a grove?"

Roberto laughed too. "In Italy, *Si*. Do you think you might like to buy my house?"

"*Claro*," she said. Returning to English, "it will be nice knowing someone here also speaks English. Now about the price?"

"The price is $5,000 American."

"A little high, *signore*. What about $2,000 American?" Maud smiled at him.

They settled for a figure in between. Signore Lunardi also told her that he and his wife were her closest neighbors, and when he found out Maud was a painter, he was ecstatic.

"Mama mia, artista, che bella signorina."

191

April 19, 1921

Dearest Maud,

It's spring again. You have been telling me so much about Tuscany; I thought I would try my hand at describing this lovely community where George and I have settled. Glendale has become an incorporated town. How different it looks from when I arrived here with Mother and Daddy. Now there are more homes and few boarding houses. George and I live on a wide tree-lined street. The trees stay green all year round. In the spring, the acacia trees have beautiful clusters of yellow flowers. But they make me sneeze. Our house is only two short blocks from the center of town. So convenient, when I have to go to the market or butcher shop. We also have a pharmacy about three blocks from here, owned by someone who graduated from Glendale Union High School where I took my secretarial courses. It is nice to see shopkeepers one knows. Glendale is a friendly place - a very modern suburb of Los Angeles. Our church is across the street, The First Congregational. That's where we had Evie and Steven baptized. I never told you before, but when Evie was baptized, she kept saying 'flowie' 'flowie' until the minister gave her one from the huge arrangement on the altar. See, I told you she takes after you in her love of flowers.

While you paint your beautiful canvasses, I peruse cookbooks and magazines looking for tempting recipes. I asked George for a new sewing machine at home, so I can try my hand at making clothes from more intricate patterns. The shop doesn't have enough room for me to be creative. And I don't want to manage a larger store. I use Butterick patterns mainly, but I do love Vogue. They bring designs from Europe. You know me, of course, I have to embellish everything I sew. We have a wonderful fabric store on Brand which is our main street. I use them for fabric when I design dresses for the store. Of course, I get a wholesale price so it works well for Mama and me. One day, my clientele will be large enough so the fabric salesman will come to me. All my work is custom even though I may use a pattern at the beginning. Does the name Nell Shipman sound familiar to you? She grew up in the house next door to George and me. Her real name is Helen Barham, and now she is a star on her own, writing movies, and doing all kinds of interesting things. She actually asked me to design and make some clothes for her. I was extremely flattered, but I knew I didn't have the time. I told her I would help her select some patterns and fabric and find her a good dressmaker. I think George would have been unhappy even though he says I'm as good as the movie designers. I don't know about that, but it's fun. I really love designing and sewing beautiful clothes. I have two mannequins at the store, and George also bought me one for home. It's so easy to make the children's clothes. I don't know why, but I also find it relaxing to make shirts for George. He likes them too.

Our town trolley travels Brand all the way to downtown Los Angeles. I take the children for rides. Los

194

Angeles is the largest city in California, over 100,000 people. Although George prefers to drive, I'm not so adventurous. We do have a new Buick sedan, and it is quite luxurious. Since we have so much good weather, we are becoming picnic enthusiasts – either just us, or with friends and their families.

I love you, dear friend,

Lillie

CHAPTER 17

*M*aud spent a delightful summer readying her new
cottage. She named it 'Monte Bella'. She never tired of
traveling to Rome to buy larger pieces of furniture, and
loved wandering the streets of Florence looking for
accessories to give her new home character. She
shopped in the smaller towns of Cortina, Pisa or Lucca
for vegetables in open-air markets. Whenever she went
to Rome, she would go up the Spanish Steps, and eat at
one of the little *trattorias* nearby. They all had outdoor
patios where she could sit and enjoy a coffee and
pastry. Her tastes were elegant but simple. She loved
oriental carpets, upholstered furniture covered with
bright pillows. She wanted nothing in her home to
remind her of Boston, except the pictures of her
parents on her dressing table. On this table, she also
displayed photos of Lillie and George; the wedding
portrait Lillie had sent her, and photos of Evie and
Steven, her godchildren. Maud also had a small picture
of Priscilla, Neil and herself when the three of them
were on board ship. It seemed a thousand years ago.
She never stopped loving Neil, and was glad she and
Priscilla remained good friends. If all went well, Priscilla
and Kenneth would come next spring for a nice visit.

Through Roberto and Maria Lunardi, her
neighbors, she found a competent gardener and
handyman. Paolo had a green thumb, and within
months, Maud's garden filled with golden yellow, and
rust shaded chrysanthemums, bordered by pink and

197

purple asters. It even contained a small vegetable patch to grow the ubiquitous zucchini.

"And lots of salad greens," she told him.

To thank Roberto and Maria, her new neighbors, she painted a canvas of red, yellow, and rust chrysanthemums in a terra cotta bowl. The flowers sat on a table set by a window, so the painting showed the beautiful landscape outside. Everything about the picture was painted with painstaking accuracy. It didn't look like a painting. It came alive. Maud was pleased with the results.

"Maud, I can see our olive trees and the old brick road." Roberto exclaimed. "You even put in the roof of our house with the chimney. And part of our vineyard. You are amazing. We are honored." Roberto couldn't have been any more effusive in his praise. He was absolutely delighted, as well as he knew Maria would be.

Maud had turned one of the downstairs rooms into her studio. She had Paolo put in a large window and French doors. All this gave her wonderful north light, and in warmer weather, she threw them all open and painted on a small terrace overlooking the valley below. She also could see a small section of her garden. The blues of larkspur and delphinium spiked above orange and yellow zinnias and purple and magenta snapdragons.

Maud's painting was prolific. One could feel the breath of life and color on each canvas. Her agent, Freddo Pucci, had become a godsend.

"You're ready for more coverage, Maud. I'll see that you are shown in a gallery in Rome." Soon he added galleries in Milan and Florence. Then Paris and London.

Maud couldn't believe her good fortune. Before too long, people clamored to purchase Maud Driscoll Italian landscapes or her luscious florals. She made many new friends. As time passed, she and the Lunardi's had many dinners together.

"Maud, now Maria and I, we do something for you." It was an end of summer dinner party.

"Cocktails at eight? I'll be there with pleasure."

The air was still warm and delicious, so the party began with gathering for wine and merende on the terrace overlooking the Lunardi's vineyard which covered the hills and valley around them. Maud never tired of drinking in the beautiful scenery below the terrace.

Maria served crostini with marinated sweet red peppers, and skewers of melting cheese and crunchy bread cubes. The Lunardi's cellar provided the wine. Around ten, everyone entered the dining room for roast chicken with rosemary, roasted potatoes, and zucchini, shredded and fried in butter, with garlic. Then a beautiful green salad with lettuces that came from Maud's garden. Cheese and fruit, and zabaglione completed the meal.

At dinner, Maria had seated Maud next to an American businessman from Virginia. Maud found him delightful. Andrew Lewellyn was about ten years her senior.

"What brings you to this part of the world?"

"Well, one thing I do is broker wine. Roberto and I have been friends for many years, and when he told me he started producing wine, I wanted to see if it was good enough to import to the U.S."

"So what do you think?"

"I may be prejudiced, but I think it is pretty damn good. Where are you from, Miss Driscoll?"

"I don't think I've hidden my Boston accent that well, sir. And you are certainly no Yankee."

"No ma'am, born and bred Virginian. At your service, Miss Driscoll."

Maud could just picture the deep southern bow in front of a large southern plantation.

"Have you seen the Gardner Museum in Boston?"

"Oh, Mr. Llewellyn, do you know you are the first American I have met in Europe who has heard of it, yet alone been there?"

Their conversation could have continued for hours, but the party broke up, and Maud left. As they talked, Maud realized that besides his being such a delightful dinner partner, they both had a love for art.

"I've been admiring the beautiful painting you gave to Maria and Roberto, Miss Driscoll."

"You must call me Maud."

"My first name is Andrew. I would love to see your studio sometime, Maud."

"Whenever you like."

A few days after the party, Andrew arrived on Maud's doorstep with a large bouquet of summer flowers.

"You invited me to see your studio, so here I am. However, it looks like I'm bringing coals to Newcastle." He grinned.

Maud smiled and laughed. "I love flowers, Andrew. I never can have enough."

Handsomely dressed in a white linen suit, holding his straw boater in one hand, and the aromatic bouquet in the other he said, "I hope I am not disturbing your concentration, Maud."

Maud set her palette down and wiped her hands with paint remover. Laughing again. "Well, if you can stand to see me looking like this. Welcome, Andrew. I'm delighted to see you. Anna is fixing lunch. Will you join me out in my garden?"

"I'd be honored. Would you take these flowers from me so I can breathe?" About to sneeze, he managed to curtail it.

"Thank you so much for your thoughtfulness. Come and sit down."

Anna had prepared a salad of greens, and pasta with fresh shellfish she had purchased at the fish market that morning. A bottle of white wine from Roberto's vineyard had been chilling, making a delicious accompaniment. For dessert, Anna served the tiramisu she had been planning for dinner. She also served fresh peaches from the garden and some Gorgonzola cheese. Anna liked her employer's guest and wanted to do everything she could to make his visit memorable.

"Anna, you have a set a bad example for me. How will Signora Maud have dinner with me, if you cook better than any restaurant I know?" Anna smiled and waddled back into the kitchen.

"Well Maud, do you think you could stand a restaurant dinner, and then the opera as an incentive to go out with me?"

"I would love it, Andrew. When?"

"Tomorrow night, if that is not too short of notice."

"Oh no, I can manage that."

The conversation continued from one topic to another.

"Maud, I'm sure you've been to the Met in New York. I love the impressionists."

"Yes they are wonderful aren't they? I had the distinct pleasure of knowing Claude Monet when he lived in Paris many years ago."

Andrew told her he had been in the wine business, but had to set it aside, because the President had called him into his service.

"Last year, I came to the Peace Conference in Paris representing the United States for President Wilson. I accompanied Frank Kellogg for the signing of the Peace Treaty." Maud's eyes widened, impressed. "I was actually enlisted to hold the fountain pens!" They both laughed and then went on to other subjects. He told her of some of his other adventures.

Andrew stayed and stayed the afternoon.

"Andrew, I really must get to my painting while it is still light. Please don't think me rude but this has to be finished and sent to the states. I need at least a week before it will even be dry, maybe longer, depending on how thick the paint is."

"Could I take it for you, Maud?" I need to go to Washington DC for a few days, and I will be gone for about a month including my travel time."

"Are you sure, Andrew? I don't even know you. That seems like an awful lot of trouble. It is for my best friend and her husband. It needs to go to California."

"I hope you will get to know me better, Maud. I promise to take good care of it. Just get it wrapped for me, and I will mail it when I arrive in the states. It's my pleasure to do something for such a beautiful lady, who serves me a meal on a moment's notice that is fit for the gods." They both laughed together.

Several months passed with Andrew and Maud seeing each other whenever he came to Italy. It did not take Maud long to realize their relationship seemed more than friendship. Each time Andrew returned to Italy on business, their partings became more difficult.

One blissful evening, Maud and Andrew stood on the patio. He put his arms around her, hugging her and kissing her. Maud responded with equal ardor.

"How good it feels to be in your arms. Hold me closer, Andrew. I've missed you terribly."

"Maud, I don't like leaving you. I have fallen head over heels in love with you, and I want you to become my wife."

"My answer is yes. Oh Andrew, you have made me the happiest woman in the world."

"Would you like to be married in the states?" I own some beautiful acreage near Monticello in Virginia. I would like to give you the property as a wedding gift."

"It would certainly make it easier for my family, and I don't want to be married in Boston."

"I can understand that."

"But Andrew, darling, please come sit with me in the living room. There are some things you should know about me before you decide you want me as your wife."

"Whatever you're going to tell me doesn't matter."

Maud hoped he meant it, but she plunged right ahead almost as if she couldn't help herself. "I had a baby when I was twenty-two. I had to give him up for adoption because his father was fatally stabbed in a pub by a drunken patron. We never married, and my parents didn't want me back in Boston, unmarried and pregnant."

"Oh, you poor darling. What a terrible ordeal to bear alone."

Immensely relieved at his response, Maud then told him about Priscilla and Kenneth, both of whom she would like Andrew to meet.

"They helped me so much."

Maud proceeded to tell Andrew about her marriage debacle with Ted and how she ran away from Boston to Italy.

Andrew put his arms around her, holding her close. "It's all right, my darling. You're a survivor. Look at you now. You're beautiful. You're charming. You're successful. I love you."

Andrew was so accepting of her past life, it made Maud love him even more.

"Andrew, I remember a small church in Washington D.C., just off Connecticut Avenue. I think it's Episcopal. Do you think we might be married there? My parents could come down on the train. I don't want them motoring alone for that distance. Daddy is getting too old."

"Of course, my darling."

Maud made arrangements to shut down her little Italian villa. Selling it was out of the question. It had been her refuge, and a glorious place to paint. She knew when Andrew went to Rome on business, they could always come there for a vacation. Anna agreed to stay on the property. Paolo would continue to maintain the grounds, and the Lunardi's also were given a key.

The wedding was supposed to be a quiet affair, with a small supper at the Willard afterward with only Maud's parents there to celebrate the occasion. But Priscilla telephoned she and Ken were going to the states, and could they be present at the wedding too? So Maud also asked Lillie and George, but it was impossible for George to leave as he was in the midst of a very heavy trial. And Lillie didn't want to come alone, although George had said she should.

"Maud, I can't believe I'm talking to you on the telephone. It's amazing. I'm so sorry I won't be there to see you and Andrew married."

"Oh, Lillie, I'm sad about that too. I just wanted you to meet everyone. And to give you the biggest hug imaginable. Lillie, I'm going to put Priscilla on so you can meet her – at least over the phone."

"Hello Lillie, I'm very happy to meet you. Maud has talked about you since the day we met. And I remember that wonderful apron you made her for Christmas while we were at Wellesley."

"Priscilla, that was so many years ago. It seems like a lifetime. Maybe one of these years we will meet in person, and I will see my dear friend again."

Ken and Andrew hit it off immediately, and Priscilla and Maud had so much to say to each other. The foursome spent an extra few days together in Washington D.C. after Maud's parents returned to Boston. For their delayed honeymoon, Andrew and Maud went to look at the site where they would build their home. Andrew already had a lovely home on the property, but he wanted to give Maud the world which included a home in her own style. Maud could just envision what she wanted, a typical Southern mansion with porticos, and columns, wide porches, and a double-sided stairway in a large entryway. Andrew let her have free rein on what she wanted to do including finding the architect and crew to build her dream house. Maud had antiques in storage she wanted to use to decorate, but she accompanied Andrew on a few of his business trips to France where she purchased fabrics for draperies, and bought accessories to add to the ones they already had. With Maud's eye for color, Andrew knew they would have a showplace worth public display in magazines or newspapers. Andrew continued to pursue his international business interests, but he loved politics. His friend in Washington wanted him to take a more active role in partisan government politics. He and Maud talked about it often, and the lure of Washington was becoming more attractive than business. Once Andrew indicated he would be receptive to running for office, he accepted the nomination to run for the fifth congressional district in Virginia.

With Maud's assistance, the two of them waged a strenuous campaign. Maud's graciousness as a hostess and Andrew's candor as a candidate couldn't help but see him elected to office. Maud arranged teas, cocktail parties, dinner parties, and managed to see that Andrew shook the hand of everyone they met.

"Darling, you should be the one elected. You worked so very hard to put me here."

After the election, he and Maud purchased a lovely home in Georgetown so Andrew wouldn't have a long commute and a place where she enjoyed being hostess. Andrew also saw to it that Maud had a small studio, so she could paint.

At Christmas time, Andrew and Maud spent the holidays at their home in Southern Virginia. Andrew had located a large Christmas tree, and with the help of their gardener, set it up in the living room. Maud and the maid spent hours decorating it with ornaments from Italy and Germany.

"Maud, I would like us to take flying lessons," he told her in a quiet moment.

"Oh Andrew, that sounds like great fun. But I will let you learn, it's not my forte."

It soon became his passion, and each afternoon in good weather, he flew before returning home. He bought the latest Piper Cub and had it painted fire engine red.

"Maud, President Harding has asked me to consult with some of his cabinet members. He wants me to be in the Department of the Interior."

"Darling, that sounds wonderful, but won't you have to give up your congressional seat?"

They sat in their library having evening cocktails. Andrew picked up a canapé. "Yes, I really would rather stay in Congress, but I don't think I can turn him down. What gives me concern is there are too many of his, what I would call rowdy boys there, and I don't want to be saddled with finding myself on the wrong side of the president."

"Maybe the president wants you there as a watchdog."

"I'm not so sure about that. You know he appointed Albert Fall to be Secretary of the Interior. Fall is talking about taking all those oil leases and giving them to people like Harry Sinclair. I suspect he is taking kickbacks, and bribes or even worse. Sometimes, I think my life might be in danger, if I were to go to the president and tell him what I think is happening. He's really naïve as to what is going on around him. President Harding thinks everyone is on the up and up, especially if they are friends."

"But Fall is a Cabinet Secretary, do you really think he could do something like that?"

"Honey, I think he's an absolute thug."

"What are you going to do?"

"I don't know yet, but I will do something. It's really troubling me."

Andrew, well-known in the Capitol, his reputation was that of an honest and forthright congressman, as well as an astute businessman. Even though he spent a great deal of time with Maud at their home in Virginia, after he accepted President Harding's offer, he realized the new government was not as reliable as it should be. His consultation with regard to the Department of the Interior, and to some Oklahoma oil leases, made him aware without even going to Oklahoma to see the properties, something was wrong. As yet he didn't have enough proof to go public. Not having cabinet status, he wasn't privy to necessary information. But he felt the President had some very unscrupulous men surrounding him. He wanted to tell President Harding about Secretary of State Fall, but since they were close friends he was uncertain as to the consequences.

March 11, 1922

Dearest Maud,

George and I love reading the newspaper clippings you've been sending us. How I wish we could have been at your wedding. I'm so thrilled you're pregnant! How do you like living in Washington DC again? Andrew's work must be exciting and so stimulating. To actually be on the president's staff. I imagine all those gala balls are so splendid. I am turning green, dear one. I can tell everyone I knew you when you were a little girl with red braids and rosy cheeks. Are you still painting?

Besides my dress salon, I have become a club lady. I guess that is what one would call it, but you would be so proud of me, Maud. I marched in a suffragette parade, and Dr. Jessie Russell and I have become very good friends. Even George likes her. She can be so opinionated; but she's very progressive, even though she is a Republican. Through her, I was asked to join the federated women's club, and after she served two terms as president of the Los Angeles County Equal Suffrage League, I followed her as president. Politics has connected me to influential Republican men and women around the state. The reason I sought or value her friendship was because I also believe women need to continue to organize separately from men even though we work alongside them in some political milieus. But I also believe women shouldn't be self-serving or self-seeking in our political actions. George calls me his little politician. He's very happy for me I think, because I have found something with intellectual ramifications that interests me.

I am finding politics fascinating, and I have to say I'm sorry about prohibition, because George and I enjoy our evening glass of wine – and now we can't even buy it. George is talking about going to a place called Cucamonga; (it's about thirty miles east of Glendale), and buying grapes, bringing them home and making wine in our basement. I imagine you saw a lot of that in Italy. By the way, we so enjoyed the wine you sent us from there.

We have a wonderful theater here that shows Charlie Chaplin films. George and I almost love more to listen to the musical accompaniment rather than watch the screen. But Chaplin is funny. And I love the clothes Gloria Swanson and Lillian Gish wear in their films. You can just imagine clothes are becoming more and more glamorous. I have put my sewing skills to good use, and people tell me I'm just as good as any designer in Hollywood.

You know, Maud, I wish I could have gone to college. All the women I meet today are so well-educated. Even though I read everything in sight, it still isn't enough for me. Maybe someday. I keep it in my heart as part of my wishes. But I have a wonderful husband, and a wonderful family, and they do take up the majority of my time.

Oh, Maud, George and I have your beautiful new painting hanging in our new dining room. Yes, we bought a new home, Spanish style architecture, and moved to a different section of Glendale - larger rooms, lots of trees, more property. We love it. The common phrase of our dinner guests is what a beautiful painting. George and

212

I agree. They are very impressed when I tell them the artist is my best friend.

I can't believe it's been over twenty years since we've seen each other. One of these days, George says we may just show up on your doorstep. We do have a new telephone number now. It's Citrus 21. I'm so glad we can talk and at least hear each other's voice. I'm beginning to think I'll never leave California, even for a visit. Oh, my life is so dull compared to yours. Yet I am happy and almost content. George is a wonderful husband, and he, the children and I are all fine and healthy.

I must close now - ironing is piling up in my basket. Now that would be a luxury - someone to do all the family ironing. It's going to happen. George says I don't need to work so hard, especially now that we have a new home to decorate. My dear George.

I love you, Maud.

Lillie.

P.S. I still want us to correspond.

April 25, 1922

Dearest Lillie,

I lost the baby. It was a boy. He only lived a day. Something was wrong with his lungs. I wonder where my first child is, and if he's happy. Maybe I'm being punished, Lillie. I wanted a baby so much. Right now I'm so depressed; I can't even think to write more than a few words. Andrew is sending me to the Saratoga Spa for a month's recuperation. He will come up every weekend by train. I wish you could be with me. I don't even feel like painting. I can't sleep. I just want to lie in a bed in a dark room. But, oh it would be so wonderful to sit and talk with you. I have political ideas too. And please forgive me for being so short in my letter.

Hug everyone for me. Kisses too. I love you.

Love,

Maud.

CHAPTER 18

A few months after Maud lost the baby, Andrew unexpectedly needed to travel to Italy on business. He also planned to see the Lunardi's. It was a trip that couldn't be put off. Maud and he expected Lillie and George to come and visit them in Washington, but Andrew wanted Maud to accompany him to Italy.

"Darling, the Lunardi's will be devastated if you don't come. I truly want you to come with me. Roberto isn't well, and I know seeing you would perk him up considerably. Lillie and George will understand. Perhaps we can go on a short trip to Greece. You've never been there, have you? And I promise you, I'll take you to California to see the Patterson's next year."

"Of course, my darling. Is it still all right with you if the Patterson's stay in our home? Gazetta can come in the day, clean and do whatever is necessary to keep the house in order."

"Please, do let them come here. I know I've disappointed you, springing this on you at the last minute."

"You couldn't help that, my darling. I'll go with you, of course."

When Maud and Andrew returned from Europe, she found a thank you letter from Lillie, waiting for her on her dressing table.

CHAPTER 19

"Lillie."

"Maud is that you? You sound so strange."

"Andrew's gone. He's dead."

"Maud darling, how did it happen? I'm devastated for you."

Maud began crying into the phone. Through her tears, she answered "In an airplane crash."

"Dear God. Maud, George and I are so sorry for your loss."

"The funeral is next Saturday morning."

"Did Andrew crash his plane?"

"We think someone tampered with the engine so it would crash and kill him."

"You mean he was murdered?" Lillie was almost speechless.

"Pricilla, Ken and I believe so." Maud tried to dry her tears and become stoic, but it didn't work.

"Is your mother there with you?"

"No, Priscilla and Ken happened to be here on a visit from England. They were staying with us when he was killed."

"I'm so glad you have someone close to you. I don't think you should be alone."

219

"They'll stay with me until after Christmas."

Lillie called back again on Christmas day.

"Maudie, dearest, won't you please come stay with George and me? The children would love to meet their Aunt Maud."

"Oh Lillie, I can't believe he's gone." Maud could feel herself tearing up all over again.

"I can't either, Maud. You have George and my deepest sympathies. Do you still believe that someone tampered with the engine?"

"Yes, I do."

"You must feel absolutely devastated, you poor darling."

Lillie was receiving simple yes's and no's from her questions. And President Harding, he won't help you?"

"He's absolutely washed his hands of the whole thing. He wouldn't even see me or talk to me, except at the funeral."

"Oh Maudie, how isolated you must feel. Is there anything we can do to help?"

"I just want to return to my home in Italy. It's where I've spent my happiest times."

"I know how badly you want to leave Washington now. Will it be difficult to sell your home in Virginia?"

"I don't think so, Lillie. I so appreciate your love and concern."

"Maud, George and I would love to have you come to California. You know how much we love you."

"Thank you so much, Lillie. I'll be fine. It's just good to hear your voice. I will go back with Priscilla and Ken to England, and then on to the continent. You know I'm a survivor."

"Yes, I know that. Just remember how much your friends love you, and if we can do anything at all, we will."

"I know Lillie. I'll write to you as soon as I get settled."

March 1924

Dearest Lillie,

I'm back in Italy now. I can't thank you both enough for all your concern. Now I can look objectively at Andrew's death, and no, I don't think his airplane crash was just an accident. He had been telling me about all the rumors flying around the capitol, and he felt many of them were true, especially any rumors regarding the oil leases in Oklahoma. He had only started his investigation when his plane crashed. Several of his former colleagues in the House want me to file a lawsuit and start an investigation, but you know Lillie, I just want to mourn privately. If they want an investigation, they have my blessing. I'm certain Andrew would want them to also. Me, I'm too overwhelmed.

After President Harding died, President Coolidge didn't want to or wouldn't help me. Kenneth told me two of the men Andrew was suspicious of, Harry Sinclair and Edward Doheny committed suicide, and I'm sure former Secretary of the Interior, Albert Fall will go to prison. I hope so. In my heart of hearts, I feel he had something to do with Andrew's death. But, as I said, I'm just too worn out now. As soon as I can dispose of the property in Virginia, I hope to make this move to Italy permanent. I'm so much happier being an ex-pate. Hopefully, there will be no more war. I want you and George to come visit me. I love you, dear friend. Thank you for being there for me. Love,

Maud

April 12, 1924

Dearest Maud,

George and I were happy to read you're living in your little villa again and painting is occupying most of your days. A party at a Baron's? Royalty? That sounds like something you read in fairy tales. You wear beautiful clothes, attend parties that make your world seem unreal while I wear an apron and use a vacuum cleaner. I did get a part-time housekeeper though. Oh, Maudie I really shouldn't complain. I have my club life. George and I go out often. Los Angeles has a wonderful symphony. And I do get to wear nice clothes now and then. What do you think of me in the picture I've enclosed? I actually designed the dress myself, and I have received numerous compliments. It's a pale gray, and George bought me a gray fox collar to wear with it. Fox cuffs too. I'm wearing my hair in a French twist, with spit curls at my ears. How diverse our lives have become. Please forgive me for complaining. My life is really very complete. Evie is going to college this fall. She won a full scholarship to the University of Southern California. We are so thrilled for her. It seems like yesterday when she was born.

George and I found a piece of property and decided we would like to build a house. The lot is covered with pine, oak, and sycamore trees. I'm sure we will have to remove some of them in order to build. It's on a small hill and overlooks the entire valley of Glendale. It's in a new area just being developed.

The children are all healthy. Even though you have never seen Evie except in pictures, she has many of your traits including the fact she loved to draw as you did.

225

Now she is interested in writing. At least before she starts college. She studied French and German in high school, so maybe she will get a degree in a language and teach. She's very undecided at the moment. All I know is she has peripatetic feet, and says, "Mom and Dad, I really want to travel. I will figure it out, somehow." I really think she wants to come and visit you in Italy. I would love to have her do that, even though I can't come. And Steven, I hope he will take after George and become a lawyer.

Love,

Lillie

October 11, 1928

Dearest Maud,

It's hard to believe. My first-born has decided to test her wings and go off to Washington D.C. I'm not certain exactly what her job is, as she hasn't elaborated on it but she seems to be enjoying it. She's working for Senator Johnson from California. It's quite an honor for a young woman. George and I are so proud of her. See, the world is modernizing. From what she says in her letters, she's interested in all her surroundings, and learning about D.C. She still hasn't mentioned a man in her life. I guess I should be happy because I think she is too young. Of course, a mother always thinks her daughter is her baby.

Evie told me she has a very nice apartment on Seventeenth Street. It's a block or so from Connecticut Avenue, so bus transportation is close by. George asked her if she wanted to have a car there, and she said no. I wish you were still in D.C. so she would have family near. But, I know you are enjoying yourself in Italy, and it's about time. George and I worry about you almost as much as we worry about Evie. Evie says she loves visiting all the monuments and museums. She told me she and a girlfriend went to New York for a weekend, and stayed in the Algonquin Hotel and went to the theater. She said the hotel was full of celebrities, and it was such fun just people watching. She recognized Tallulah Bankhead, Alfred Lunt, and Lynn Fontaine. Can you imagine? "I get to visit there vicariously as Evie's descriptions are quite vivid. Steven is just fine, and will be a senior in high school this year. He wants to go to Stanford. We would love to see him go there as the law school has a fine reputation. George and I send you our love. Much love,

Lillie

CHAPTER 20

Tuscany, Italy

Giovanni da Neri, owner of the neighboring villa was charming, a few years older than Maud, he had been widowed during the First World War. He was a hardy specimen of a man, muscled from all his work in the fields with his grapes. In spite of his title, he was down to earth, and approachable. Had he been given the choice, he probably would never have used it. Giovanni stood about 5 feet 10 inches tall, brown eyes, and his once black hair was now prematurely graying around his temples, skin ruddy from all the sunshine. da Neri also respected Maria Lunardi, Roberto's widow. Roberto passed away about five years earlier; shortly after Maud and Andrew had made the trip to Italy to visit him. Giovanni had purchased all the land from Maria and had built his new house on the highest point of the hill. Maud had been in Washington with Andrew when all this occurred. Although captivated by Maud, da Neri kept his distance as she was newly widowed.

Maud, content to be his friend and be seen in his company, was relieved Giovanni made no advances toward her.

Maud had started to paint again, and prolifically. She reconnected with her old agent Freddo Pucci. Freddo couldn't wait to plan a large one-person exhibition for her.

"In Paris, of course, if it wouldn't upset you."

"Yes. Yes, Yes, Freddo."

229

Maud would paint all day in her studio, stopping for a quick bite of lunch that Anna would bring to her each afternoon. Even the food looked like a painting so artfully placed on a yellow, orange, and cobalt blue majolica plate.

"Anna, you're going to make me fat with all these beautiful dishes. The ravioli is scrumptious. Are the vegetables and lettuce from the garden?"

"Si, Signora Maud. I picked them this morning."

"Baron da Neri has invited me out for a picnic on Sunday afternoon. I hope the weather is as beautiful as today."

"Do you want me to press your silk pants and blouse?"

"Would you please? I think the black pants, and the pale yellow blouse with black trim will be just perfect. I'll wear my new straw hat."

Maud thought about all the times the Baron had taken her out or they were both guests at the same party. He was so solicitous to see she was comfortable in her surroundings. It had been almost four years since Andrew was killed in the plane crash. She began to have feelings for Giovanni. Knowing how romantic an Italian man could be and not feel anything but the romance of the moment, she wasn't sure she should be going out with him so much. He filled a place in her heart that had been empty for a long time.

"I truly never thought I would fall in love again." She was having a monologue with herself. "I loved Neil. I bore him a child I couldn't keep. I know he placed himself in harm's way so someone would kill him. Ted was certainly the mistake of the century. I wouldn't have married him had I had any idea he was homosexual. And Andrew, my dear love, who brought me so much joy, taken away from me at a turbulent time in the American government. I'm so glad all those miserable men paid the price for killing my husband because of their greed. He had such a great future in government. Giovanni is different than any man I have known before. He's charming, but a man of the earth. I think I will just have to wait and see."

It was a mid-summer Sunday. The day was warm, a cloudless sky, and the vineyards were heavy with clusters of grapes hanging from their green branches, just waiting for the sugar to be at its best. Maud planned to meet Giovanni at his home because he had to be out supervising his workers in the morning. She left Monte Bella with about a thirty-minute drive to reach Giovanni's home. Maud had asked Paolo to put the top down in her little Alfa Romeo. *Windless day. Shouldn't mess my hair.*

As the car rounded the curb a large truck approached. It didn't stop. Maud's car was clipped on the side, and it went hurtling, rock and fenders screeching as they met. The car flew over the side of the road throwing Maud from her car where she lay crumpled in a heap. Her hat landed on a patch of grass about ten feet away from her. The truck went barreling on.

Meanwhile, Giovanni anxiously waited for Maud to arrive. When she was about two hours late, he called Monte Bella.

"Anna, when did la signora Driscoll leave?"

"Signore Baron, la signora Driscoll, she left over two hours ago. She's not there? She was so happy about the picnic today. You go find her, Signore Baron."

"Angelo, come quickly," yelled Giovanni. Angelo Cimino, his foreman came running. His little boy Dario was with him.

"I need to take my car to go and find la signora Driscoll. She was supposed to be here over two hours ago. You and Dario come with me."

They all climbed into Giovanni's Mercedes, and began to back track towards Maud's home. When they came to the curve, just a few miles from Monte Bella, they saw the overturned smashed sports car. Giovanni immediately stopped the car, and the three of them got out and began looking for Maud.

Dario went over the little rise where Maud had been thrown. "She's here. She's here." He excitedly yelled to Giovanni and his father. Giovanni and Angelo came running. When they came to her body, she made moaning sounds, but not saying anything intelligible.

"Don't move, darling. I'm going to get you to the hospital."

"Angelo, help me carry la signora to my car. Dario, bring me the lap robe in the back seat. There may also be one in the trunk. Hurry now. Both of you help me put her into the back seat."

Maud dozed in and out of consciousness. The doctor had given her medicine to relieve the pain. He had put her arm in a cast. "She's lucky only her arm was broken. She could have been killed. Baron, we will have to wait a few days to see if there was any head trauma. It doesn't look like it, but I want to be sure."

Giovanni never left Maud's side. He ate and slept in the hospital until she regained full consciousness. He held her hand, and whispered to her. Fully awake, she looked at her surroundings – green hospital walls. She saw Giovanni asleep in a chair in the corner. Several large bouquets of flowers filled the room.

"Giovanni. Giovanni, what happened? I feel very strange."

"Oh Caro, you were in a terrible accident. Your car rolled over into the ditch, and you were thrown from it. Can you remember anything that happened?"

"A big truck came barreling down the road, and never stopped. What about my car? Is it repairable? How long have I been here?"

"Three nights you have spent in the hospital, Caro. Today is the fourth day. Now we can ask the doctor when you may return home. I'm so pleased you are going to be just fine. I couldn't live if I knew you had been killed in that accident." He went close to her bed, and took the hand of her good arm. "Caro, I love you so much. Do you think you would be happy to be married to me?"

"I've fallen in love with you too. But I can't marry you like this, Giovanni." She smiled. "I'm in a hospital gown. My left arm is in a cast. How can I marry you, darling?"

Giovanni gave a big laugh. "Just so you will, Caro."

"I'm not Catholic, Giovanni. I've been married before."

"Yes, I know, Maud, but when you are well, we will go see the priest at San Giovanni Church. He is my cousin. He will tell you what to do. There should be no problem since you are a widow. All you will have to do is talk with him a few times, and sign the registry."

"Will you come with me?"

"Of course, my darling."

"I spoiled our picnic."

"It doesn't matter. We will have lots of others."

"I can't have children."

"It's alright. We will have each other."

The doctor wanted Maud to spend two more nights in the hospital. On the day she could leave, Giovanni took her home. Happy to be home and in her own bed, Anna couldn't have been more solicitous or helpful.

"Giovanni, I'm going to need another car. Would you please take me shopping for one? I think I'm through with sports cars. How about a small Mercedes?"

Giovanni laughed. "As soon as you feel able to move about easily, we will go."

Three months later, Maud and Giovanni stood at the altar of San Giovanni Church, the oldest Catholic Church in Lucca and recited their vows. Maud had visited this site many times before she had even met Fr. Umbertod da Neri. The church was an historical treasure, and she had sketched pictures of the inside. The sun illuminated the stained glass windows. Maud and Giovanni decided they didn't want another wedding except for the needed witnesses. After the grape crush, they would give a large reception to tell everyone they had been married. Maud looked radiant. Her arm had healed perfectly. Giovanni had driven her to Florence to buy her a magnificent trousseau.

For her wedding, Maud decided on a luscious pale lime green silk suit with matching lime green straw hat and veil. Her shoes were the finest Italian beige suede leather. She carried a bouquet of two huge white peonies surrounded by baby's breath.

They couldn't travel far on their honeymoon, as much work needed to be done in the vineyards. Angelo couldn't do it alone. So they drove to Viareggio, a coastal town where Giovanni had reserved a hotel suite overlooking the sea. He and Maud were content to walk the beaches, and wander the seaside area rich with beautiful gardens and flowerbeds which were a riot of color with rust, burgundy, gold, pink and white chrysanthemums. The leaves on the trees were turning also, indicating it would be fall and crush time very soon.

Crush season, the time the grapes are harvested, never lost its fascination for Maud. She watched the workers in the fields, cutting the clusters, filling the box with the grapes, and then carrying it to the end of the road where the grapes could be loaded on a horse-drawn cart to the area for the actual crushing. Even Father Umberto was there to bless the harvest. So much had to be done by hand. Giovanni and Angelo worked side-by-side straining the juice, letting any stems and skins remain on one side of the strainer, and the juice dropping into a waiting vat. The vats were filled with the juice, and would be set out to age in the cellar. The skins would be crushed again, and the remaining juice put into another vat. This would be the *picholo* they would drink every night at dinner.

November 10, 1928

Dearest Maudie, or should I say Baroness da Neri,

I can't believe you live in that palace. It looks incredible, and the countryside absolutely breathtaking. George and I would love to come, take a ship to Genoa or Venice, and then hire a car and driver to see you in Lucca. He has said we can come next year. We are waiting with eager anticipation to taste Giovanni's wine.

One of George's clients is old Mr. Brand himself - yes the main street is named for him, and he is the mayor of Glendale. He is quite an eccentric old bird. He constructed himself a house and named it 'El Miradero' and built an airfield in front so his buddies can come and visit. He throws these lavish parties. George and I have been to several. And the people we have met! Would you believe I met Amelia Earhart, who flew her own plane here, and Charles Lindbergh? I know you must meet celebrities every day, but this was new for me. And you know what? They are just like anyone else. Now, if I met some movie stars - that would be exciting. They lead such glamorous lives, at least that is what I read in those movie magazines when I have my hair done. I can tell you George is very proud of me since my clothes looked like they come from couturier salons. Well, the patterns began as Vogue but I made my usual changes. I made a chocolate brown faille suit trimmed in black braided cord I hand sewed and decorated on the front and the sleeves. It was very smart, and I had a new brown cloche with a small black cord decoration to match. You would have been so pleased to see how I looked. George and I even made the papers, but

237

you could hardly see me. Otherwise I would have sent the article.

One night a week, George and I play duplicate bridge with several other couples. Do you know how to play? It's a marvelous game. I do enjoy it. It makes me think.

It is so easy to drive a car since highways are being built all over California. George and I have been taking weekend trips about once a month, jaunting all over the state. One of the newest phenomena in California is swimming pools. We're getting ready to build our dream house and will also put in a pool. I certainly wish someone would design a bathing costume that didn't make me feel like I would sink to the bottom every time I went in the water. Maybe that is a future project for me.

George and I are meeting with the architect next week. You have no idea how excited I am.

Love,

Lillie

P.S. The children are thriving.

September 10, 1928

Dearest Mom and Dad,

Oh, why didn't anyone tell me how wonderful and exciting Washington D.C. is? I love working here. I only wish I could tell you more about my job. I work in the Senate office building. Senator Johnson's office is by no means luxurious, but I'm awfully busy. It's been an interesting time. If he doesn't run for re-election, I think I will still find another job here.

I am making a lot of friends, and have been seeing about as much of the countryside as one could imagine. Virginia is absolutely magnificent in the springtime so I am told. I can't wait to see all the daffodils. Of course, a picture, unless painted wouldn't do it justice. Too bad Aunt Maud isn't around so she could do it. I wonder if Aunt Maud painted them when she lived in Virginia. The open fields sound just like something beckoning her. She would sit right down, set up her easel and paint. Every once in a while I hear Uncle Andy's name mentioned, and how sad it was he died so young. I don't hear anything more than that, but I begin to wonder too, if he was murdered. There has been a lot of cleaning up as you can well imagine with all the scandals over the past few years, The Teapot Dome being the one most often mentioned. Mr. Fall finally ended up in prison. I

know Aunt Maud would like to know that. Dad, I hope
you aren't working too hard, and that you and Mom are
having fun getting ready to build the house. I'm so excited
for you. I love you both with all my heart. Love to Steven
too.

Evie.

P.S. I've already made plans to be home for Christmas.
Can't get away that long for Thanksgiving. Just thought
I should let you know.

September 30, 1928

Dearest Evie,

We are so happy you are enjoying yourself in Washington. It is an exciting place. Dad and I loved visiting there. It feels like there is so much power around you. Of course, you must really feel that working in the Senate.

Evie, you just won't believe what Brand Boulevard looks like now. Mr. Brand has actually made it a tree-lined street, all the way to the front gate of his house. And if that isn't enough, he built an airstrip in front for private planes. Dad and I were invited to one of the parties. Oh Lord, Evie, such a crowd of celebrities. They fly in their private planes, and then stand in front of them while photographers shoot pictures. I suppose it is good publicity. I think it's a waste of film. But I suppose it's necessary. We have many interesting films now at the Alex Theatre, and lots of previews. Dad and I enjoy walking downtown to see all the movies. We pass many shops - you know how much I love good clothes, and they are in abundance. Lillie's is keeping me more than busy.

Best news, Steve was accepted at Stanford University, and he leaves next week to start his first year. Dad is letting him take the Ford up to school so he will

241

have transportation. I will be terrified until he calls me and says he has arrived safely.

Dearest child, we miss you so very much. Take care of yourself. And I am sending you a heavy winter coat. I made it from a Vogue pattern. I think you will like it.

All our love,

Mom and Dad

October 10, 1928

Dearest Mom and Dad,

As you know right now, I'm working for the reelection of Senator Johnson from California. It's very intellectual and challenging work, and my journalism classes are really paying off. I'm writing a lot of his correspondence, and just doing many interesting things. Yesterday I was able to go into the Senate chambers and listen as he promoted his latest bill. It was so exciting, because I helped write his speech.

I'm sure I told you I won't be home for Thanksgiving, but I will have two weeks at Christmas. Can't wait to see all of you. The coat hasn't arrived yet, but I'm waiting with bated breath. It's getting cold here. But all the excitement of politics is worth it.

How does Steve like Stanford? I've seen some pictures of the campus, and it looks absolutely wonderful. I bet the first thing he bought when he arrived was a bicycle. That campus looks huge. He can't drive the car everywhere.

Love to everyone,

Evie

November 9, 1928

Dearest Evie,

    I was overjoyed you liked your coat. Dad thought it would be absolutely beautiful on you. Thank you for all your compliments. Yes, I do love to sew beautiful things. We'll go shopping and make ourselves some wonderful dresses for the holidays.

    Dad and I will meet your train in Pasadena. It's so much easier than going to Los Angeles. Steve may be with us also, as he is supposed to arrive the day before. We have everything in readiness for the two of you. Would you like to have a party?

All our love,

Mom and Dad

January 29, 1929

Dearest Mom and Dad,

Can't believe it's been a month since I returned to D.C. My lovely coat is keeping me nice and warm. Even though it is cold, I still find Washington as exciting as ever. It was so good to speak with you on the office telephone yesterday. I'm getting a phone for my flat. Seems to be a necessity in my life these days. What did you ever do before you had a phone?

Dad, I'm going to buy a little MG roadster a friend of mine is selling because she is moving to another post. It's very cute. The mechanic says it is in good condition, and I promise I will be very careful with it.

Virginia is such a lovely state. I hope to just go explore on weekends when it becomes warmer.

Senator Johnson remembered my resume noting I speak, read, and write German. I do but I'm sure it's pretty darn rusty. A group of dignitaries is going on a goodwill tour to Europe, mainly to Germany. Senator Johnson asked if I felt comfortable enough to translate. I stammered yes, and the next thing I knew I was asked to go along as a translator. Interestingly enough, I'm supposed to act like I don't speak any German. A most unusual request, but I won't question it. So I get to go on a month's junket to Europe. I would love to visit Aunt Maud, but I don't think we will be in Italy. Aren't you excited for me? Much, much love from your daughter,

Evie

September 10, 1929

Evie darling,

We were thrilled to receive all your postcards from Germany. I can't believe you saw one of Aunt Maud's pictures hanging in a gallery. Well, yes, I can. She is a fabulous artist, even was when we were young girls.

We are getting excited about building the new house. The lot has been cleared and what they call graded.

Dad and I are looking forward to a beautiful yard for entertaining. We plan to put in a brick barbeque for cooking outdoors. (The plans are from an article I found in a magazine.) They look smashing, and I think we will put in an arbor also. Do you know what wisteria is? It's a lovely light purple. Can also be pink or white but it has a heavenly smell and the blossoms hang down in bunches in the spring. Then, when it is finished blooming, there is an abundance of dark green foliage. Makes for nice shade and a lovely place to play cards during the summer. Enough about flowers.

Steve is doing fine in school. Dad and I are so proud of him. He made the Dean's List. He told Dad he would like to join him in his practice when he graduates from law school so the firm would be Patterson and Patterson. Won't that be wonderful? I'm so proud of my children. I'll have to go to college just to keep up with you.

All our love,

Mom and Dad

CHAPTER 21

December 8, 1929

Evie nervously held the receiver.

"Oh Mother darling, are you and Daddy coping a little better today?"

"Yes Evie. We are managing, though it's very hard. We are going to lose the lot and the almost completed house we were building."

"I've been crying ever since I spoke to you yesterday. Is Daddy doing okay?"

Lillie wiped the tears from her eyes. "Yes honey, we'll be fine."

"I'm just glad he survived his heart attack. I'm so sorry you lost the house. I didn't even know Daddy was in the stock market. Do you want me to return to California so I can help you?"

"Evie, that is so dear, but it is not necessary. Steve should be out of school in a few months. Then I'm sure all will be well. Daddy's associates at the firm can handle everything until Steve gets here."

"I know you will survive. Can I send you some money? I can do it today."

"Oh Evie, honey, that is so sweet of you. We aren't that bad off. It's not like your father worked on Wall Street."

"Well, I just want to be sure you're okay."

"We'll be just fine, Evie. You are a darling for calling again. I know your Daddy would love to speak with you, but he is sound asleep." *It's better Evie doesn't know how terrified I was.*

"We have turned our den into a bedroom because there is a bathroom just off of it. Much more convenient for your father. He doesn't have to climb stairs. I can actually hear him snoring," she laughed.

"It is good to hear you laugh, Mom. I'll call you soon. Love to everyone. Bye."

August 2, 1930

Dearest Evie,

You know me and letter writing. I had a few minutes this afternoon and wanted to get a small note off to you. I am happy to report that Dad is doing well, and he and Steve are busy finding office space for him. It's going to be larger than before because they will need the room when Steve graduates from law school. There are several new buildings on Brand Boulevard, and also on Glendale Avenue near the courthouse. I think that's probably where they will end up.

Even though we lost the house, Dad and I are still planning to find or build another. That is our dream. I just want him to stay well and healthy. The doctor said since he survived his heart attack, he should live to a ripe old age. I hope so. He doesn't run around a tennis court anymore, but he and I have taken up a new sport, golf. Would you believe it? I'm learning how to play - with the help of a golf pro. Steven convinced us we should join the country club, so we did and now, when we have the money again, we will buy or build near it. They have a wonderful swimming pool where we can sunbathe, and the food is delicious. I'll have to do an incredible amount of swimming in order to stay thin with all the good, but of course fattening items on the menu. Instead of dropping off after the stock market crash, Dad's practice has absolutely burgeoned. I think it's because Glendale is growing so much. One of these days, when you return for a vacation, we should have our new home.

Any more trips planned for you? No man in your life? Let me know everything, my darling daughter.

All my love, and Dad's too.

Mom

CHAPTER 22

Evie's translating skills did not go unnoticed. One day, she received a phone call from Taylor Barnes in the state department who said he would like to visit with her at her earliest possible convenience.

"Can you come tomorrow afternoon? I can see you after you finish at your office. Would you be available to meet for dinner?"

Evie was intrigued by this last comment.

"I can do that."

"I will have a car call for you at 7 P.M. Please dress for a formal dinner. May I have your home address?"

"Formal?"

"Yes, my dear. I'm sorry I cannot tell you any more than that."

Evie was extremely puzzled by the phone conversation. She hung up shaking her head. I wonder if I should have accepted. I never should have given out my home address. I'd better tell the Senator. Then she was called into her boss's office.

"Evie, please close the door, then come and sit down."

Evie sat in the chair across from the Senator.

"I know all about your telephone call. I think your life is about to change. I just want you to know it has been an absolute pleasure working with you, and you will always have a place on the hill, should you want to return."

"Where am I going?"

"Evie, I'm not allowed to tell you more. You cannot and must not speak to anyone about your dinner engagement tonight."

"But, I don't know anything yet."

"I know, my dear, but please, you have my permission to leave the office now. Take anything you want to keep, because I don't think you will be returning tomorrow morning."

"But can't you tell me anything?"

"All right, the only thing I can tell you is you have been tapped for a very secret project because of your facility with the German language. You can't even tell your family."

"Oh, Senator Johnson, my head is spinning. I have no idea what it could be. I know you were instrumental in my translating documents, and for my trip to Germany, what now?"

"Everything will be explained tonight." The Senator stood and gave her a big hug. "Good luck and Godspeed, Evie."

Evie packed her large carry all with the few things she thought she would want, and thankfully, no one was in their office suite at that moment, so no explanations were necessary. She took a taxi to her apartment. It was 2:00 P.M. in the afternoon on a lovely autumn day in 1938. She dropped her bag on the sofa, removed her hat and gloves, and walked into her bedroom.

Well, she thought, I guess I can wear this navy dinner dress Mom made for me. It really is beautifully draped. And the shawl that matches it. Hopefully, I won't have to do much walking.

At 7:00 P.M. a long black limousine parked in front of Evie's building. Her doorman rang her apartment. Evie took one last look in the mirror, checked her makeup and hair before she grabbed her purse and gloves, closed her door, and walked to the elevator. Her mouth was agape when she saw the size of the limousine.

The chauffeur held the door open, tipping his hat. "Good evening, Miss Patterson. I'm Martin. And I promised the big boss I would take very good care of you."

"Thank you, Martin." She stepped inside and sank into the luxurious leather seat.

Minutes later, they stopped outside a large iron gate, waited a few moments, and then were admitted.

Evie looked out the window and gasped. They were driving up the main entrance to the White House. Underneath the port-cochere, Martin turned off the motor and came around to open the door for her. Evie was awestruck. The White House lights glowed in every window. She noticed how clean the windows were. The white looked so white, and the shrubbery with lights in them, looked black green. The front door opened, and she was welcomed inside.

"Miss Patterson, will you please join the others in the Blue Room." The man who met her at the door gestured with his arm as he led her down the hall. The door opened and sitting there was President Roosevelt, and other men she recognized but had never met.

"Mr. President." Evie was about to ask if there hadn't been some mistake and they were looking for another Patterson. But the President smiled.

"Miss Patterson, thank you for coming here under such mysterious circumstances, but I cannot stress enough the secrecy of this meeting, although you are welcome to tell anyone you dined at the White House as the guest of Senator Johnson. I'd like you to meet the others, as you soon will be coming in constant contact with them. This is Secretary of State, Cordell Hull; Harry Woodring, Secretary of War; Homer Cummings our Attorney General, and last but not least, Claude Swanson, Secretary of the Navy."

"Gentlemen, I'm so honored." Evie could have said much more, but had a hard time believing she was in the White House, in a room with the President. *I need to catch my breath. In my wildest dreams I never thought of having dinner with all these powerful men.*

"I'm confused. Senator Johnson had me clean out my desk," she was speaking directly to President Roosevelt, "and told me something is about to change my life forever."

"Very true, young lady. You have been chosen to be part of an elite group of Americans who will be part of a spy network."

Evie blanched. "What?" She couldn't believe what she heard.

"We know you speak German," continued Harry Woodring, "and we believe we will be in a war soon. If not this year, the next, but we will be involved for certain. The United States is the only great power with no intelligence service. We are putting together an elite group of men and women who can provide special services to the war department."

"What is it you want me to do?"

"Well, from now on, you will be working at the White House," said Woodring. "If anyone asks what you do, you work with protocol. That is your cover. However, what you will really be doing is working in our code room, listening to German broadcasts, translating them, and providing reports to the President through me. We want to monitor any German conversation you hear, whether it's on a bus or in the ladies room." Woodring smiled and continued. "You will also be asked to courier documents to and from wherever you are sent. We don't want to chance any of these messages being intercepted. You make a perfect cover; young, pretty, and business-like. We will not send you on any dangerous missions. At least we hope not. You probably won't travel outside the United States, but you will go to our major military installations. Does that sound like something that would interest you? You will be performing invaluable service to our country."

"Of course, I would do anything to help the United States. But I would like to know if I can have an outside life. May I see my parents and family in

California? May I travel on vacation? And of course, may I date?"

There was a loud and friendly laugh throughout the room.

"Of course you can, Miss Patterson. You just can't tell people what you do as you could compromise our entire secret service network. All you can tell them is that you work in the protocol office deciding who will sit where, at what banquet, how the seating will be arranged for a conference, and so forth. I'm certain you can be very inventive in your stories. Just keep them straight. But I don't need to tell you that. And, Miss Patterson, we have reason to believe your former German teacher is a spy for the enemy, so whatever you do, stay away from her. If she contacts you, be polite but too busy to see her."

Evie looked surprised. My German teacher? Is she here in Washington D.C. now? I thought she went back to California. At one time, she asked me to translate several documents for her. But they seemed innocuous enough. Like grocery lists, or children's toys. She just said she was too busy and could I help her out."

"She is not who she purports to be," the Secretary of War emphatically stated. "Those were probably letters she was going to decode," Woodring continued. "She is on our spy list. Hildegarde Krueger never became a citizen, and the Attorney General feels she is a huge security risk and is looking to deport her."

An audible gasp could be heard coming from Evie. My mousy little German teacher is a spy?

"Come, my dear," said the President. "We have many more important things to discuss. Let us have a good dinner, then I will have Martin drive you home."

That night when Evie returned to her apartment, she pinched herself. She called her parents and told them about her new position on the protocol team at the White House, and she would be working there from now on.

The days and months flew by. Evie loved her work, and she had become more than proficient in her responsibilities. She seemed to have a flair for refining ideas and distilling complex information to simple explanations. Her cohorts loved her for her sweet temperament, and easy-going attitude, even though what their jobs entailed caused stress and nightmares in many.

The date was December 6, 1941. Evie had seen the Japanese ministers leave the Oval office earlier that afternoon. As she compiled her reports later, she felt uneasy. Sleep was fitful that night, as Evie tried to get comfortable on a cot in the ready room in the basement, glad she would be in Glendale for Christmas and getting a break from work.

CHAPTER 23

January 1942.

As the country was recovering from its deep
depression, World War II became a reality. Men shipped
off to war, leaving behind wives, children, and families.
The women stepped into the breach to earn a living for
their families and help the men by manufacturing war
materials, building aircraft, tanks and other machines to
help them win the war.

Peter knew he wanted to do something to be
involved, even if it meant leaving Michael with Molly.
Peter went down to the recruitment office to see if he
could enlist as an officer. Michael at thirteen and loved
the school he attended, for its comprehensive art
program: his first love. Peter did not realize how bad his
eyes were until the recruiting officer rejected him after
his physical.

"It says here you speak German?"

"And French." Peter added.

"Mr. Wells, I'm sorry we can't use you in the
active service, but I sure could find an interesting desk
job for you. We are desperate for translators."

"I'm an architect," volunteered Peter, "but I
would be more than happy to do translation for you. I
haven't spoken German since the Great War, but I'm
sure I could be up to speed very quickly. I want to do
whatever I can to help my country. I saw what
happened in Europe during the First World War."
Peter's mind momentarily drifted back to the last battle

he was in. "I lost my parents and our home. I walked all over France to escape the Germans."

When Peter left the recruiting officer, he made a phone call to Matt and told him what had happened.

"Peter, I have a friend in Washington, Harry Woodring. If you are determined to do something for the war effort, let me find out if you can get something in D.C. You might as well be where the action is on the home front. I guess this means you want to dissolve our partnership too?"

"Not really, Matt, but I just don't know what this will do to it. I want you to be free to bring someone else on board if need be. I just know I have to do something to help out the United States. You may be my business partner, but you are also my best friend. With a war going on, I will be feeling useless if I can't help to win it."

"Before you sign with the army, let me see what I can do."

"Thanks, Matt."

A week later, Peter boarded the corridor train for Washington from Manhattan. He rested his head, and soon he transported himself back to 1917...

Pieter saw himself inching his way through the tall reeds, even though the tide rolled in. It was the only way to stay safe. Mont Saint Michel towered in the distance, but he had no desire to go there either. A very tired Pieter burrowed in the reeds away from the tide and slept until daybreak.

The next day, he needed to travel in a different direction to head towards Paris. It wasn't his ideal solution to join the Germans, but if they found him, he had to have something plausible to say. Because he spoke German, his language skills might hold him in good stead. Pieter thought maybe the French Resistance might be able to use him because of his fluency in German, but he had no idea where to look for someone who might be a member.

It would be a long trek to Paris. He had thought about heading towards Bernay, but so much destruction and death surrounded the area, he decided against it. He remembered his father telling him about the guns placed on specially constructed steel cars. The French had painted the cars and guns in strange mottled colors so the artillery wouldn't be recognized by the Germans. It hadn't been enough. So many townspeople were being slaughtered anyway.

It seemed to Pieter the number of soldiers walking down the road became fewer and fewer. They all appeared to be congregating around the beleaguered town of Arras. Pieter saw the bullet-battered signpost, indicating where he was. Without a map, Pieter was navigating only by the geography he remembered from his father.

The next little village he saw had also taken a lot of mortar hits, and almost in ruins. Pieter crept along using his instincts to keep him safe. On the outskirts, he spied German tanks hidden in the heavy brush. Caution kept him from going any closer. Maybe the soldiers were going back to Germany. Looking at the camouflage made him think otherwise.

What's that? He thought he heard a cry. It could be a bird. No bird. Haven't seen or heard a chirp in days. I'm sure they've flown to safer tree branches.

"That sounds like someone in pain," Pieter told himself. Pieter listened as he took a drink of water from a stream, filled his canteen, cupped his hands in the water and splashed his face. He heard another moan, but couldn't tell where it was coming from. Pieter looked around and then saw a fragment of fabric dangling from a fallen tree. *Could someone be hiding behind it?* The material didn't look like any German uniform he'd seen. With caution he moved in the log's direction and saw a soldier belonged to the piece of torn fabric. Then he saw an American insignia. The soldier needed help. *I must find a place to hide the two of us from the Germans. If they find us we could be taken prisoners, or worse yet, shot and killed on sight.*

Wary of the Germans in the vicinity, Pieter grabbed the soldier under his arms and using all his strength moved him inside a clump of bushes. Large and dense enough, the foliage would hide them both. He laid the man in the center of it. Pieter then returned to the log, removed the piece of torn fabric and retraced his steps, erasing all signs of where he had dragged the body.

Sam's mind began to wander as he lay hidden in the foliage. He knew a bullet pierced close to his heart, but his army training told him it also made a clean exit through his back. The wound wouldn't kill him if he could make it back to a dressing station – if someone could clean and bandage it. That 'if' loomed large. In the last battle, he had been separated from his men during heavy gunfire. It would be a miracle if one of his men returned to the area. This latest siege had lasted several days. Sam knew someone had moved him to safety. He also knew the bushes kept him well-hidden because he could hear voices speaking German. Sam struggled to remain conscious.

Where am I? I need water. I chewed my last piece of hardtack. Papa? No, it's Frank. I'm in a tree in our backyard. I see Frank's lips moving. I can't hear him. Lillie, what are you doing here? You should be at work. Why are you crying? Why is Mama crying? Papa is lying in his bed. I can smell Mama's roses.

Pieter watched Sam. His mind raced. *How can I help him?* Pieter had never seen so much blood. He listened as Sam rambled. He didn't understand a word. Pieter wished the weather were warmer. Winter arrived early, even before fall had time to shed leaves from the trees.

An icy blast swept through where Sam lay. A few snowflakes fell over his body. Sam's mind played tricks on him. His thoughts were jumbled. His delirium grew more pronounced.

I'm in a car and...lord I have a flat tire. Frank help me. Come find me. Mama will be worried if I'm late for dinner.

Sam saw his family in the cold mists of his mind, but reality returned in moments of lucidity, as he hallucinated.

Hours later or was it minutes, he didn't know. But another person stayed in the bushes with him. Had he found him? Had he moved him? Was it the enemy or a friend? Sam remained motionless.

"Soldat. Soldat." Pieter felt the soldier's body again and checked to see if he was still breathing. *"Je ne parle pas anglais.* I don't speak English," he told him. "I'm Pieter. I'll try and help you."

A semi-conscious Sam opened his eyes to see a scruffy teenager sitting beside him. "Sam, I'm Sam." He pointed to himself. "I don't speak much French."

"You are covered in blood. You must be badly hurt."

At that moment Sam and Pieter heard heavy footsteps. Words of German followed. Pieter put his finger to his lips indicating Sam must be quiet. Pieter heard they were looking for someone.

"Nein, nein," Pieter heard them say.

Those Bosch must not find them. A rustling in the bushes, and Pieter thought the soldiers were standing next to and then were on top of them. A bayonet pierced through the foliage, once, twice, then again and again. Someone lunged his bayonet through the bushes towards the ground. One thrust almost sliced Pieter's arm. *"Niemand ist hier,"* One of the Germans told the other soldiers no one was hiding in the bushes, and they should return to camp. Sam and Pieter could hear the heavy boot steps and voices grow fainter and fainter.

The two of them breathed a sigh of relief, but still with caution. Sam pointed to his bloody shirt. Gesturing to the canteen Pieter carried, Sam showed him his wound. In pantomime, Sam made a gesture towards the canteen and then to his wound again. Pieter realized Sam was asking for water to wash the blood off. He had filled his canteen right before he found Sam, so it was almost full.

Pieter had never seen anyone who had been shot. Dressing a soldier's bloody wound would be a true test of his mettle. The soldier kept pointing at his gear he'd been carrying. Pieter reached for the bag and Sam nodded yes, indicating Pieter had what was needed. He opened Sam's army-issue bag and found medical supplies. He searched for a clean cloth to dress Sam's wound. Pieter opened another layer of the bag and saw bandages, syringes, and several small boxes. Pieter tore away Sam's shirt, poured the water he had on the wound and cleansed it. Then he took several bandages and placed them on top of the cleansed flesh. Sam pointed to one of the boxes marked with a content label of sulfa. He gestured the sulfa powder should be placed on the wound first.

"*What's he trying to tell me? Shake that yellow stuff on him?*" Pieter watched Sam's hands. Pieter nodded okay, and covered Sam's wound with the powder.

Weak as he felt, Sam knew Pieter had saved his life. There would be time to be grateful later.

A hungry Pieter and an exhausted Sam lay in the foliage, hoping another American soldier would come by. They remained in their hiding place until morning. Sunlight began to appear through the trees, and they heard footsteps. *More Germans?* They sucked in their breath. Then with the recognition of an American uniform, they both breathed easier. Sam saw the sergeant's stripes.

"Give us a hand." Sam called.

"Captain, we all thought you were dead."

"Might well have been. Thank the young man here, he can follow my hand gestures. Doesn't speak English but caught on fast. Did a damn fine job, but I need a doctor to check for infection. Get me to the closest dressing station."

The sergeant nodded at Pieter. "Captain, can you walk on your own?"

"I don't think so. I've lost a lot of blood. I feel weak." Sam gasped for breath. "Are we close enough to a station to get a stretcher? I believe you and Pieter here are strong enough to carry me back."

"Yes sir."

"Rustle up some chow too. This young genius and I haven't eaten in several days."

Sam pantomimed as best as he could to describe a stretcher. He pointed to Pieter to stay with him until the sergeant returned with a stretcher so Pieter could help him transport Sam wherever they were taking him. The sergeant would return with food for them to eat also. Pieter grinned at Sam's pantomime, indicating he understood.

The sergeant looked at Pieter. He saw before him an unarmed scrawny freckled young man with a speck of red coming out from underneath his black cap. He tried to be kind in his gruff voice, "Well, what do we have here?"

Pieter pointed his finger at himself. "Pieter, Pieter, *Francais, Francais.* Thank you."

"Yeah kid," the sergeant answered.

"I want to be American soldier." Pieter kept telling him in French.

The sergeant gestured to Pieter to come along and help him in transporting Sam. Pieter gave him a big smile and sigh. He put his knapsack over his back and stepped behind the gurney the sergeant brought. The two of them lifted Sam onto the gurney. The sergeant seemed to know the terrain. It didn't look like Pieter remembered it – trenches dug everywhere, trees stripped of their leaves. A trusting Pieter helped transport the wounded Sam. Pieter surmised the sergeant knew the pathway, and did not show any kind of fear. Pieter's head burst with thoughts of America and Americans.

Ever since he had been a little boy, he had wanted to build beautiful buildings and houses, different from the ones he saw in Paris while studying at L'Ecole des Beaux Arts, the premier school for architectural studies in all of France. Somehow his parents had accumulated enough money for him to study at L'Ecole. He thought the funds might have been in the letters his father received each month from a Paris law firm. But they had ceased to arrive after the German invasion – in fact no mail whatsoever was getting through. It didn't matter anyway. The Germans would have confiscated it all.

Now Pieter had another mystery to solve. What were the documents he found hidden inside his father's journal? He knew his father kept all his important papers inside that book. He couldn't wait for some time to sit down and study the papers he discovered.

The three of them traveled on a well-worn path next to the river. The reeds and willow trees seemed to have survived. Pieter thought they had walked for well over an hour, with the sergeant saying nothing. He wondered if there were Germans still in the vicinity, or if the sergeant didn't like to talk. Pieter tried to emulate his stride with enthusiasm as they carted Sam. Soon they arrived at a makeshift campsite. The sergeant and Pieter took Sam to the field hospital. Pieter stayed with Sam.

The colonel came to see Sam and talk with Pieter. The colonel realized Pieter also spoke German. Pieter explained to the colonel who he was, where he was from and what he wanted to do.

271

"Colonel, my parents were murdered by the Germans. My father executed in the town square, our house destroyed by bombs. I want to join the army," Pieter rattled off in French.

"Son, I think you're too young to join the army."

"I'll be eighteen next month."

The colonel knew he could use someone who spoke both German and French. "You've suffered enough at the hands of the Germans, but I still can't make you a regular soldier.

"I'll volunteer my services. Could you give me food? I'm so hungry." Pieter told him, gesturing to his mouth and stomach.

The sergeant and the colonel had a good laugh. "Of course, Sarge will see you get something to fill that empty belly of yours."

The next day, the colonel came to Sam's bedside for a meeting with the captain of another unit that was hunkered down about three miles outside of Arras. Pieter then accompanied the colonel as the officers were interrogating some prisoners picked up near the village.

When Pieter saw them, he remembered these were some of the same men he had spent the last two days evading. Pieter realized the German soldiers were not telling the truth when they answered the colonel's questions. Pieter turned to the colonel and whispered about the camouflaged tanks he had seen while hiding from the Germans. He proceeded to tell him how many and how they were hidden in the brush. He also confirmed what the other captain thought. The Germans were amassing an offensive to the south of Arras. That explained the thinning of the ranks in the area Pieter and Sam had been found by the sergeant.

The colonel realized the Americans would be walking into a trap. He interrupted the captain and told him what Pieter had witnessed.

Pieter's information proved to be invaluable. As they ate dinner that night, the captain came over to Pieter, and told him so. An overjoyed Pieter patted his stomach. He felt full for the first time in many days. He was with the Americans, his newly found friends...

Peter's body jerked. The train had come to a halt. Peter felt drained by his reverie, but he picked up his bags and exited the train. Descending the staircase at the D.C. terminal, he noticed someone holding a placard with his name on it.

"Peter Wells. I'm Harry Woodring's assistant. He asked me to pick you up and bring you to his house in Georgetown."

"Thanks, these are my only bags."

"I'm Harold Greenwood, and very pleased to meet you, Mr. Wells."

"Nice to meet you also." Another new adventure would soon begin.

Peter secured his luggage in the trunk, then climbed in the front seat next to the assistant. Peter looked from right to left as he was driven down the tree-lined streets of Georgetown. The brick homes with white wood trim on the windows, and sycamore trees that were just beginning to bud for spring. He fell in love with it all. He saw a house of painted white brick, with a 'for sale' sign in front. The shutters were either black or dark green. *Could be either*, Peter thought. *Nice lines, interesting garden.* He could see the cherry blossoms beginning to bud, and the wrought iron fence. *Wonder what the inside looks like.*

"Glad to meet you, Peter. Matt had a lot of good things to say about you."

"Thanks, Harry, glad to meet you also."

"We are so in need of men of your caliber. You'll be part of the Secret Service, and you'll have top-secret clearance. Whatever you learn can go no farther than these walls. We will use your architectural ability as a cover. We want you to decode messages, and any communiqués in German and French. The Germans have a machine like a typewriter, and we are trying to break the codes. We call it Enigma because that is what it is – an enigma to anyone who has been working on decoding it. Allen Turing in Bletchley Park has been working on cracking the code for years."

"Allen Turing, Bletchley Park, who and what is that?" Peter questioned.

"It's where the English have their counterpart to our Secret Service. They are years ahead of us. We want you to go to London so you can be brought up to speed. You'll meet Turing in London.

"Tell me about the machine."

"This damn thing is ingenious – a mechanical ciphering device based on rings and cylinders. The main unit consists of a keyboard, like a typewriter, the scrambler unit and the lamp board. The encoding is done on the scrambler unit. It holds a number of rotors with twenty-six contacts, representing the alphabet, left and right of the rotor. Each left contact is connected to

274

a contact on the right by an internal wiring scheme. Rotors are connected to each other by sliding contacts. A reflecting rotor mirrors the connection backwards. We believe once we can crack the code, we will shorten the war by years. I'm told the concept is as old as time itself. I'm just giving you the explanation given to me."

"Sounds complicated as hell."

"Yes, that's why it's taking so long to crack the codes. We have some but not all of them. Those Germans are sophisticated in their approach to codes. We have to come up with something ourselves."

"Harry, I'm no engineer – and my mechanical abilities run at the low end of the scale."

"I wouldn't worry about that, Pete. Besides the translations, one of your other responsibilities will be to make frequent trips to New York. We have an interesting little enterprise in the Rockefeller Building. You and I will be learning as we go along. We are trying to build a formidable secret service agency, and you will be in on the ground floor. Can you shoot a gun?"

"Just the ones I used during the last war. I haven't touched one since."

"There's a shooting range in the bowels of the White House. You will make good use of it until you become proficient again. An instructor will assist you."

"Harry, you do know that when the war is over, I don't want to continue in this type of work. The only reason I am here now is to do something to help America win the war. She's been very good to me."

"I understand completely, Pete."

Peter asked Harold to drive him by the house that had intrigued him so he could look at it once more. Peter wrote down the phone number from the 'For Sale' sign.

"Nice house," said Harold.

"Yes, when I have time, I think I'll go look at it. I certainly would like a house to live in rather than an apartment.

At their meeting the next Monday, Peter had news for Secretary Woodring. "I saw a lovely colonial house a few days ago. I liked it so much I bought it yesterday. It's one street over from you. I want to set up an architectural office inside. I've noticed people have home offices in Georgetown. Also, I'm going to bring my son and his nanny down here, unless it's not allowed."

"Hell no, Pete. You should have your family with you. And the office would be a perfect cover. In fact, a courier could bring you papers in architectural containers, but they would be for translations." Woodring paused, thinking. "That might work very well. A courier coming in and out might be suspect, but someone delivering architectural drawings and you bringing them back might not draw so much attention."

Peter moved into the house and began to renovate it. On a regular basis, a messenger came and went without raising suspicion. One day, a different messenger brought the papers.

"Hi, I'm Evie Patterson, and I'm so happy to meet you."

"Hello, how nice to see a pretty face instead of a dour young man. Please come in. I'm Peter Wells." Standing in the doorway was a petite young woman with sandy blond hair and an engaging smile. She looked very studious in her glasses. Her suit was tailored navy blue, and she wore a crisp white blouse underneath it. Her shoes were low heel pumps. She looked stylish and yet so business like. *Wow.* Peter thought. *This is the first time since Sybil left I have really looked at another woman.*

"I was told you bought this house, and I've never been inside."

"Is there some reason you would have been?"

"Well, the house once belonged to my godmother and her husband who was with the Department of Interior. My parents stayed here – once – in the early twenties. My godmother's husband was killed in a crash while flying his plane, and my godmother moved back to Europe. During Harding's administration, it was rumored her husband may have been murdered. I actually have never met her. I only know of her through letters and what my mother has told me about her."

"Do you mean Andrew Llewellyn?"

"Yes."

"How interesting. I bought the house from a corporation so I didn't know who the previous owners might have been. I wish we could talk more now, and I could show you the rest of the house, but a client is coming shortly, and I need to get these papers out of the way. Where should I return them?"

"Would you like to bring them to the White House? If you have never visited there, I could give you a tour. My title is Assistant of Protocol. This is my card. I'm Maud Evelyn Patterson. Evie to everyone."

"That would be wonderful. How about around 4:00 P.M.? Where do I go?"

"To the main gate, and ask for me. Then you will be escorted to the front door."

"See you tomorrow. And by the way, my name is Peter." *What an attractive lady. I wonder if she is attached.* Peter thought he might ask her to dinner after he delivered all the translations.

CHAPTER 24

Evie became the usual courier to the Georgetown home. She and Peter met on a regular basis but it wasn't until a late spring day the following year Peter invited her to come for Sunday brunch at his home. "Evie, we never seem to have any time to visit, and I promised I would show you the house. I have a very dear woman cooking for me, and I'm sure you would enjoy seeing what I have done to the inside."

"Oh Peter, this is absolutely beautiful." She was struck by how charming and contemporary every room looked. It was then her eyes were drawn to a painting above the fireplace; a young red-haired woman was buying flowers from a flower seller. She studied the picture. Then the signature. She looked at Peter. "Peter, where did you get this painting?"

"I bought it when I was in Europe one year. In fact the artist wanted to buy it back from me. That's her in the picture. I've really never wanted to sell it. I absolutely love it, and the artist is one of my favorites."

"Peter, that's my Aunt Maud, the godmother I spoke about. This was her house." Evie's face flushed with excitement. "I can't believe this. It's too weird. You buy my aunt's house, and her painting is hanging in the living room. Wait till I tell my Mom and Dad. They won't believe it either."

Peter was stunned. He sat in his easy chair and looked up at the painting. "I'm absolutely floored. Maud Driscoll's work is my absolute favorite, and when I moved from New York, I thought it would look great in this spot. I'm so amazed."

"Lillie, my mother, and Maud have been friends since they were young girls. My mother moved to California without even being able to say goodbye at the train station. The two of them have been corresponding since the late 1800s." Evie bubbled with excitement.

"I met Maud Driscoll in Paris in the twenties, a few years after I graduated from MIT and when I first started working in New York. We always planned to meet again, but never did. Maybe we can now."

"Peter, this has been a wonderful brunch. I don't know when I have enjoyed a morning more."

"I have too. I hope you will return. I would like you to meet my son, Michael. He's the artist in the family. I just dabble."

"Well, I have no talent along that line at all. I've always been the student, studying something new. When I reached the age of thirty and realized I might not find someone interesting to marry, I decided to come to Washington. I worked for Senator Johnson for several years before winding up where I am now."

"You're not that old. How old are you anyway? Can I ask you?"

"Thirty seven."

"You don't look it! I didn't mean to interrupt you, Evie. Please continue. Do you like Washington?"

"D.C. is so exciting. In spite of the war, I love it here. Of course, I love California too." *I wonder why I'm telling Peter all this information about myself when we haven't known each other that long. I know he is older*

than I am, but only by a few years. I know he has a son,
but he never spoke of a wife. I want to ask him these
questions. Maybe there would be time. Another time.

Months passed and Evie began to wonder if it
was fate that brought Peter and her together. She
found him so attractive, and was happy every time she
saw him, and sad when she knew she wouldn't. He was
a charming man, and she felt herself falling for him in a
way she had never expected. If it was love, then she
was fully in it.

"Evie." It was a Sunday afternoon, and they
were walking around the neighborhood in Georgetown.
"You know I wasn't born in the United States. I became
a citizen in 1926, a few years after I graduated from
MIT."

"No, Peter, I never realized that. I've wanted to
ask you many questions, but I didn't think it was my
place."

"Oh, Evie. You can ask me anything that you
want."

"Michael," she said. "You never talk about his
mother. Does she ever see him?"

"Sybil didn't even want to hold him when he
was born. She decided a career in Hollywood more
exciting than an architect husband and a baby boy."

"Oh, Peter. I'm so sorry. I feel sorrier for
Michael."

"He's a great kid. And Molly has been with us since the day I brought him home from the hospital."

"Does he know who his mother is?"

Yes, I have told him. But he has no desire to meet her, even though she is quite famous now."

"Famous?"

"She's the well-known costume designer for the movies, Sybil Meecham."

"That's amazing and weird. My mother adores her designs and is always copying them. She makes clothes professionally, not just for me, or for herself and friends. She has quite a flair for dressmaking and design. She owns a very successful dressmaking business. I had better tell her to stop copying Sybil's designs."

"That's okay. We have nothing to do with Michael's mother, and I rarely go to the movies, so I wouldn't know one way or the other."

"You said you weren't born here. But you have no accent, Peter. What was your childhood like?"

"Difficult, would be the easiest way to describe it. I don't know exactly where I was born. I was adopted by a Swiss couple. My parents always seemed to have enough for my education when I was young. When World War I broke out, I found myself running for my life. Impossible for my father to get materials for his embroidery and lace factory after the war started, we moved to France. We ended up on a dairy farm in Normandy. They sent me away so I wouldn't be drafted. The Germans were crawling all over the area. They shot my father in our town square. They virtually murdered my mother because when she was ill, they wouldn't let her see a doctor. I think her appendix burst. I took what I could find from my home. A neighbor gave me some cheese and bread. I had my knapsack, and a few mementos, and that was it."

"How absolutely terrifying for you."

"I was at that fearless age of seventeen. All I was interested in was joining the Americans, or the French Resistance."

"And what happened?" Evie listened attentively.

"Well, I couldn't speak much English, and I hid out from the Germans. Then I met an American soldier. He had been badly wounded. I helped get him to a field hospital helped by the gruffest sergeant you ever would want to meet. In fact, I took this soldier to the field hospital twice."

"And?" Evie couldn't wait to hear the rest of the story.

"In my fractured English I told him my name, and I wanted to be an American soldier. We had a tough time communicating, but I helped the sergeant transport him by stretcher. Sam, who was a captain, took me under his wing. I taught him French. He taught me English. We got to be pretty good friends. He wanted me to go back to California after the war. He even wrote his sister about me, and gave me his address while he was recuperating at the hospital. I wrote him, but the letter was returned with addressee unknown."

"Oh, how sad. I'm so sorry. So how did you get to the U.S.?"

Peter recapped his entire story of how he arrived in New York to the time he arrived in Washington D.C."

"That is an amazing story."

Evie and Peter sat down on one of the park benches.

"Evie, do you feel I am too old for you?" Peter changed the subject.

"No, of course not, Peter. I don't think you're old anyway. My father is fourteen years older than my mother. She used to work for him as a secretary."

"I'm not the most romantic of souls, but I love being around you. You're so enjoyable to be with. But I also have a son to consider. He's fifteen now and has two more years of high school. I'm not sure where he plans to attend college. But his grades are good. I know he likes you."

"Oh, Peter I think he is a delightful young man. But let's face it, we are not exactly in a situation where we can be romantic. We're at war, and our jobs are vital to the American cause."

"I know, Evie, but it would be awfully nice to come home to you every night, or for you to come home to me for that matter."

"Are you proposing to me, Peter Wells?" Evie felt butterflies in her stomach, but her heart was soaring.

"I guess I am. Evie, would you do me the honor to become Mrs. Peter Wells?" Peter put his arms around Evie, hugged her, and explored her face with kisses.

"Peter," she sighed, "if you would let me breathe, I would say yes."

"Oh dear Evie, I promise to make you happy. Where do you want to get married? And when?"

"I was planning to go to California for Christmas. That's only a few months from now. Why don't you and Michael and I go, and we will have a quiet wedding at my parent's home in Glendale. How does that sound?"

"Wonderful, but I would bring Molly, and ask Matt and Jessamyn to come too. Do you think the boss would give us enough time off?"

"It's three days to California from Washington, if we take the train. So that's six days. We could ask for two weeks. It's only the middle of June – that gives us six months if we make the request now."

"I'll talk to Harry on Monday. Maybe I can ask him to scare up some extra gas and food ration coupons. Your Mom will need sugar and eggs for cake, and with all the mouths to feed, she'll need some coupons for meat too."

"You know Peter, Mom and Dad are amazing. They have the best victory garden you could ever imagine, and they share their produce with all the neighbors. They grow carrots, radishes and onions and other root vegetables plus lettuce. The neighbor next door grows all kinds of fruit and berries. The neighbors behind them grow squash and melons, and the neighbors across the street grow corn, peas and beans. They have no shortage of vegetables or fruits. And the woman who cleans for Mom sells her eggs from her chickens. I think she would rather have butter and flour instead of more eggs, maybe some meat if it could be located."

"I hope generations after us will realize how precious freedom is, and what sacrifices have to be made to keep it. You could be making a lot of money in the corporate world, and I could be building more skyscrapers, and not buildings for the war effort. War is hell. Look at what I went through in France. We lose a lot of men, but they know what they are fighting for, don't they? Guess I've climbed on a soapbox, but it is so important to me."

"I don't think you're on a soapbox. I feel the same. My family does too. If my brother Steven didn't have flat feet, he would be in the army now. As it is, he is an air raid warden and his specialty is poison gases. I've watched him in exercises. It's not fun. But if it protects us, I'm all for it. Honey, let's go back to your house, and I can call Mom and Dad and tell them our news. Mom will make my dress. She can get the minister from their church to marry us. It might even be warm enough in December to hold the reception outside. If not, we can just use the living and dining room. I hate to ask lots of people, especially in wartime."

"I know. I'll leave those details to you. I'm not very good at that kind of planning. Michael will be my best man."

"I have been in Washington for so many years I don't really have any particularly close girlfriend in Glendale. It would hurt too many feelings if I asked someone from here. If I asked one, I would have to invite the rest." Evie paused thoughtfully. "I know she is getting old, but do you think Molly might be my matron of honor?"

"I think she would be very touched."

"Anyone else you want to invite?"

"Just Matt, Jess, and Molly."

"Then with Steven my brother, my Mom and Dad and the minister. That's ten of us." She pondered. "That sounds just perfect to me."

CHAPTER 25

𝒫eter and Evie were thrilled with the two weeks off. How miserable it must be in Europe. Fighting in snow. She thought about all the hardships soldiers faced and was grateful for the beautiful December day when the entourage arrived in Glendale. Peter arranged for two limousines to pick them all up at the train station in Pasadena.

"Peter must be very well-connected to get those two automobiles," Lillie said in an aside to George.

"Oh Mom, Dad, you both look so wonderful. This is Peter and his son, Michael. And this is Molly Harcus, and Peter's good friend, Matt Hood, and his wife, Jess."

"So nice to meet all of you," Lillie said, beaming. "I took the liberty of getting you some rooms at the California Hotel. It's the best Glendale has to offer, but I thought you would rather be closer than luxurious."

"Wherever you put us will be just fine, Mrs. Patterson."

"You must call me Lillie."

"Thank you, Lillie."

The wedding was in two days. That would give Peter and Evie enough time to fill out all the necessary paperwork and have blood tests.

Peter stood in the Patterson living room, looking at family pictures. On the piano was a photograph of Maud, whom he recognized, and it sat with other family members. Peter looked at a picture of a soldier in the silver frame. He picked it up and studied it. "If I didn't know better, I would swear this was Sam. But it couldn't be. That would be too strange," he mumbled. Peter had a most puzzled look on his face. He cocked his head to the left. Flashed in front of his eyes, the grizzly details of the blood and the gore. Peter nostrils smelled burning flesh.

"Are you enjoying our rogue's gallery, Peter?" Lillie asked, bringing him back to the present.

Peter snapped back to reality. "What did you say?"

"I asked if you were enjoying seeing all the family pictures."

"Oh yes, but this looks like someone I knew a long time ago." He nodded to the picture. "But it couldn't be. Who is the soldier?"

"That's my brother, Sam. He served in France during the First World War."

"Sam, Sam Doty?" He had chills waiting for her answer.

"Yes, my brother was Sam Doty."

Peter's cheeks were wet. His hands were icy cold. He felt shivers down his spine. "Oh, my god, Lillie, I bet you don't even remember. I'm the redheaded boy Sam wrote to you about. He wanted to bring me to California after the war."

290

Lillie dropped into a chair next to the piano, her hand to her throat, tears in her eyes. She could hardly speak. He knelt beside her. "Mrs. Patterson, Lillie, are you alright?"

"Oh Peter, please tell me about Sam," she said when she could speak. "What did you know about him? He came home from the war and began medical school. In 1922, we had a terrible epidemic of influenza. Sam in helping so many others couldn't help himself. He died in the hospital. Sam wrote me about a Pieter in his letters, but the name was Pieter Weiler."

Peter took both of Lillie's hands into his own. "When I came through Ellis Island, they couldn't read my handwriting, so I became Wells. When I got my citizenship, I changed my name officially to Peter Wells."

"And now you will become my daughter's husband, and a dear son-in-law to me. How happy Sam would be! Evie was just a young girl when he died, so I don't know how much she remembers of him. It's almost like – like having a part of Sam come back to us. Oh, Peter, I'm just overjoyed." Lillie removed her glasses and wiped her tears.

"Sam was a great friend to me, and is responsible for me learning how to speak English. I tried to find him after the war, but the letter was returned address unknown."

"I saved every letter ever written to me, and I know I have the one Sam wrote to me about you. I'll find it and share it with everyone at dinner. We have a surprise for the rest of the family." Lillie stood when Peter did, hugged him and wiped away more tears.

That night at dinner, Lillie read the letter amidst tears, laughter, and a joyous celebration. She read part of the letter…. "Pieter Weiler is a courageous young man who has suffered a great deal. Miraculously, he found his way to our camp, and has been invaluable helping me with German translation and teaching me French, while I teach him English. He's like my younger brother. I want to bring him back to California with me…."

There were also many champagne toasts to the happy couple. They even let Michael have a few sips, and he stood and made a small touching toast.

"Dad, I never even thought about you marrying again, but I am happy for you. And Evie, if I am to have a stepmother, I couldn't ask for anyone nicer. Welcome to the Wells family."

"Why Michael, that is the sweetest thing I have ever heard. Thank you. You are one great kid, and I'm proud to be part of the family. Come here, you, and let me give you a hug." He did and received a big hug and kiss that reddened his face to match his hair. Very embarrassed, he kissed her back on the cheek.

"Thanks, Mom," he said with a touch of sarcasm.

CHAPTER 26

Evie was a vision in white in the dress Lillie had made for her wedding. The house was filled with huge white pompom chrysanthemums and red poinsettias. Lillie had raided her garden as well as those of several neighbors to find all the red and white flowers, carnations, baby's breath, white hydrangeas and red roses. Lillie's friends made certain there would be no shortage of flowers. Evie's dress was made of parachute silk that draped and clung to her body. Lillie had hand-tucked pleats and embroidered the neckline with hand-sewn seed pearls down the left side of the entire gown. The pearls fell in lovely cascades over Evie's slender figure. Her headpiece was a crown of fragrant white orange blossoms. She did not wear a veil. The ceremony only took a few moments, and they were man and wife.

There would be no honeymoon for now because of the war, and in two days, they would return to Washington. Evie would keep her apartment as a clandestine meeting place for their spy network, and if anyone needed to stay there, Evie had twin beds in the bedroom.

Evie and Peter were a terrific team, and after marriage, their work also seemed to go seamlessly. They spent a great part of their time translating papers. Peter still had a thriving architectural practice, but of course nothing grand was being built, and he couldn't talk about some of his projects to the outside world, or even to Evie for that matter.

One evening, Peter led Evie to his office. "Evie, we have to sit and talk about something very important. Not even Michael knows this, and you must not tell him."

"Goodness Peter, you are so serious. Of course I would never tell Michael anything unless you wanted me to. What is it?"

"Darling, you know I'm not just a translator, don't you?"

"Well, I know you are a wonderful architect."

"That's not what I mean. When I'm not at work, have you wondered where I was?"

"I know I am unhappy and sad when you aren't around. But, no, I really have tried hard not to wonder. With my desk constantly full of translation to tackle, I guess I have been preoccupied."

"Well, I want you to know, because I've been on little excursions for Harry Woodring. I travel to New York weekly and other places. I can't tell you what else I have been doing because of its sensitivity. I wanted you to be aware of as much as I'm able to tell you. In case I really need to be clandestine, I don't want you to think I'm ignoring you. I really can't tell you when I leave, how long I will be gone, or when I will return because I don't want you to ever have to lie to anyone. Hopefully, I won't be making many more trips, because now I have you to think about. However, plans are in the works I believe will end the war, at least in Europe."

A few days after Peter's strange, partial confession, President Roosevelt died in Warm Springs. Peter and Evie were at President Truman's inauguration. Shortly after, they were called into the Oval office. The new President seemed well aware of Evie's and Peter's role in the war effort. He asked them to join all the gentlemen at the conference table. All the men except Peter and the President were in heavily decorated uniforms. All appeared to be from different branches of the service. Evie was the only woman present.

"Scrambled eggs to excess," thought Peter.

Documents in German, and various maps were placed on the table in front of them.

"Peter, all these papers were smuggled out of Germany through one of our agents and brought directly to me."

Peter was thinking to himself, "I hope Evie doesn't realize I'm the agent the President is speaking about."

"We are planning a massive offensive the first week in June, and I want to be sure we are aware of all the German positions. What is the best place to land the LST's? Can you answer that? How quickly can the two of you decipher these?"

"Mr. President," Evie offered, "I think Peter and I could decipher all of it right here in about one half hour. Is that fast enough?"

Peter adjusted his glasses and picked up one of the documents. "Sir, this states fortification will be at a maximum with heavy artillery, and should the enemy be able to land, they should be stopped at the cliffs. I saw the area myself when I was there a few weeks ago."

Evie managed to keep a straight face when she heard Peter's words. She never realized he had been sent to the front as a spy.

"The harbor at Arromanches is about the easiest landing place. The Germans have stone bunkers above the cliffs. The ocean is a sharp drop off a cliff below Arromanches – they have a perfect view of the ocean and the surrounding beaches, anywhere the Americans or British might choose to bring in troops."

"Anything else, Peter?" One of the generals was speaking to him.

"Well, sir, before the First World War, I used to play on those beaches. There are high cliffs all around, and if you must use a frontal assault, a lot of men will be lost. Is there any way to come in from land rather than the sea? I'm not a tactician, just a translator with another dimension, but I'm not qualified to answer you as a military person. I can only tell you the roads are narrow – the beaches right in that area are rocky, and you will have no cover. Arromanches is a small town on the harbor. I would think it would be the easiest place to bring in troops. However, I am quite sure the Germans will reach the same conclusion also. There are a couple of other spots north of there, but if I were going to have to land, Arromanches would be my first choice."

The general spoke to the other men at the table. The men stood, and the general called for his aide. "This information needs to be transmitted to London immediately – in high priority code. Attack preparations need to be solidified as soon as possible. Thank you so much, Mr. And Mrs. Wells. You have translated some very valuable information for the war effort. The American government thanks you, and when we are victorious and the war is over, you will be properly thanked again."

Peter turned toward the president, "Thank you, Mr. President."

"Thank you Peter and Evie for what you did this afternoon. President Roosevelt was right when he described your translation abilities." President Truman then dismissed himself from the room.

Later that night in bed, Evie moved close to Peter. "Peter, you have prowess in other directions also."

"What do you mean, darling?"

"Michael isn't going to be an only child anymore."

"Oh Evie, oh my dearest darling, oh how wonderful." They hugged and hugged and kissed. "When?"

"I just saw the doctor this morning. He says February or early March. What a year 1945 will be for us."

"Evie, have you had any thought about what you would like to do after the war is over?"

"Hopefully, I can stay home and be a mother. But Peter, I don't think you want to stay in Washington anymore, no matter how much you love this house. I know you are not content with the type of architecture you are doing? Do you want to go back to New York?"

"No, my darling, I don't. Matt is retiring, so there is no reason to return there. We will always visit each other. Michael will be going to college next year. Do you realize there will be an eighteen year difference between our children?"

"They will both have been raised as only children, so they can be spoiled rotten if you want."

"Evie, I have some thoughts about what I would like to do after the war. See what you think about this. I know there will be a huge influx of new families, and they all will need to be housed. I think I would like to buy a piece of land in the suburbs of Southern California, design a couple of model homes, then build them and sell them to the returning G.I's and their families. It would be like designing our own little city. Housing developments will be burgeoning all over. Buyers will need new schools, utilities, streets, landscaping. All this would be included in the price of the house. I could design a house where there would be three or four bedrooms, two baths, and no larger than 1600 square feet. If each house sold for between $4,000 and $8,000 tops, we would have a cost of about $800 in the house including the land. Do the math, Evie," Peter got excited, "I bet we could put twelve or fourteen houses on an acre, and buy parcels of twenty to thirty acres. Evie, we could be groundbreakers in the housing industry. I know Paul Williams and Wallace Neff are the two big California architects, but I doubt they would ever want to try something like this."

"Peter, that sounds absolutely fantastic. I bet Steve and Dad would know where we could buy some acreage. And Mom says Steve is one of the area's top real estate attorneys. Won't we need a lot of capital? Dad and Steve are comfortable, but I'm not certain they would have enough to invest."

"I have more money than you know, Evie. That is not a problem. We just need the property. Steve could participate as the lawyer. And I need you to help me find construction people, help me in the office, and be my right hand. Maybe we should put together our own construction firm besides. Once Michael finishes college, he can decide whether he wants to join us or not. This entire venture will be a Wells project."

"I like that."

'But we can't say a thing until the war is over. I believe we would be viewed as greedy vultures if we started now."

"There's tons of property out near the Los Angeles airport, a place called Inglewood. Dad has a brother out there who owns a chicken ranch. He is getting on in years and may want to sell the property."

"Good," said Peter. "How are you feeling, darling? Have you given any thought as to where you want to deliver? I don't like telling you that you are an older mother."

"I know I'm going to be an older mother, but I'm healthy as a horse," Evie continued. She touched his hand. "I doubt the war will be over before this child is born. Maybe right here in this house with a doctor and a good midwife. When I see the doctor at my next appointment I will ask him. It might be safer at home than in a hospital. Not too many babies are being born there these days. And darling, I repeat, I'm as healthy as a horse."

"I know that, my sweet. I don't want anything to happen to you."

CHAPTER 27

Lucca, Italy 1943

Giovanni and Maud were extremely happy. The grape vines Giovanni had planted were producing a fine quality of grape for wine. Maud painted in the studio Giovanni had built for her. But the aggression of Hitler, and the alliance with Mussolini, made them both shudder. Rumor of war was the constant topic of conversation. Mussolini, who at first said he would remain neutral, aligned himself and his country with Hitler and Germany.

As an American citizen, Giovanni wanted Maud to return to the United States, but Maud wouldn't leave without him. Finally, Giovanni successfully negotiated passage by ship out of Genoa and, after much persuasion, she agreed to leave. It would be an arduous trip as the accommodations on board would not be at all what she was used to. Maud wanted Giovanni to come with her so he would be safe. But it was too late. Maud's escape route to Genoa had been closed and now heavily patrolled by the Nazi invaders.

Maud saw German soldiers in tanks, in jeeps and on foot, commandeering the village people, taking down the Italian flag and raising the menacing black and red swastika. She carefully maneuvered her car to a back road and returned to the villa.

Even though Giovanni spoke fluent English, the only way for him to get out would be with false papers. At this juncture, he wasn't even certain he could find someone to falsify documents for him.

With the German army advancing, Giovanni had been afraid they wouldn't get out in time. And he was proven right. It was winter – the wrong time of year to flee through the Dolomites to Switzerland, so Genoa had been their only option. Now that route had been closed to them because the Germans heavily guarded all the roads and allowed no one to pass.

"Maud my darling, I think we had better bury all your jewelry and good silver. Otherwise it will be confiscated I'm sure, especially after what I have been hearing on the radio."

"Where can we put it?"

"I thought of putting in a false bottom in the wine cellar, then putting a large vat over it, so that it would look like part of the cellar."

"What can I do to help you?" Maud thought about her beautiful jewelry she had collected over the years, and wondered if she would ever be able to wear it again.

"I also hate to do this to you, but I think you should close down your studio, and let me put the paintings in hiding also. I want you to put your good clothes in trunks, and leave them in our bedroom. We will move to the caretaker's cottage, taking only the barest necessities. I don't want the Germans to know we are the owners of the property. And I want you to stay out of the way. If any of them come here, I'm afraid what might happen. You are so beautiful; they are not gentlemen. They are monsters!" He touched her hair and caressed her cheek.

"We will become the caretakers, the owners having left for parts unknown."

"I never would have thought of that. How smart you are, Giovanni. I will start cleaning out the cottage today."

"We will still be the da Neris, and we will no longer be the Baron and Baroness, but Giovanni and Maud, and darling, keep that red hair hidden at all costs. No more English."

"Oh Giovanni, I'm scared. I love you so much." Maud was not just scared. The Germans terrified her and what could happen to the two of them. She knew she had to keep a brave face for Giovanni. "I just want to get through this safely. I'm not a very good cook. Do you think we might be asked to be the servants of the Germans?"

"It is possible, my love. You've watched enough in the kitchen to know how to make pasta, or roast a chicken. And I know you make wonderful salads. We will be just fine."

It took Giovanni and Maud almost two weeks working day and night with a couple of neighbors they could trust, to put a small cellar room in, fill it with Maud's jewelry and paintings and the house silver. Giovanni also added some of his treasures. The room was then closed up, and the vats moved on top of it, securely fastened as part of the floor.

Maud took some linens, two pillows, and used a blanket as the bed cover. They had a small bathroom with a tub, and she brought what soap she had for laundry. She would now have to wash by hand. Giovanni put up a small clothesline for her. She moved a few flowers she liked best, and some herbs from the garden. This would be no picnic. Once everything had been completed, Maud would spend her days with Giovanni, helping him tend grapes, and working in the cellar making wine.

Maud thought about the war and about her own son. She prayed he was safe and happy even though she didn't know his name or where he might be after all these years. Her heart was heavy – not knowing.

Unfortunately, they didn't have to wait long for the onslaught of the Germans. The soldiers ruined part of the vineyard by running tanks and other vehicles through it because of the narrow road. When the Germans discovered the empty house, they commandeered it as a command post. Since neither Maud nor Giovanni spoke German, it was impossible for them to understand their captors. One day, another troop of Germans arrived with an officer who also spoke Italian.

He ordered Maud and Giovanni to come to the dining room of the main house. A non-Italian speaking soldier dragged Giovanni from the cottage along with Maud. Maud was so frightened she was afraid they would be killed.

"I am Colonel Fritz Ludendorff, and I'm going to be staying here for the duration of the war," the

German officer said when they stood in front of him. "You two will do my cooking, cleaning and anything else I might want. Where are the owners of this villa?"

Giovanni shrugged. "Gone, Colonel, I take care of the vineyards. I help make the wine."

"Wine? Wonderful. Show me the cellar. What kind do you make?"

"A red wine sir... Colonel."

"What is your name?"

"Giovanni, Colonel."

"And the woman with you?"

"She is my wife, Colonel. Her name is Maud." He didn't add anything more. Giovanni worried as to what the colonel might do.

"That's not an Italian name."

"No sir, her mother named her for the lady she worked for."

"Well, from now on she will do the cooking, and cleaning and serve. I require breakfast at five, and dinner at six in the evening."

"Colonel, we don't have food to cook for you. We don't have food for ourselves."

"I will see that you have a kitchen full of anything my men can find. You may feed yourselves from that, and eat in the kitchen."

"Thank you, Colonel, sir."

"Now show me that cellar."

The Colonel walked from one end of the cellar to the other. He saw the several vats with their bungs. "Get me a glass so I can taste this."

Giovanni brought him one of the cellar glasses, and he opened the bung to pour a small taste of wine.

"You are a good winemaker, Giovanni. I want all this bottled and put in the dining room. What is there, on the shelves?"

"Very little, Colonel. A truck came over a month ago, and took all the wine away."

"Bottle all this for me. You won't need the vineyards anymore. I'm going to have my men burn them. Please realize this isn't my order, it's from my superior."

Giovanni turned for a moment, and wiped tears from his eyes before he turned back again. His life's work would be ruined.

"One of my men shot a cow this morning. He was a butcher before he went in the army. There will be about twenty of us for dinner this evening. He will give your wife enough meat to feed us. And some potatoes too."

"Yes, Colonel, I will tell Maud. Giovanni couldn't wait to get out of the cellar and back to the cottage where Maud sat, shaking.

"Oh Giovanni, I don't know how we can do this. Look at me. I'm frozen in this chair."

"Well, darling," Giovanni put his arms around Maud and pulled her close to him. "I love you so much, Caro, but right now you must put on your apron, tie your scarf around your head, and hightail it to the kitchen. The illustrious Colonel wants you to cook dinner for twenty tonight."

"Oh, my God, how can I? No food, no nothing."

"One of the colonel's men shot a cow and butchered it this morning. He will give you the meat to cook, and also potatoes. He said we could eat in the kitchen. He wants me to bottle all the wine and put it in the dining room. He doesn't know what good wine tastes like. And, oh my darling, he's going to burn all the vineyards. He said it was his superior that told him he had to burn everything in sight. I don't know what we will do after all this is over."

"Let's just get through it first, and tonight when we are in bed, I will tell you what I think we should do."

Maud had done her best to make their bed a comfortable one but she was so tired as each day went by, she couldn't have cared less. She thought she could have slept on a stone floor if she needed to. One night when Giovanni had gone to the cottage before she had finished the dishes, she was left alone with one of the officers. Maud did not like his looks and couldn't wait to complete her chores. The tall blonde approached her from behind, grabbed her shoulders, turned her around and kissed her roughly, his day-old beard digging into Maud's skin. Maud wanted to scream but his mouth dug into hers as he held her arms. He undid his pants fly and tore her dress off. It was at that moment, she was able to let out a blood-curdling scream. Another soldier came into the kitchen and began to laugh.

"Hans, you want some help?" He squeezed her breasts.

"For her age, she looks like a pretty good piece, if you ask me."

Maud was terrified. Even though she didn't speak German, she knew what they were planning. There was no one to help her. If she fought, they might shoot her. The other soldier moved her to the kitchen table and held her down.

It was then the Colonel walked into the kitchen. "What the hell do you think you are doing? We may be the conquerors, but that gives you no right to rape this woman. If you come near her again, I will have you both shot." He helped Maud up. "Get to your cottage!" He almost screamed it at her.

"Colonel, we were just having some fun."

"That's not the kind of fun you're allowed. No wonder our enemies hate us so fiercely. They think of us as animals. And you have given them the perfect reason. Remember, we are supposed to be aligned with Mussolini. You're both confined to quarters, and as soon as I can transfer you both, I will. Now get out. Heil Hitler." They both saluted back at him and quickly left.

Maud gave the Colonel a look of gratitude, ran out the back door, down the path to the cottage, opened the door and flung herself into Giovanni's arms. She sobbed uncontrollably. "Giovanni. Giovanni. How much longer?" Maud related what had happened in the kitchen.

"Maud, I will never leave you alone in the house at night again. Oh my precious, I'm so sorry."

"We both have had our sorrows today. Let me tell you my plan." Maud lay in Giovanni's arms, snuggling into his chest. She whispered in English.

"Maud use Italian, you can never tell who might be listening."

"Do you know my friend Lillie; I have had since our childhood in Boston?"

"Yes, I remember the letters you used to receive from her."

"She lives in California. It is a place where they grow grapes. I thought maybe you and I could move to California, and buy vineyards and start a winery. I remember reading about a place called the Napa Valley. A lot of Italians moved there at the turn of the century. As much as I have grown to love the villa, with all that has happened, I don't think I could bear to live here when the war is finally over."

"Oh Maud, now I have nothing, only what is in the cellar. What can I offer? I won't have any money, I'm sure. I'll be as poor as the little mouse that runs in our vineyards. This property won't be worth anything without the grape vines. It will take years before the land will be producing grapes again."

"Giovanni, now I have something to tell you. I have plenty of money for the both of us. I own property in Boston I can sell. It belonged to my parents. They left me a good deal of money. It's in a bank in Boston. I also have a stock portfolio but I've paid no attention to it. I'll sell that. Whatever it takes, we will get to the Napa Valley. I will sell all my jewelry if I have to, but I want to see us have a new start." Her voice was filled with courage, and it gave her new hope. "Lillie says California is beautiful, and the Napa Valley is described as the closest thing to Tuscany."

"Oh, Maud you are the dearest wife imaginable. How was I ever able to find you? It sounds absolutely wonderful. What a magnificent dream to live for. It keeps my hopes alive. Thank you, my darling." Giovanni's heart was warm to the core with love for Maud.

"This is something we both can live for."

"Your suggestion is wonderful." *I haven't told Maud about the little town church toppled and the priest shot. I need her to keep her hope alive. I feel we won't get out of the war alive the way vineyards and homes are being destroyed and plundered throughout the Tuscan landscape. .*

"I want to be able to paint again. I miss it so much."

In September of 1943, Mussolini was convinced to join the Germans, and he established a Fascist government. This coincided with the occupation of the da Neri villa by the Colonel and his staff. Giovanni and Maud thought they would never be able to leave but in February, they woke up to the sounds of much activity in the courtyard. The colonel was loading a truck with everything he could ransack from the villa. All his men were helping. By the time the sun was up, it was quiet again. It was 1944.

A liberated Italian army now fought alongside their new American and British allies against the Germans. The Germans were forced to abandon their hold on Lucca. That freed the property from the enemy. Giovanni and Maud went inside the villa where Giovanni broke down in tears.

Maud decided it best to remain in the cottage. Even though she was afraid to be alone.

They didn't know what might happen because they had no means of communication. Giovanni thought he might sneak down to the village.

At that moment, her thoughts turned to London and Priscilla. It was 1939 when they had last spoken. Her family had been growing each year. Kenneth was in Parliament, but still a member of the British Expeditionary Forces. Priscilla had a child that would almost be as old as her baby. *I hope my boy is alive and healthy. Goodness, her oldest could be a father himself. Priscilla could be a grandmother.*

Maud's mind began to wander. It was the first time she had any thoughts other than survival. When the Germans left, they removed all the telephones and wires. At least they hadn't blown up the house. Maud looked out the small cottage window.

"Isn't that the neighbor's son?"

They joined Dario Cimino outside where they hugged, happy to be alive.

"Dario, where is your family? Is everyone alright?"

"Si, Baronessa. We are all fine. We had been living in the fields in a storage cave on the hill. We hid the cave opening with bushes. When the big fire came, we thought we would all die, but God was good and spared us. Even the brush that covered the opening was not burned."

"Do you know what has been happening? We have been virtual prisoners on our own property."

"Si, the Americanos, they are coming. I heard about it when I went to the village. The Germans are nowhere around now. After they destroyed our little town and killed our priest, they left. I am going to become an American. I want to go to America."

"I don't blame you, Dario. It's nice knowing I am an American, and as soon as the war is over, I will return to America with the Baron."

"Can I go with you and the Baron? I will help you all I can."

"Let the Baron and I discuss this, Dario, and we will have an answer for you soon. Right now, it is too premature to make any decisions. The war isn't even over." Maud thought taking Dario with them an excellent idea, especially since Dario was so familiar with grape tending. He might be of great assistance to Giovanni. The two of them were not young anymore, and young, strong arms could be of help. She and Giovanni would speak about it later.

CHAPTER 28

𝒫eter had one last spy mission for the War Department. He had to tell Evie, since he could be gone for several weeks, and wouldn't be able to contact her. He knew it would be dangerous, and was worried about her and the impending birth of their baby.

"If I'm not back in three weeks, contact Harry."

"Oh, Peter, the baby is starting to kick, and it being winter, I don't want to drive myself anymore."

"Darling, I will ask Harry to let the War Department provide you with a chauffeur. It's the least he can do for us."

"When do you leave? May I pack a suitcase for you?"

"I won't be leaving from the house, and what I need will already have been packed for me. Don't ask me any more questions, sweetheart. I don't want to have to say I can't answer them. Tomorrow is the big day, so let's have a nice dinner together, and relax this evening. We will both go to work as usual so nothing will look amiss." Peter hugged and kissed Evie and patted her tummy. "I know you're going to be a little girl, with bright red hair, and your Mommy's blue eyes."

Evie laughed. "Are you a great seer, lover? How about scrambled eggs and toast and jam? We can have a bottle of wine with it. That's about all the larder will bear at the moment."

"Oh, for a good steak. Can't wait till we are at peace again and can eat normally."

"Peter, this time I'm so frightened for you. I think about the people in Europe that have nothing. I won't complain, but I want the war to end too. I'm tired of living in cold weather. I do miss my family. I never thought I would say it, but I think I will be happy when I'm no longer connected with politics, and you will be home for good."

"Well, my darling, while I'm away, you write a letter to your parents and tell them our plans. Tell them you will probably be having the baby at home here, unless we find out differently from the doctor. Molly may want to come down and take care of her when she is born, like she did with Michael."

"Peter, do you think Molly would like to retire in California? I think it would be good for her bones."

"I'm sure she would, Ev."

Evie stood over the stove. She took a little olive oil and put it in the frying pan. She cracked six eggs, and whisked them in a bowl with a bit of water. When the oil was hot, she poured in the eggs and stirred. Happy to have some homemade blueberry jam to accompany the eggs and toast, she took two of their nicest plates, and served their meal on those.

Peter opened a bottle of red wine and filled two wine glasses. The table was set near the window that overlooked the garden. She and Peter ate their dinner, holding hands.

"I could do this every night, Evie. I love you so much."

"I love you too, Peter, and I will be waiting for you when you return. Don't be long."

The days seemed interminable to Evie. Inundated with extra work, she had to complete Peter's work also. Harry called her several times to make certain she was okay. Not having to worry about finding a parking place or driving a car did help. The War Department asked Harold Greenwood to do her chauffeuring. Glad to be of assistance, he had enjoyed Peter's acquaintance ever since the first day he picked him up at the train station.

Michael came home to visit, and to talk about where he wanted to go to college. He stayed for several days, which also helped Evie to pass the time quickly and more comfortably. All Evie could tell Michael was that his Dad was on a business trip. Michael seemed to understand completely, and offered to do anything that Evie might need.

"Even grocery shopping."

Evie laughed at him. "Michael, you are priceless. Have you ever been inside a grocery store?"

"Only when Molly or Dad offered to buy me a piece of candy," he answered with a facetious laugh.

Peter in the meantime was having a different kind of trip. When he left Washington DC, he was taken to New London, Connecticut where he boarded a submarine. It was his first experience below the water.

315

He was afraid he would be claustrophobic, but he adapted. The quarters inside a submarine were cramped. The walkways narrow, and there were no windows. He had to watch his head wherever he walked. He was amazed to find the decks so clean. The sailors constantly swabbed them. Peter could almost see his face in the crystal clear glass gauges. The brass was highly polished, as was the chrome. The captain gave him a tour.

"We've got all the modern artillery; ten 21-inch torpedo tubes, six forward, four aft. We've got twenty-four torpedoes on board, one deck gun and two machine guns. The sub has two props."

"I'm impressed, Captain." Peter's destination was London. "How many sailors on board?"

"We have six officers and fifty-four crew members. One of our officers is doubling up with another one so you will have a private cabin. My orders are to get you safely to London."

"Will you be bringing me back to the states?"

"That's the plan, Mr. Wells."

I can't wait to take Evie on a tour of Europe. We'll go hunting for antiques and Maud Driscoll paintings. I will take her to dine at the best restaurants in Paris. It will be the honeymoon we never had.

Peter made his way through the naval shipyard to the nearest phone box. He called the phone number he was given before he left Washington. "Mr. Jones, this is Mr. Smith."

316

"Hello, Mr. Smith. We've been expecting you. Would you meet me at 10 Downing Street at 11:00 hours on Thursday?"

Peter answered in the affirmative, thinking, *this is the first time I've been to the Prime Minister's residence.* It was only a brisk walk from his hotel to where he was supposed to meet "Mr. Jones". A butler opened the door and ushered him into a side conference room.

"I'm sorry you will not be able to meet the Prime Minister today, Pete, but he has given us permission to have lunch here, and enjoy a little conversation after we finish our business. You have the papers for me?"

"Yes, I do, Sir, and I trust they will be helpful to the British for the invasion. Our president doesn't keep me privy to what the dates and times are, but I find if I can translate, and tell him about the geography, it is helpful."

"I know it must be, Peter. You have been invaluable to the Secret Service."

"Thank you, Ken."

"I'm sorry to do this to you, Pete, but we need to send you back in again. We need more corroboration as to where to bomb."

"Do you think I will be away longer than three weeks? My wife is due soon, and I would like to be home then."

"I don't blame you. Hopefully, you will be through in just a few days. We're going to fly you into

317

Switzerland, and you will ski to a shack where we have operatives in Germany. We are afraid to transmit anything more for fear of them being found. If anything goes wrong, just get back to where we dropped you."

"I hope you have a map of the area. I haven't skied in Switzerland since I was a child."

"We have a nice surprise for you. Someone will be waiting to take you there and to get you out."

"How will I know him?"

"We will give you a specific greeting to use, and he will be waiting for you. Before the war, he worked as a ski instructor. He is now living in the rectory of the local Catholic church."

"You mean he is a priest?"

"Well, he was on his way to becoming one, but he never was ordained. Anyway the old priest took pity on him, and he works around the church doing odd jobs. It's a marvelous cover, and the priest doesn't have to lie when he says he has gone to another village on an errand. He has been one of our best agents. I'm not sure whether he will enter the priesthood after the war. We'd like to encourage him to come to London and work for us."

"Interesting, Ken. When do I leave?"

"What did you leave at the hotel?"

"Just the suitcase you supplied me with."

"Pete, inside the suitcase there's a ski outfit with an extra heavy parka and gloves. You'll need it.

This is an extremely dangerous mission. I hate sending you when I know your wife is expecting your child, but we don't have anyone else with your capabilities."

"Don't look so glum, Ken. What am I to bring back?"

Ken's voice was adamant. "Some transmissions too dangerous to relay, and if anything goes wrong, get out immediately. That's an order. The people manning that shack know what a slim chance they have for survival. I don't want you in the same kind of danger. It's horrific enough what we are asking you to do. You will have Germans to deal with every step of the way. And you need to travel light so all I can give you is this revolver. Don't let it out of your possession. I know you know that already. I'm giving you an extra round of bullets. I just pray to God you won't have to use them. Here is your German passport. I still gave you the first name of Pieter. I think the last name Ludwig is innocuous enough. Once you return to Switzerland, Rudi will see you get to the plane and out of the country and back to London. Once you are here, call me at the usual number, and we can meet shortly after."

"What if I don't get back?"

"Pete, you might want to write up a short will and give it to me before you leave. I promise if anything happens to you, your wife and children will be provided for."

"I know nothing will happen, Ken. But I thank you. And I'll be back in London before you know it."

"Then I will see you get on that same submarine and head back to New London."

319

"Sounds simple enough."

"I can assure you, it's not a simple task we are asking of you. I had the clothes put in a suitcase. Give me the key to your room. I will see everything is taken out of there, and delivered back to us, just in case we need you again. Now, before you go, let's go have a good meal. You deserve it."

CHAPTER 29

Somewhere in Switzerland, 1944

𝒫eter stood on the tarmac of a small airstrip somewhere in Switzerland, near the town of Montigny. He was on a level piece of ground in a lovely valley between two mountain chains. Tall green pine trees glistened with snow, pristine white drifts covered the ground.

"There is so much snow, I'm amazed the pilot was able to land!" But the landing strip had been cleared of anything white to show the hard dirt underneath. Peter would be skiing into Germany. That was all he knew. With all the snow, it would be difficult to keep his bearings. The terrain was unfamiliar. Peter had changed into the ski clothes Ken had provided. He was glad for the heavy black turtleneck sweater he had been wearing. He laced up his ski boots, and as he left the plane, the pilot wished him well.

The cold in D.C. doesn't compare to this, he thought. This is absolutely raw. Peter followed the pilot's directions and after about a two-mile walk, he saw the little church that had been described to him. It was too cold for anyone to be outside, so he doubted anyone had seen him. I forgot how cold Swiss winters can be. He noticed a small building behind the church he presumed was the rectory. He walked through the courtyard, past a small cemetery, and stood on the front stoop. He knocked at the door, and a tall man in his late thirties or forties opened it.

"Hello, I'm looking for Rudi," said Peter in his best German.

"I'm Rudi, what can I do for you?"

Then Peter gave him the secret code phrase. The man answered him and Peter replied.

"Ken sent me."

"Oh, you must be Peter. Please come in. I bet you're freezing. How about something hot that's supposed to taste like coffee?"

Peter laughed. "Anything hot would be welcomed. Ken had some good words of praise for you, Rudi. I'm glad to have you along on this junket. I don't have the slightest idea where I am."

Rudi smiled. "You'll spend the night here, Peter. We leave before sunup. But, if it's bright enough with the moon and stars, we'll leave tonight."

"Whatever you say. How long of a trip do we have?"

"Well, if we don't run into trouble, we should be out and back within eight hours. I've packed us some cheese and bread, so that should keep us going. You look like you are pretty fit. That's good. We go over some rugged terrain, so we can keep away from the Germans."

Peter thought about Evie and Michael, and the new baby coming. He hadn't been on skis for a while, so even though he was in top physical condition, the tough trek challenged him. He and Rudi didn't even talk for fear of an echo. After about two hours, Rudi waved his arm to signal Peter to join him.

"I'm glad for the stop," Peter whispered.

Rudi whispered back. "There's a small German camp just on the other side of this hill. We need to avoid it at all costs. I don't want them chasing us. We have crossed the border into Germany."

"What do you suggest?"

"Cross-country on the top of the ridge for another three miles, then go down the hill."

"You lead."

Rudi nodded yes, and skied off. Peter followed in his tracks, so if anyone saw them, it would appear there was only one skier. The sun was now high in the sky. The only thing not white on either Rudi or Peter was necessary sun goggles. An hour passed before Rudi made another gesture to stop. He put a finger to his lips. Then he pointed. Below were several dogs, and then behind them, several German soldiers on skis. It wasn't a happy sight to Peter. He gestured a 'now what?' to Rudi and Rudi pointed to a small crevasse in the mountain that seemed free of snow.

They made their way to the crevasse, and Rudi leaned against the cold rock. Heavily armed soldiers walked the perimeter. Peter had his pistol, and Rudi had a pistol and rifle he pulled out from his ski pack. Peter didn't say anything. They could hear the soldiers talking and the dogs making noise below them. Neither Rudi nor Peter said a word. Hopefully, the soldiers would pass without the dogs picking up their scent. They waited what seemed an interminable amount of time. Then Rudi motioned for Peter not to move. Rudi edged his way over to the crest of the hill, crouched down and looked over. Thank God. No one appeared in their sightline and their tracks led in the opposite direction.

"Let's go, Peter, before they return."

In the distance, Peter could see a roof, with smoke coming from it. When they were close to what appeared to be a chalet, Rudi stopped short.

"What's wrong?"

"I don't like it. You wait here and let me go check."

"You're the boss on this trip, Rudi."

Once inside the chalet, Rudi discovered an empty building. He stuck his head outside and motioned for Peter to come ahead. Inside, they could see whoever had been here had left in a hurry.

"Peter, did they tell you what you were supposed to get?"

"Maps of German troop movements."

"I think those maps might be what they burned in the fire."

"Oh God, those papers were so important."

"Well, the Germans could have torched the place but they didn't. They're probably still looking. The maps could be hidden anywhere. What would you do if you had to hide something? You might start a fire to make the enemy believe you had destroyed whatever, so they couldn't get their hands on it."

"I'm thinking the French Resistance would do something clever, but they're not here." He laughed quietly. "Those Germans will be back to look again. I'll put a bet on it. Where in this place would one hide documents? It's probably someplace very simple."

"I'd put them under a floor board, behind a loose brick – even in a book. Let's start checking." They searched any place covered in brick, all around the fireplace and hearth. They tested all the floorboards. They removed the small rug and looked under it. Nothing.

"Maybe there's a book with a false inside."

"Those shelves have about fifty books on them. Let's get to it."

Peter started reading all the titles. Translating from German made it slower than he would have liked.

"Rudi, look at this title." Peter had pulled a green leather bound book from the shelf, 'The Road Home'. "Sounds like a perfect title." Peter opened the book to discover papers and maps folded into a false bottom. "Pay dirt."

"Great. Now let's get the hell out of here, while we still have our heads."

Peter took every paper and map, stuffed them under his heavy sweater, and part of his underwear. He put the book back where he found it. They had just shut the door and put on their skis, when they saw the Germans in a grove of trees about 300 yards away.

"Shit, Peter, let's make tracks. If the Germans start shooting, keep going, that crevasse we were in is about the only place to hide."

They quietly began shushing over the snow. One of the dogs barked. Bullets flew wildly in their direction. Peter felt something sting his collarbone and shoulder. When they reached the crevasse, Peter realized Rudi was badly wounded. He had slumped down in the snow, grabbed his stomach and moaned.

The Germans probably were looking in another direction when they left the cabin, but the dogs barking started the barrage of bullets. One or two of them had ricocheted and hit Rudi.

"Rudi, you're hit." Peter took a handkerchief from his pocket and held it on Rudi's stomach wound, trying to stop the bleeding. "I'm not going to leave you here, but I don't think I can carry you."

A bullet had also creased Peter's shoulder, and it needed tending.

"Rudi, your wound needs attention. Can the priest get a doctor? I'll bind you up with whatever I can use."

At that point, Peter pulled off his top layers to his undershirt, ripped it in pieces and carefully wound the makeshift bandage around Rudi's body. *Damn it, he won't stop bleeding.*

"Think you can make it?"

"Damn sure. I sure as hell don't want to stay here."

As strong as Rudi was, the loss of blood was taking its toll on an ashen Rudi.

Peter saw the drops of blood on the snow, and he carefully covered them so the path to the crevasse wouldn't be discovered. It was a very slow trek back to the church. Afraid Rudi wouldn't make it, Peter took his skis off and then Rudi's. He looped his belt around Rudi's waist so he could support him better. At the very last, he had to almost drag him. Finally, on friendly soil, Peter's adrenaline pumped to capacity. It took them another three hours to arrive at their destination. By the time the two of them reached the rectory, Rudi had lost a great deal of blood.

Peter's shoulder ached. "Thank you, God." An exhausted and cold Peter laid Rudi on his bed, went and found the priest.

"Father, Rudi is badly hurt. Can you get him a doctor?"

The old priest nodded yes, put on a heavy coat and hat, and left the warmth of the room.

Peter felt for Rudi's pulse. He had no color at all. His eyes were closed.

"Rudi, stay with me. Don't you go dying on me. Ken wants you to come to England after the war and help him. He says you are the absolute best, and he wants to recruit you." Peter kept talking to Rudi, but heard little response.

The doctor and priest arrived. The doctor checked for a pulse to find Rudi's breathing shallow, then shook his head. The priest put his amice over his shoulders and administered the Last Rites to Rudi. The priest held up his hand, and made the sign of the cross.

"En nomina patri, filia, et spiritu sancti," the priest intoned.

Peter knelt by the bed, and held Rudi's hand until the very end. He had forgotten all about his own wound until the doctor noticed Peter's bloody shirt. It didn't take the doctor long to remove the bullet, and then bandage him.

"A few more inches and you would be joining Rudi," The doctor commented.

"I know, doc. Thanks." When the doctor finished with Peter, the three of them carried Rudi's body to the icehouse behind the rectory. They would bury him in the spring.

The old priest gave Peter some hot soup and a bed to sleep in for a few hours.

The next day, Peter trudged down the road to the airstrip, slower than his usual pace because of the pain to find the pilot waiting for him.

"Do you have any painkillers?" Peter's shoulder was throbbing. The pilot handed him a bottle. "Thanks, man." Peter took two pills and put two more in his shirt pocket. While in the air, Peter changed his clothes, and put the papers he rescued into the suitcase along with all the ski clothes and shoes.

Back in London, he made the designated phone call, and within half an hour, he sat having a brandy with Ken.

"Well, I was told it was a little hairy for you. Tragic about Rudi. He was such a good guy." Then changing the subject, "How's the shoulder, Pete?"

"A little on the painful side, but the fact I'm going home, lessens the pain."

"I'm glad your mission was successful. The Navy told me your sub is docked in Liverpool. I'll get a car to drive you. I bet you will be happy to get back home. Someday, my wife and I would like to tour your country. But as soon as this bloody war is over, I'm going to stand for another seat in parliament to represent Essex, the area where I live."

"Wonderful on both counts, Ken. I'm sorry I won't be here to vote for you. All I can say is I will be glad to get back to Evie, and my son, Michael. It's been a pleasure to meet you, and let us pray this war we've been fighting in Europe and against Japan over. I can't think beyond Europe even though Japan declared war on the U.S. in '41."

"Mr. Churchill said Japan woke a sleeping tiger. I know he's right. Now with America's help England will prevail."

Six days later, Peter walked into his home in Georgetown. Evie ran to him and smothered him in hugs – as well as she could. Her tummy, swollen with their baby now protruded a great deal more than when he left a few weeks before.

"Oh, Peter, I am so glad you're home."

"You have no idea how glad I am to be here."

She saw the bandage on Peter's shoulder.

"I had a little run in with a stray German bullet." He laughed as he kept her fingers entwined in his hand. Evie looked at him.

"Peter you are being so cavalier. What happened?"

"Evie, I really don't want to talk about it. I lost a man on this venture." Peter's face looked so sad.

"Oh, Peter, I'm so sorry."

"He saved my life."

"I'm very grateful to him, whoever he was."

"A young man who had been studying for the priesthood before the war."

"My poor darling." Evie put her arms around Peter.

"These tragedies happen in war. It's alright sweetheart." He hugged her back. "It's over. At least I was able to get him back to his own country."

They continued hugging and kissing.

After his return, Peter still felt the effects of his wound. He was glad to have a few days relaxation before reporting to Harry. His shoulder bothered him, and he was not sleeping well. He began to have cold sweats at night, and would wake up calling for Rudi.

"Don't die on me. Don't die." Then he would see Sam's face, and he would cry out. I'll get you to a field hospital. Surreal images of Rudi and Sam's faces superimposed each other in his dream.

Peter re-lived every moment of his last assignment, as well as being a seventeen-year-old boy in France, saving his friend in the German onslaught, and losing Rudi in his last mission.

"Peter, wake up! You're having a bad dream." Evie was solicitous and her voice soothing.

One night Peter woke up sobbing. Evie put her arms around him and held him as tightly as she could.

"Darling, it's all right. You're safe now."

"Evie, I think I've cried for everyone lost in the war. I've cried because I never found Sam again. I cried because I lost Rudi. I've cried because I am safe. It's been a watershed. I know I will be just fine when I go and see Harry tomorrow."

CHAPTER 30

Washington D.C., Spring, 1945

*O*t was now summer and the war in Europe essentially over. Harry Woodring told Peter his service for the United States government had been completed, although they would love to have him remain in the Secret Service. He could stay on as an aide to Harry or just continue his architectural practice. "Your choice Peter," Harry told him.

"Of course the Secret Service would love to have you as a permanent employee. Your service has been invaluable to the U.S. Government."

Buoyed by Harry's comments, Peter said, "Harry, I'll get back to you after I speak with Evie."

And when they spoke, she said, "I can't imagine loving any house as much as this one. It's where I fell in love with you and where we first lived."

Since rationing, Evie had a hard time finding a crib for the baby when she and Molly stopped in an antique store one day, and hidden in the back corner, she found a very old brass bassinet. It surprised Evie it hadn't been commandeered in a scrap metal drive as so many old beautiful pieces had. But she and Molly had it delivered to the house, where they cleaned and polished it so much Evie knew her face could be seen in the railings. Evie found someone with a sewing machine who made them a mattress cover. She filled it with the softest materials she could find. Molly knitted a blanket, and Evie crocheted one. By the due date, her baby would be living like a prince or princess. Evie's doctor found an experienced midwife for her, and would deliver at home.

Evie had purchased everything she thought she would need to give birth, and the midwife had come to live with them until her delivery. It was three o'clock on a blustery March morning, when Evie poked Peter.

"Peter, my water broke. I know it's time. Please go wake up Mrs. Beaton."

"I'm on my way, sweetheart." Peter quickly dressed, and ran down the hall to bring the midwife.

She's taking over like a drill sergeant, Peter thought, *but I'll do whatever she tells me.* Mrs. Beaton sent Peter to the kitchen to start boiling water, then to get some clean sheets and towels from the linen closet. She deftly changed the bed where Evie lay, making certain she was as comfortable as possible. Peter timed her contractions. When he first started, they were about five minutes apart. Now, they weren't even two. Evie perspired profusely. Peter went to get a cool washcloth from the bathroom to wipe her forehead. Mrs. Beaton continued to time the contractions. Molly joined them in the room. They were now less than one minute apart.

'Evie, when I tell you to push, push hard. It will all be over soon."

Penelope Anne Wells didn't take long to arrive. She was just perfect. And Molly didn't know who acted more excited, the mother, the daddy, or her. Mrs. Beaton cut the umbilical cord, wrapped the little girl in a blanket and handed her to her daddy.

"Oh, she's just beautiful, Evie."

"Peter, she has your red hair."

"Your little girl is just beautiful. Thank you for letting me deliver her. I called the pediatrician, and he will be here this afternoon to look at her."

"Thank you, Mrs. Beaton, from all of us."

"After the doctor arrives, he will drive me back to my home. If I can leave you for a little while, I'll go pack my things."

"There's no hurry," said Peter. "Don't feel like you have to rush off."

"I don't, Mr. Wells. I have another baby to deliver."

Michael also arrived later in the day to see his new sister. "Dad, was I ever that small?" Everyone laughed. "Dad, I came to talk to you because I know you and Evie will be moving soon. I will have just finished my first year at Georgetown, but I would like to come to California with you."

"Oh, Michael, we'd love that," said Evie. "Where do you want to go to school?"

"I'd really like you to come into business with us, Mike. Think you would have a great future, son."

"Dad, I've been thinking about that too. As much as I love studying art, I think it would be more practical to study business. I'd like to transfer to Evie's alma mater."

"That would be wonderful, Mike."

"I've already sent for, and completed all the forms and mailed them back. Plus, I have my acceptance."

"You're way ahead of us, son. When does the semester start?"

"Late September, Dad."

"Well, you've given us the impetus to move sooner. However, we can't do anything until the war is over. I know you can go stay with Lillie and George, or even Steve would probably take you in."

"I thought I might live on campus, Dad. If that's okay with you?"

"Of course, Mike. In the meantime, you need to continue your studies until the semester ends. Then come and stay in your room here. You can help us get boxes packed. Harry tells me if everything goes well, we should be out of the war within the year."

Harry wasn't too far off. On August sixth, a devastating experimental nuclear bomb fell on Hiroshima, Japan, and on August ninth, the United States dropped another nuclear bomb on Nagasaki. A few days later, America declared the war officially over. People danced in the street, church bells rang, and gas rationing ended.

Peter and Evie just hugged each other harder and harder.

"It's over, Peter," Evie said trying to catch her breath between Peter's repeated kisses and crushing hugs. "If I were still pregnant, darling, Penny would have been born right here and now."

Peter laughed. "It's so good to know we're free."

"Mother has been so worried about the lack of news about Aunt Maud and Giovanni. No mail, nothing."

He smiled, "I'm sure they're safe, and your mother will hear something." Changing the subject, "Mike is heading off to California soon. Since gas rationing is over, I thought about letting him drive a car, but I'm going to play it safe. He can buy one when he gets there. I'm sure Steve or your Dad will help him."

"I know they will."

"Honey, when are you going to officially resign from your job?"

"Well darling, since you are also retired, I thought you might come with me, and we could bring Penny for everyone to see what a beautiful child we have."

"I'm happy to go with you, but I think you are crowing a bit, Peter."

"Darling, I know I am."

September 9, 1945

Dearest children,

Dad and I couldn't be more thrilled that you are moving to California permanently. Michael joined a fraternity on campus, so, although he lives there, most of his personal belongings are sitting in your room, Evie. He seems to be thriving in California and is becoming what I hear him called a Big Man on Campus. Of course, in order to stay current, I think the term is BMOC. So far, he has brought over two different young ladies for us to meet. They were both nice, but I don't see any future for them with Michael. I have to be very prejudiced when I say he's too smart for them. Let's just say they were not up to him intellectually.

Peter, you should be so proud of that young man. I couldn't love him any more if he were my own grandson. I know George feels the same way. We can't wait to hold our baby, Penny. When are you coming? What can I do to help you?

And Peter, do you and Evie know where you want to live? Do you want me to do any house hunting for you? Are you going to rent or buy? Peter, I'm sure you already know Steve and Dad have optioned several pieces of property they think would serve as good places to put up a lot of new homes. I hope you and Evie will want to learn to play golf and join us on the golf course. It's such a wonderful game.

Dad is feeling just fine, Evie. And the doctor concurs. Steve has taken over his trial practice, so that relieves him of a lot of stress. My arms are around all three of you with lots of love and kisses and hugs from Dad and me.

Mom

September 9, 1945

Dear Lillie,

Although you don't know me except for that brief phone call when Maud married Andrew, Maud asked me to get a letter off to you to let you know she and Giovanni survived the war intact. Their property in Lucca however, was completely destroyed. She and Giovanni are coming to England to stay with Kenneth and me until they have recouped enough strength to travel to California. I know Maud wants to tell you herself what their plans are, so when she arrives here, I know she will send you a letter of her own.

My family is all well, thank the good Lord, and I have a new baby granddaughter, Lavinia. Someday, I hope Kenneth and I will travel to California to meet you, or that you will come to London and visit us. I feel like I have known you all my life.

With affection,

Priscilla Colchester

October 1, 1945

Dear Priscilla,

I can't thank you enough for letting me know about Maud. George and I have been so worried about her and Giovanni. You and I both have something more in common. I, too, have a new granddaughter. My daughter, Evie, who was born right after Maud married in Boston, (remember when I couldn't come?), just gave birth to a baby girl, her name is Penelope. We call her Penny, and I haven't seen her yet. Peter and Evie have been living in Washington D.C., but their plan is to move here as soon as they can arrange to do so.

I can't believe all the people I hold near and dear to me will be moving to California. George and I are overjoyed. Thank you again for the wonderful news.
Lillie

CHAPTER 31

*I*t was the end of October before Peter and Evie could wind everything up in D.C. Parties and celebrations kept them in a whirlwind. They were awarded medals by President Truman at a ceremony in the White House.

Once all the fanfare died down, Peter and Evie worked in earnest to shut down the Georgetown house and move to California. They decided to leave all the major pieces of furniture in the house, and purchase new furniture when they had a new home of their own. Evie brought in movers who packed and crated everything they wanted to take, then shipped via railway where it would be delivered to a freight office close to Glendale.

Once she and Peter checked everything was ready to go, all their personal belongings were taken out of the house. Peter made certain the paintings were exceptionally well packed so they wouldn't be damaged on the long trip across country. Even Molly's belongings were packed in a crate.

It would have been possible to go by air now that passenger planes were available, but Peter thought Evie and the baby would be more comfortable on the train. He arranged for two drawing rooms that gave space for Molly and the baby in one, Peter and Evie in the other. A kind porter made it possible for them to eat meals without having to subject the baby being moved from car to car.

Three days later, they were in Pasadena, and just like the time they first arrived together, Peter arranged for two cars to take them wherever they wanted to go. This time, Peter booked a cottage at the

345

Huntington Hotel in Pasadena. Here they would have a fully-equipped kitchen and furnished home for all of them to be comfortable until they decided where they wanted to live.

"Evie, I'm going to see if I can buy us a car today. We need transportation. I'll be back in a few hours."

Peter returned driving a new station wagon. "Well, what do you think?"

"It's perfect, Peter. We can even put a bed in there for Penny."

"Evie, you and Peter both know I'm getting a little old to take care of Penny." Molly and Evie were sitting at the kitchen table drinking tea. "You need to have someone much younger than I am. I love what I have seen of Pasadena, and I think I would like to settle here."

That night, Evie repeated her conversation with Molly to Peter. "She's been with you a good long while, since Michael was born, and he's going to be twenty-one very soon. Have you given any thought as to what you might do? I don't think she has much money to live on, darling."

"Evie, what I would like you to do is to take Molly shopping for a duplex or apartment. There seems to be a lot of them going up these days. Whatever she finds, we will either buy the building, or if she wants a little house, we can do that also. Then we will pay her a monthly stipend for as long as she lives. I owe her everything including my sanity. I don't know how I would have survived after Michael was born if she hadn't been there. She's been a true rock to the Wells family. We will tell her at dinner tonight what we would like to do. I'd even give her one of the houses we are

346

planning to build, but I don't think the area would be the best for her. Pasadena is more developed, and has good transportation, since she has never learned to drive."

Molly couldn't believe what she was hearing. Tears of happiness flowed. "You people have truly been my family. You will always be my family."

"The same is true for us, Molly dear, and tomorrow, Evie will take you shopping for a little house or duplex, whichever you would like. Don't worry about anything except living there. I know there are some lovely little houses just off Lake Street that might suit you perfectly."

"You and I will start looking tomorrow, Molly."

Molly and Evie drove up and down every street near Lake each day to look for houses, and became very discouraged. In fact, Evie wanted to tell Peter to let Molly have the house of her choice when the next development was completed. They were on their way to go shopping when Evie turned down a little lane paralleling Lake Street. Molly couldn't believe it. A sign.

She was overjoyed when they actually saw a 'for sale' sign on a small cottage, with a beautiful yard filled with flowering shrubs and rose bushes. They went up to the front door, and rang the bell. After being shown the home, Evie realized Molly had found her place of refuge. She asked the price of the home, and without quibbling or negotiating, told the owner they would take it.

"I can't believe I will move in here in less than three weeks." Molly was pinching herself with happiness.

Lillie spent several hours designing and sewing dresses for Penny. As soon as she wore one for a few weeks, the sides had to be adjusted to fit Penny's growing body. Her granddaughter weighed twelve pounds when she arrived in California, now she tipped the scales at almost twenty.

Lillie loved having her at home and taking care of her. Peter had rented an office, large enough to have an architectural room for drawing plans, a separate desk for him, a desk for Mike when he was working during his vacations, and a reception area where sometimes Evie would work when she was there. Most days, Evie took care of Penny and loved to wheel her in her carriage all around the neighborhood. Steven, Peter, and George went out to look at several pieces of property shortly after the Wells' arrival, and now a few months later, they were watching sewers go in, electric lampposts and sidewalks being laid. Every day, someone would be out at the first project overseeing the progress.

The day the project completed and opened to the public, lines of veterans and their families formed along the sidewalk, waiting to buy homes. Peter was ecstatic. When the day ended, they were all at the Patterson's where Lillie had prepared dinner for them.

"You've sold out the entire project. Now what are you planning to do?" Steve asked.

"Get started on another project. With our success on our first one, I think we should try to do two. The San Fernando Valley seems to be the ideal place after all the driving I've been doing around here."

"I think you may be right on that score, Peter." George pulled out some paperwork that was on the sideboard. "I have a client who wants to sell 100 acres in Van Nuys. He's asking a fairly reasonable price. Shall I tell him you'll take it?"

Peter responded by nodding yes with a big grin on his face.

Evie looked at everyone and laughed. "What," she asked, "are we going to do with all this money we are making?"

"Honey, I thought you wanted to turn the house in Georgetown into a museum. Lillie, do you think Maud Driscoll might be interested in having some of her paintings there on permanent display?"

"Oh Peter, what a wonderful idea. What do you think, Mom?"

"We don't even know if she is still painting. But I had a letter from her friend, Priscilla, who told me she and Giovanni are surviving. The Germans confiscated all their property and burned the vineyards to the ground. Every piece of furniture in their home ruined, the wine vats depleted. No salvage they could rebuild upon. Can you imagine, everything, just everything gone?"

"Poor dear souls, what are they going to do?"

"I know they're planning to move to the U. S., but as yet I don't know where. The obvious place would be the family home in Boston, but I think Maud is ready to move on. And what would Giovanni do there? He certainly couldn't make wine in Boston. I know she will write me as soon as she arrives in England."

April 10, 1948

Dearest Lillie,

It has been so long since I have written to you, and even longer since I have seen you. So much has happened in my life. Giovanni and I are fine, thank God. Unmentionable, terrible things happened during the war in Italy. I was on my knees thanking God when Germany surrendered. All of our property in Tuscany is gone, at least for another couple of generations.

I guess Priscilla already told you that. One thing I can say is my clever husband and I figured out a way to save my jewelry, some family heirlooms, and all my paintings. I haven't painted in five years. I miss it so.

Priscilla and Ken were so kind to invite us to stay for a few months at Bodicea Hall, their home in Essex, so we could recuperate. Priscilla is a grandmother to four-year-old Lavinia. She was born during an air raid. At least no one heard her mother cry out with labor pains. Lavinia is adorable with her blonde ringlets and blue eyes. Sorry to make light of it, but I wish I were fortunate enough to have a grandchild, but right now I'm just grateful to be alive.

Everything Giovanni and I own has been crated up and brought to England, kindness of Ken. Giovanni was completely wiped out, and I can't get at my money until I return to New York or Boston. There is nothing for me in Boston. I just want to sell the house and put the proceeds in a bank. Mother and Daddy left me an heiress, so whatever I have will go to rebuild Giovanni's and my future.

I saw a magazine article several years ago before the war about the Italians that had settled in Napa Valley, California and were making wine. So that is where we plan to go. Can you believe it? We'll be neighbors! Are Napa and Glendale far apart?

But let me get to the point. Giovanni and I are going to need a good lawyer. Would George consider helping us? We want to buy a winery, or build one, if we can't find what we want. A young man who worked for us in Lucca is also coming with us as our ward. He is a wonderful vineyard worker and knows a great deal about vines and rootstock and all that.

Could you ask George for me since I've never met him personally? You can write and let me know at Priscilla's. And when we arrive at the Waldorf where Ken booked a suite for us, I will telephone you.

Oh, Lillie, do you realize we may get our Thanksgiving together yet. I have missed you, dear friend. And I have so missed the freedom we have in America.

Love and a thousand hugs,

Maud

April 30, 1948

Dearest dear Maud,

 After all these many years, it is so good to hear from you. And I need to underline that a good many times. I am grateful to know that you and Giovanni are alive and well. I am beside myself with joy because you are moving to California, and I am going to see you. But, I think you forgot your geography. Glendale is about 500 miles from Napa Valley. I live in Southern California. Napa is in the north. But I don't care. We will get to see each other, and that is all that matters.

 George says he can't run around as he thinks you need a lawyer to do, but we are offering our son, Steven, who has earned quite a reputation for his skills in real estate law. Steven isn't married yet, so has offered to accompany you to the valley, even drive if you would like. He went to school in the north, and used to do a lot of weekending there, he now tells us.

 So much is happening these days, I don't know where to begin. George and I have a granddaughter also. Her name is Penelope Anne. She was born March 15, 1945. She has red hair, just like her father. But Maud, she was born in Washington D.C. in the house you lived in with Andrew. I can't wait to tell you all about this. Oh, my dear, Maudie, please hurry to California. Anyway, Peter, Evie's husband bought it when he went to work in D.C. during the war. They still own the house, although they live here now. Peter is an architect, and is building small tract homes for the returning soldiers to buy. He and Evie are on their third project now, and all the homes are being sold before they are even completed. Of the building boom continues like this, the San Fernando Valley will be completely Wells tract homes. I kid you not. Peter has a son, Michael, by a previous marriage, and he is general manager of the entire outfit.

I think Peter and Evie would like to fly to New York and meet you there. Peter has something he would like to talk to you about before you come to California. I hope it will be all right with you. I told him you would be staying at the Waldorf, so that is where he booked rooms for him and Evie.

Oh, Maudie, there's so much to sit and talk to you about. Letters just don't do justice for us, but at least it's been better than nothing. And you have no idea how thrilled I was when I picked up the letter with your handwriting.

I have missed you, dear friend.

Love, love, love,

Lillie

Maud and Giovanni, with the help of Dario Cimino who had come to America with them, packed the newly purchased Cadillac with all the suitcases they were able to take in the car. Their visit in New York was a whirlwind of eating, shopping, and visiting. To meet Evie and Peter had been incredible. As they sat in the Wells' suite, Peter and Maud relived their former encounter.

"Peter, I have to ask you when you were born."

Taken aback when she heard the answer, Maud said, "Children, I think something very significant is happening." She trembled at this point.

"Caro, are you all right?" Giovanni had seen her afraid before, but this was something new.

"I think I'll be fine. Sit down next to me while I talk. This is something I've held so close to my heart, I'm almost afraid to tell it now."

"It's all right, Caro." Giovanni kissed her cheek and sat down beside her.

"I need to tell you about my life when I was an art student in Paris. I was very much in love with an Englishman, the brother of my college roommate. His parents had him betrothed to a girl he didn't love, and didn't want to marry. But the father was adamant. Neil must marry this young woman, but Neil had asked me to marry him and to keep it a secret from everyone. That is why I went to Paris in the first place. So we could be nearer to each other. I didn't want to return to Boston."

355

Evie and Peter sat on the sofa together across from them, holding hands. They couldn't wait to hear what was coming next. Maud continued.

"Once we arrive in California, I will show you a picture of Neil Wescott. Peter, Evie, I became pregnant by Neil. Then I received a letter from him telling me he had to marry someone else because he couldn't live without his inheritance, and all the pomp and circumstance that went with it. I was devastated. But then Priscilla came to visit me and told me Neil was dead. That he was killed in a pub brawl. It was as if he would rather have been dead than married to the other young woman. Priscilla stayed with me through the end of my pregnancy. I knew I couldn't keep my baby boy because the stigma on my parents would have been too great. Times were so different then." She was about to continue when Peter interrupted.

"Maud, what happened to the baby?"

"The doctor found a nice couple from Switzerland to take my precious child. Priscilla and I sent money each month to a solicitor to forward it to the couple so there would be sufficient money to see that he was well educated and cared for. When the Great War started, Germany had taken over the banking system in France and we were unable to send more. It was then we lost all track of my child."

"Peter," she said, hesitatingly, "Peter, I believe you are my son. You are the baby society forced me to relinquish." Maud's eyes brimmed with tears.

Everyone saw the emotion in Maud's face. Peter looked at Maud with pure love in his eyes. He stood up from the couch, taking Maud's hand; he knelt in front of her.

"If that is true Maud, it would be an incredible coincidence. One of the only items I was able to save when I fled the Germans was a small baby picture. I had bright red hair. Do you really think you could be my biological mother? My mother and father received money from France every month. There couldn't be two stories so exactly alike. It may be why all these years I have felt such a connection to you. Right before the war started, we moved to Cieux, France where my uncle owned a large dairy. My father was in the embroidery business, but it was difficult to buy thread and machine parts, so he closed down the factory. He and my mother were murdered by the Germans. It was a very sad and difficult time for all of us in France. I made my way across France and found an Army attachment. More coincidence, I was taken under the wing of a Lieutenant Sam Doty. The day before Evie and I were married, I saw his picture sitting on the table in the living room of Lillie and George."

"Lillie and I were stunned. We couldn't believe it because I had a different name then. I changed it when I began my career. It took several years and a lot of determination to find my way to the United States."

"Peter, Peter... Peter." It was about all Maud could say. So Peter began telling his story again. Tears of joy streamed down her cheeks as she listened.

"I started collecting your paintings in the twenties when I graduated from MIT. Does this mean I

have to give you the painting of the flower vendor?"
Peter laughed and hugged her.

"This is so precious to me. I'm overcome with happiness. We must call Lillie now, and tell her our wonderful news."

Peter picked up the telephone next to him on the table. "Operator, I would like to call Glendale, California. The number is Citrus 21... Yes operator, I will hold." Peter waited a few minutes on the line.

"Lillie, this is Peter. ...Yes, we are all fine... Evie is sitting right next to me on the sofa... We are with Maud and Giovanni. I'm going to put Maud on the line now. Evie will talk with you later."

"Lillie."

"Oh, Maud, I can't believe I'm really talking with you, and that I'll be seeing you soon."

"I have some wonderful, some amazing news for you." Maud answered.

"Tell me." Lillie replied anxiously.

"I think you had better be sitting down. I don't want you fainting."

"Good Lord, Maud, what is going on?"

"You know I had to give up my child in Paris?"

"Yes, I remember, and I burned the letter just like you asked."

"Lillie, I believe Peter is my son...my baby, the joy of my heart, the son I couldn't raise because of the

358

attitudes towards unwed mothers. When the war came in 1914, the money Priscilla and I were sending to my lawyer toward my child's well-being could no longer be forwarded to any bank because the Germans would only have confiscated it." Maud's words were tumbling out faster and faster.

"What kind of proof do you have, Maud?"

"I showed Peter a small picture I have of him, right before he was adopted. He had bright red hair and a lot of it. Peter says he has a small picture of him a little older with bright red hair also. He told me his parents received money from a bank in France every month. That was until the war. Then the money stopped. Lillie, it has to be him. It couldn't be otherwise – two babies. Both with red hair? Both adopted and raised in Switzerland? Both receiving money each month. Peter has to be one and the same."

"Maud, that is the most incredible and wonderful news. I'm so happy for us, because we are all really related. Peter and Evie's daughter is your granddaughter also. Could anything be more splendid or special? Oh, Maudie dear, I can't wait to see you."

"I feel the same way. Let me put Evie on the phone now. We'll see each other soon. I love you, dear friend."

"Hi, Mom, isn't this the most perfect news? What could be more special? Oh, yes, Peter is absolutely overjoyed. He and Maud are holding hands, and neither one will let go." Evie laughed as her eyes surveyed Peter and Maud whispering to each other.

"Mom, will you give Dad a great big hug and kiss for me? And of course Penny, from both her Mother and Father. Is she behaving? Tell her Daddy and I are bringing her some wonderful new treasures. Lots of love and hugs and kisses from us all. See you soon. Bye."

After the phone call, the room filled with uncontained excitement and frivolity. Peter then called down to the front desk and ordered not one, but two bottles of champagne for all of them to celebrate their discovery. "Now Maud, Aunt Maud, Mother, we have something else to talk to you about. I'm sure Lillie told you I purchased the home in Georgetown you lived in with Andrew Llewelyn. I've made several architectural changes, but I think you will like them. Evie and I would like to turn it into the Maud Driscoll Museum of Impressionism. The house is sitting empty now, but we thought we would talk to someone at the National Gallery who could recommend someone to curate and manage the property."

At this point, Maud couldn't speak. Giovanni had his hands on her shoulders caressing them. He leaned over and kissed her gray hair. "Caro, what wonderful things happen in America? I am so happy for you."

Maud reached up with her left hand, and touched Giovanni's hand. "I know my darling. My heart is racing."

The thought of having her former home in Washington D.C. turned into a museum housing her paintings overwhelmed her. She could not have imagined anything more wonderful. Maud couldn't stop talking about it to Giovanni as they traveled.

"Giovanni, can you imagine? We will have to take a trip there soon. But first, we will find vineyard property in Napa. And Steven will look at property with us. Do you have the feeling Peter would like to be part of the winery also?"

"Si, Caro, I'm certain he does. It also seems money is no object. Do you know I have already thought of a label for our wine - Baronessa? How do you like that?"

"Oh, Giovanni, I think that would be wonderful." Maud sighed. "My darling as much as I loved our villa, it is wonderful to be back in the United States, to be safe and know no enemy will be coming into our home and destroying it. Where will we meet Steven? Did Peter tell you?

We are going to drive to a place called St. Helena. Peter says there is an accommodating small hotel there. He has already spoken to a realtor, and he will be meeting us with Steven. I am so glad Dario knows how to drive and has a license, even though it is a foreign one."

"That is something we will have him do right away. Get a California license so he can chauffeur you around. Dario is a lot younger than you are, and I'm certain can relieve you of a lot of anxiety," Maud said.

"I know you are right, Caro."

During an uneventful trip across the continent Maud reminisced about the letter she had received from Lillie so very long ago, when she first took the train from Boston to California.

"Certainly no cowboys or Indians to cope with." When they stopped in Albuquerque for the night, the only Indians she saw were in the hotel lobby gift shop selling their handmade turquoise and silver jewelry. Maud purchased a beautiful squash blossom necklace for Lillie.

They spent two nights in San Francisco at the Fairmont, then traveled north. They took the ferryboat from Benicia to Vallejo. Once they left Vallejo, the landscape markedly changed. There were fields and fields of yellow mustard, and small vineyards on each side of the road. Little farmhouses were scattered, standing at the end of a long dirt road that would stop at the front door. Red winged blackbirds sat screeching to each other on the fences. Giovanni noticed everything including the red-barked trees on the hillsides which he would learn later were madrone. Groves of olive trees lined each side of the highway. Giovanni marveled at the scenery on Highway 29.

"You know, Caro, I would like to buy hill property, with some flatland where we can build a home. Maybe a replica of our villa in Lucca."

"Oh, Giovanni, are you sure?"

Dario drove up the main street of St. Helena.

"There's the hotel on your left, Dario. If you go around the block, we can park right in front. Would you please bring in the suitcases for us? Oh." she exclaimed,

"There's Steven. I'm sure of it. He looks like Lillie and George from the pictures she sent me."

"Hello, hello and welcome." Steven recognized Maud also. When the car came to a full stop, Steven opened the door and helped Maud out. "I feel like I have known you for years and years." He gave her a warm hug and a peck on the cheek.

"Oh, Steven, so do I. This is my dear husband, Giovanni, and driving is Dario Cimino, the son of a neighbor. He is now our ward. Dario is very good in the vineyards."

Dario gave him a smile, and nodded his head.

Steven presumed Dario spoke no English. He told him, "*Boungiorno.*" and then shrugged his shoulders. After a few minutes of polite conversation with Maud, Steven turned to Giovanni.

"Giovanni, there are numerous pieces of property to look at. I took the liberty of going to Giugni's, the local Italian deli, and having some sandwiches made for us, so we can picnic while looking. Does Dario speak English?" Steven thought he'd better ask the question so he wouldn't look like an idiot, since he already said good morning to Dario in the only Italian he knew.

"Not a word."

"Dario, welcome. Would you please translate that for him? There is so much Italian spoken here, I don't think he will have any problem. But I imagine he will want to learn English as soon as possible. My Italian is nil except that 'good morning'."

363

Giovanni relayed the message in Italian, and Dario answered with a wide grin.

"Do you have any idea of the kind of property you want?"

"I want it to be partly on hills, but will want flat lands as part of the property. This valley looks so like the Tuscany we remember. I want to build a beautiful villa for my darling Maud. She has put up with so much horror and sadness from the war I just want life for her to become as beautiful as the landscapes she has painted."

"I can certainly understand that. Maud's painting is beautiful. I have lived surrounded by it all my life." Steven asked Giovanni if he would allow him to drive their car because it held more passengers. "I also want to tell you about the area." When given the approval, Giovanni and Steven sat in the front seat, and Maud stayed in the back with Dario.

"The Napa valley is approximately twenty-five miles long. At its widest point it is about five miles across, and at its narrowest at the town of Calistoga, it is only about two. I'm told the weather is very similar to northern Italy."

"It feels like it today."

The ripening grapes still hung from the vines, waiting for the hot summer sun to turn their color and sugar up. Steven took them up Howell Mountain Road to show them property on the eastern side of the valley. As Steve drove, both Giovanni and Dario shook their heads negatively.

"No, Steven, I would like to be on the other side. The soil looks as if it is much richer. It appears to be more conducive to growing red wine than the acreage we have looked at here. The view is beautiful though."

"The realtor gave me one place to show you, but it is outrageously expensive. Even the realtor made the same comment."

"Show it to us anyway, Steven," Maud said.

"We'll go see it tomorrow. I'd like to show you a little of the area on the flatlands before it's too dark."

A beautiful spring morning greeted Dario and Giovanni as they stepped from the car. The aroma of the spring lilacs wafted in the soft breeze. Maud breathed in the delicious scent. Dario and Giovanni went to feel the soil. The green leaves on the vines swayed to the dance of the wind. It reminded Maud so of the vineyards outside of their home the Germans had destroyed. Dario smelled the dirt and rubbed it through his hands.

"Buono, buono, Giovanni."

"Yes it is, Dario."

"The price, Steven?"

When Steven told him the figure, he shook his head and turned to Maud.

"Too much money, Caro. And not enough hill land. We will have to look for something else."

Disappointed, the little group returned to the hotel.

"Would you like to make yourselves comfortable in our lounge and have some wine?" the proprietor asked them.

"My, that's a good idea, thank you."

Maud took a glass of wine and a piece of cheese from the plate the proprietor set on the table. Maud sat in the comfortable settee by the rear garden window. A small newspaper lay in front of her on the table.

"That's our local town paper," she was told. Maud picked it up and perused the pages. On the inside back page were two or three real estate advertisements. As she started reading, she called to Giovanni and began to read aloud the ad she discovered.

"There's a phone number, Caro. Let's call it and see if we can see the property right now."

Steven spoke to the owner, and made the arrangements. Everyone went back to the car for a ride up Spring Mountain Road.

"I'm enchanted with the wildflowers I see; the corn lilies, and lupine, black- eyed-susans." *How wonderful those colors would look on canvas. I hope it won't be too long before I can begin to paint again*, she thought.

Giovanni nodded approval of the terrain as they drove up the hillside towards the top of the mountain. An elderly Italian gentleman who had emigrated from northern Italy right after the Great War owned the vineyards. Old enough to be Giovanni's father, the two of them got along famously, the whole conversation in Italian. Even Dario participated, talking about the soil and the types of wines they would like to produce: cabernet, Barolo as well as the heavier Chianti.

"Delighted to meet your *famiglia*. Such tragedy you have suffered."

Maud related some of their experiences during the last few years in Italy, about the vineyards being burned, and how they could never feel comfortable, or secure, even if they did rebuild all they had lost on Italian soil. They were looking for a new beginning in Napa Valley.

"Won't you come into my home?" The elderly man ushered them into their dining room, where his wife offered them a glass of wine and cheese accompanied with some warm bread she had just baked.

"I like this American custom. It is Italian custom too," interjected Dario as he helped himself to another piece of bread. Everyone laughed except Steven who could speak no Italian. When Maud translated for him, he lightly tapped Dario on the back.

"Italian or American, I agree."

"Is this your wine?" Giovanni asked.

"*Si, si, es mio.* Do you like?" He offered them a taste of his cabernet, and the *picholo* he made only for his family.

"It's very good." Giovanni answered emphatically. "Did you make the *picholo* too?"

367

"*Si*, this is the last from our harvest last year. Now I will show you the winery and the cellar. All the equipment goes with the property."

Now if they could just agree on the price, Steven thought. *It'll be too high. I know it will be too high.*

The hands gestured and the voices talked around the table for almost an hour. Then the elderly gentleman stood up, held out his hand to Giovanni and told everyone the property would be theirs.

The Bank of America just up the street from their hotel would handle the transaction. Being a lawyer, Steven was amazed at the ease and grace these two men handled the sale, all with the shake of a hand. He told them both he would look over all the paperwork to make certain all the "Is" were dotted and "Ts" crossed. They would all present themselves to the bank in the morning. Because of the late hour, Maud made arrangements to call her bank in Boston to arrange for the money transfer in the morning at the St. Helena bank.

The house on the property would be theirs also. The owner, however, did request a little extra time for him and his wife to vacate the premises. They were moving to Marin County to be nearer their daughter and grandchildren. Now there was so much for Maud and Giovanni to do, they needed to make lists to include everything. Maud called Lillie on the phone to tell her their exciting news. The house itself was quite old but would be comfortable enough until a new house was completed. Maud was thinking Peter could design and build them a house similar to the villa in Lucca.

"If we are going to call the wine Baronessa, then we will live at the Villa Baronessa." "Baronessa Vineyards. I like the sound of that," Maud said.

Maud directed a smile at Giovanni, but he didn't see it. He was too engrossed in conversation with Dario. They were compiling a list of necessary equipment purchases, and discussing what pieces of machinery on the property could be salvaged.

Steven made a phone call to Peter to tell him about all the happenings of the day. In turn, Peter called Giovanni and asked him if he could be included in this new venture.

Giovanni was overjoyed because he didn't want Maud to be footing all the bills.

"Giovanni, I can have my bank wire you $50,000 tomorrow morning, and I can add another $50,000 in about two weeks. Is that enough?"

"Oh, my God, dear Peter. That is incredible. That will give you a third interest in the purchase price. Steven has also said he wants to invest, and I think your father-in-law will also do the same. It will be wonderful not to go outside the family, so to speak, for us to have our financing. Speaking for Maud too, I know she will be more than thrilled."

"Evie and I thought we might take a few days off, and come up and see you, and the property. We thought we might take George and Lillie with us, as a surprise to Maud. Are you going back to San Francisco to stay?"

"No, the hotel although very sparse, is nice enough. I will check to see if they have other rooms available, but just come to the hotel here, and we will have found a place for you to stay if they don't have the accommodations."

"Sounds wonderful. We will see you on Saturday then. Don't tell Maud."

"Our first visit to the Napa Valley," said Lillie.

"Oh my goodness, Peter, I know Maud would love to be painting this area. The colors and scenery are magnificent."

It took all the control Evie and Peter could muster to keep from blurting out the secret they were keeping from Lillie. When Peter drove up to the hotel, he stopped the car and removed all the bags from the trunk. Evie, Lillie, and George went inside. Lillie saw an attractive woman standing at the window looking out on a back garden.

"Evie, you know what? That woman looks how I picture Maud looking today."

"Why don't you go over and introduce yourself, Mom? It might be nice for you to talk to someone who lives in St. Helena."

Lillie, who wasn't the least bit shy, started to cross the lobby towards the woman when the woman turned and looked at her. Lillie's mouth went as wide as her arms did.

"Maud, Maud, is it really you?"

"Oh, Lillie, my dearest friend. I can't believe it."
They hugged and hugged closely, then at arm's length
so they could look at one another. Each one started to
say something.

"Sorry, Maud, you go first."

"No, Lillie, you start off."

"I have to sit down. Come, Maud, sit next to
me."

"Did you know I was here?"

"Peter and Evie didn't say one word. Bless their
hearts. They insisted George and I come with them to
see the property Peter was going to purchase with
some business partners. He didn't say it would be you
and Giovanni. I should have realized it when you called
me though. I can't tell you how wonderful it is to be
here. Are you really partners in this wine venture?"

"Yes, we are the guilty parties. You will also be
pleased to know Steven is going to be an owner too. I
know Giovanni is going to ask George if you two would
like to be part of this exciting new adventure for all of
us." Maud leaned over and touched Lillie's arm in a
loving gesture.

"Your red hair is gone, but I like the silver," said
Lillie.

"I like your silver too. Where's the Boston
accent?" asked Maud.

"It's been gone a long time. Yours is too, Maud.
I just can't comprehend all the atrocities you had to

371

endure during the war. You and Giovanni must have suffered so much."

"It's over now and best forgotten. But I have my best reward, Peter. Could anyone ask for a better son?"

"No, that is for certain. He and Evie just seem to be made for each other. I know you haven't been painting for several years. But I hope you won't give it up."

"Oh no, the easel will go up as soon as there is a place to do so. I can't wait. Tell me about your Mother and Frank. Are they still alive?"

"Sadly, no. But they had a good life together. He gave her many material things Daddy could never have done. I knew both of your parents passed away. You and I are becoming of that same vintage. Hard to believe. I never thought we would grow old. At least not when we last saw each other." Lillie sighed a happy laugh.

"Time does have a way of passing. Oh, Lillie, I'm so thrilled to be here. And grateful to be an American. I could kneel down and kiss this beautiful ground. The Napa valley reminds me of Tuscany. I know it must do the same for Giovanni. But this is a new beginning for both of us."

Lillie and Maud chattered non-stop.

"I'm glad we have the telephone too. You'll never be far away again."

CHAPTER 34

Dario and Giovanni studied the hillside where they planned to set out the new vineyard. "Every slope has its own particular signature," Giovanni was telling Dario. "One must assess exposure to sun and wind."

"Si, Signore, some hills feel just right, don't they?" He answered his own question.

"It's so wonderful, Dario. We have found property that contains slopes; has nice elevation, pitch, sun, and good drainage."

Giovanni and Dario were up at the crack of dawn each morning. Dario learned to drive a tractor so he could till the land. Giovanni laid out the area on paper to show Dario how he wanted the new vineyard planted. He wanted to keep as many of the beautiful shade trees as possible, but each row had to produce symmetry with the next one. Planting the rootstock was prodigious.

Even Maud volunteered to help, but Giovanni felt it would be much too strenuous for her. Giovanni wanted to plant fifteen new acres worth of vines. Those wouldn't bear fruit for another four to five years. An additional fifteen acres were already under cultivation. He hired several young men to help. They would begin at five in the morning, stop for lunch for about thirty minutes, and then be right back to the digging and the planting. With the task completed, then the watering system had to be set in. The plants began to grow, an almost religious sight, as Giovanni looked over the land with reverence.

"It will be a few years before we can have any production from the new vines, but we can buy grapes from other growers and produce a wine from them."

"You know the soil, Dario. Are you happy to be here?"

"With all my heart. America is wonderful."

Giovanni took Dario with him to every interview and meeting he had. Dario was not only a good chauffeur, but asked some very pertinent questions. Giovanni had taken Dario to Napa to get his driver's license, so he could translate for him. Giovanni and Dario enjoyed learning about their adopted country, and the Napa Valley, talking to other vintners such as Louis Stralla. He had been leasing the old Charles Krug winery. Bob and Peter Mondavi were Dario's age, and they became good friends. The young Mondavis worked at the Sunny St. Helena winery producing bulk wine. Giovanni became a welcome addition to the winemakers who operated Inglenook, Beringer, and Beaulieu. He regularly attended Grange meetings. Over and over again, Giovanni's own methods reconfirmed the world's best grapes grew on hillside vineyards just like those grown for so many years in the Tuscan hills: similar warm days, cool nights and a long frost-free growing season.

Although advancing in years, Giovanni felt in his steps, the gait of a younger man. *I'm so blessed to have my dearest Maud and to have the loyalty and love from Dario.* "Maud, I believe Dario should inherit part of the property when the time comes. He is like a son to the both of us. We must become American citizens as soon as possible. I know Peter can tell us what to do."

"I couldn't agree more, my darling." She leaned over and kissed him.

The people in St. Helena enjoyed their quaint and charming town with its stone buildings. Extremely friendly, they went out of their way to help strangers. In some ways, it reminded Giovanni of Italy, but streets were wider, and electric street lamps lit them at night, although they weren't the modern ones, giving Main Street a glimpse of the golden days of the past.

Giovanni bought a truck for himself, and a truck for the vineyards he actually bought for Dario so he could get to and from town with ease without having to borrow Maud's Cadillac.

As the new house took shape, Peter's plans were coming into being. Giovanni felt like he and Maud were Adam and Eve, and this was the Garden of Eden. Peter had even included a large dramatic picture window in Maud's studio that overlooked the garden.

"The north light will be marvelous. Peter, I want you to build Maud and me a tiny chapel on the side of the hill. Can you do that for me? When the day comes I will no longer be here, I would rather be buried on our property, than in a marble orchard."

"I can understand that."

"I spoke to Maud about it, and she is going to plant a garden surrounding the chapel. Father Tim said he would bless it for us."

"I'll get to work on the plans right away. As long as we have a construction crew here, we might as well do it at the same time."

"Wonderful, Peter." Giovanni's eyes shone.

"I hope you're not planning on leaving us anytime soon."

"No, no plans, Peter. Just thinking ahead."

"Now, Giovanni, I see you doing all these wonderful, intriguing things to the land. Tell me what you are doing."

"Well, Peter, each acre will grow four hundred and fifty vines. At full blossom, each grapevine will grow eighteen pounds of grapes."

"That's not much is it?"

"Probably not, but it's a good production. One acre grows about four tons of grapes. But we don't want to plant everything too fast. We want to be certain the vineyard is doing well before we expand."

"I still have no idea what is going on, but the plants look healthy, and the landscape is changing in front of my eyes. It will be wonderful when we can taste the fruits of your labors."

"The cabernet grapes on the old vines will give us a wonderful beginning for our new wine. I'm looking forward to harvest time, just to smell the air. It should be heavy with must and the vats filled with the juice from the grapes. We purchased new oak barrels, as well as a stemmer–crusher, something new for Dario and me to master."

"Then I shall be learning along with the two of you."

In late September, as the field hands emptied the flats of grapes into the stemmer-crusher, Giovanni had tears in his eyes. Maud stood with him, holding his hand as the juice moved along in its journey from grape to wine. Peter and Evie were on hand also when Father Tim came to bless the harvest. The valley was awash in gold, orange, and burgundy leaves on the vines as well as the maple trees growing in various spots of the upper valley.

The colors also leapt off the canvasses Maud painted. She had been reborn. The smell of turpentine, and linseed oil were like the finest perfumes to her. Her studio, almost as large as the living room, was filled with easels and paints and paintings.

Sometimes Peter would come in and join her, and the two of them would paint in silence, Maud reveling in the joy of Peter's presence. *It is so wonderful to know this man standing next to me is my son.* Maud's thoughts were interfering with her painting. Peter was delighted by the fact he was here, painting in Maud's studio.

This year, there would just be storing in the vats, the bungs checked so they could easily be removed for tasting. Almost at the end of the harvest, Giovanni and Dario saw to it any grapes left on the vines were picked and crushed. "We will at least have some picholo for ourselves."

CHAPTER 35

*O*t would be Thanksgiving tomorrow, and Lillie was beside herself with excitement. How many years had it been since she and Maud had celebrated a holiday together? Too many to count. Evie would be here to help her with the finishing touches on the dinner. And sweet Penny, her adorable red-haired grandchild would be here also, as well as her half-brother Mike, and his fiancée Laura, and Peter, her wonderful son-in-law. Giovanni and Maud were actually flying into the Burbank airport with Dario. She and George would pick them up and bring them to their home. Evie and Peter had accommodations for all of them in their new home.

"Lillie, darling," chided George, "you will be worn out before they arrive. Let the girls we hired to help you do the work." Lillie had actually persuaded Maud and Giovanni to spend the holiday with them. She and George would love to show them around where they lived. Peter and Evie had a beautiful home in Flintridge. It sat high on a hill with a magnificent view of the valley. Evie knew Maud would love it because Peter had copied the architecture from a house he saw in San Marino, Italy.

Lillie was so proud of Penny. She was becoming quite a pianist. And she loved to entertain for anyone who would listen to her play.

When everyone arrived, Lillie declared: "This will be the best party. Everyone I love so dearly is gathered around me. Something I thought would never

379

happen. I'm so happy." The tears of joy glistened on her cheeks. Maud and Evie joined her.

"If everyone doesn't stop crying," commented George, "people will think we are having a funeral, not a party."

Everyone laughed. Peter opened bottles of champagne and started pouring the bubbly liquid for everyone.

"Lillie, this is a true groaning board." Maud remarked, "You have outdone yourself. I may be a good painter, but your art is in the kitchen."

"Hear, hear," said Peter. "A toast to the cook. Long may she reign."

"A toast to Lillie," everyone echoed.

A sumptuous Thanksgiving dinner included; roast turkey with chestnut dressing, mashed potatoes with giblet gravy, sweet potato balls, sautéed Brussel-sprouts with sliced almonds, orange cranberry salad, cranberry sauce, cranberry jelly, avocado mousse, rolls and butter, and pumpkin and pecan pies. It became a true day of thanksgiving, for counting their blessings, and being together after all the years apart.

After dinner, everyone sat down in the living room. Lillie had found some old pictures she had of her and Maud when they were young and shared them with everyone. There was a lot of laughter and gaiety. Peter asked Evie, "Where is Penny?"

"I think she took Laura and went up to the attic. Penny wanted her to open an old trunk. She had been begging Laura ever since dinner to help her. She loves dressing up in Mom's old clothes. Penny, where are you and Laura?" she called.

"Upstairs Mommy, we're coming."

It was a few minutes later when Penny came into the living room wearing an 1800's dress that Lillie had saved. Laura had actually helped Penny to comb her hair so she looked like a young girl of the same era. Lillie was the first to see her, and had to sit down in a chair because of the shock. It was as if time had been turned backward, and Maud was a little girl, standing in her California living room.

Lillie screamed in delight and excitement. "Maud, Maud, Peter, George, Evie, Giovanni, everyone. Look at our darling Penny! Maud, Penny is absolutely our granddaughter. Look at her. We have a little eight-year-old Maud Driscoll standing in my living room."

It took Maud a few minutes to recover from the shock of seeing a young replica of her girlhood. Penny looked exactly like her. Lillie had even found an old tintype of Maud sitting in a chair.

"Peter, I'm so happy I found you – or we found each other. Now, I know, my heart doesn't lie. I have another picture somewhere of me as a little girl. Penny looks like I was looking into a mirror bringing me back to when I was a child."

Peter went over to Maud, and they put their arms around each other and hugged and hugged. Tears of happiness flooded everyone's eyes.

"What's going on, Daddy?"

"Penny, darling. I know Mommy and I have told you about your Aunt Maud. Well, she really is your grandmother. She had to give me up for adoption when I was only a few days old, not because she wanted to, but because she was forced to."

"Why did you do that, Aunt Maud? Or do I call you grandmother?"

"You call me whatever you would like, sweetheart. But I had to give him away because I wasn't married, and what I had done by getting pregnant was an especially bad thing in the early 1900s. My dear friend, Priscilla, who lives in London came and stayed with me, and helped me through this tragic time. I thought I would be marrying her brother. But, their father wanted him to marry someone else. And before I could tell him about his baby, he was dead."

"Oh Grandmother, how terrible."

"Peter, I haven't had a chance to tell you this before but you have an aunt in London. Her name is Priscilla Colchester. She is the Duchess of Colchester, married to Duke Kenneth Colchester. They live in Essex. During the war, Priscilla became a nurse, and Kenneth was in the British Secret Service. I'm not certain what he did, but he worked under Churchill, and knighted after the war."

"Maud, I know Kenneth. Quite extraordinary. This is all too much for me to digest."

"Peter, how in the world do you know him?" Evie couldn't believe this conversation.

"Darling, remember when I went on all those clandestine trips? My contact was Kenneth Colchester. I had no idea he was royalty. Most of the time after business was done, we'd have a meal and a brandy. I had lunch at 10 Downing the last time I saw him, but that was in '44 – when I delivered those documents to London at the request of President Roosevelt."

"Dad," piped in Michael, "does that mean I have royal blood in me, too?"

"Not exactly Mike, we are all on the fringes. When are the Colchester's coming to California for a visit?"

"They are waiting for Giovanni and me to produce our first harvest. That should be next fall, God willing."

"Oh Maud, I can't believe all these wonderful things are happening for you. You have had so much tragedy in your life, it's time some good things arrived," said Lillie.

"Lillie dear, I have my wonderful Giovanni. We are safe after a traumatic encounter with the enemy in Italy. I have dear friends. And the frosting on the cake of my life is to know my son is alive, and well – and to realize he will be part of all our lives forever."

"It's strange, it's as if we all lived on different planes, traveling in concentric circles, but somehow our lives intertwined, even though we weren't aware of it. Paths crossed, lives changed, marriage, death. To think we might have never known any of these relationships if Peter and Evie hadn't made a trip to New York to visit you. And I believe Penny's appearance, wanting to play dress-up brought back so many happy memories of our childhood in Boston."

"Maud, somehow I can't call you mother, because even though you are biologically my mother, another woman holds that place in my heart. It doesn't mean I will love you less. I have admired Maud Driscoll all my life. I have a collection of her paintings, and guess what? I can't even sell you the picture of the flower seller. I'll have to give it to you."

Maud laughed. "I promise you will have it back someday. Giovanni and I need to return to the valley with Dario, so they can tend to the vineyards. Even though we have people we trust caring for them, Giovanni likes to know what is going on also. And Michael, you are also part of royalty by marriage. Giovanni has the title of Baron, but he is a proud citizen and will never use the title again."

"Then when he named the property, 'Baronessa', that was for you."

"True. You are my grandson, so logically you could inherit the titles. You know Michael," she continued as she changed the subject, "our wine label is 'La Baronessa'. Our first production will have a special name also. 'Monte Bella'. That was the name of my first home in Italy, and part of my refuge. It was my safe haven, where I went to paint and reconnect with my life again. So much tragedy had fallen before me. Monte Bella is a symbol of hope in my life. So dear Giovanni decided that is what we would name the first wine we produce - cabernet, from the Monte Bella Vineyard, La Baronessa Winery. I think it sounds wonderful. Your father says you are quite an artist. Maybe you would like to come up with a label for us. I would be thrilled if a family member designed our label."

"Oh Aunt Maud, Grandmother Maud, dearest Maud, I would be more than honored."

Michael, pleased with the finished results, mailed a copy of his design to them. Maud and Giovanni couldn't wait to speak with him. "Michael, it's absolutely marvelous. You have captured just the right look we wanted, a rendering of the villa, with beautiful lettering. Giovanni and I will make a trip to San Francisco to have it transformed into a label for the bottle. The next time you see it, will be at the inauguration of our wine. And Michael, you and Laura had better be here." Maud laughed.

"Grandma-aunt, we wouldn't miss it for anything."

What an occasion this is going to be, thought Maud. *I need to contact Priscilla and Ken, and see if they can be here also. We will have an enormous group just in our extended family.*

They watched an incredible procession of cars approach the winery property. Dario made certain there would be room for all of them. He and Peter had been discussing a tasting room, and if they built one, they would need to have adequate parking for their visitors. Michael managed the construction business in Southern California, so Peter could spend more and more time at the winery. He and Evie had purchased a second home in close proximity to the villa, with acreage that could eventually be added to Baronessa vineyards. Evie and Peter both were available to Maud and Giovanni. Penny was left in the capable hands of Lillie and George, making it easy for them to get away.

"I'm delighted to see you looking so well," he told Ken, "and to meet Priscilla."

"Nice to see you in peacetime, Pete. Your Napa Valley is a beautiful place."

"I can hardly believe you are actually my aunt and uncle. How much time we spent involved in secret operations during the war, all those clandestine meetings. It was only a few years ago, I told Evie I had lunch at 10 Downing Street. She never knew I was a spy for the U.S. Government."

"I'm glad to hear she didn't," said Kenneth. "Priscilla didn't know either. I think it would have frightened her to death to have known that. I can only imagine what Evie would have felt. You're a generation younger than Pris and me. Pete, you have done very well for yourself. I'm only sorry we didn't know you sooner."

"Ken, when I think about all that has happened since I met that American captain in France – it's like the plot of a novel. It doesn't seem real, but it is."

Lillie was thrilled to meet Priscilla, and to put a face to her name. "I've been hearing about you since your first day at Wellesley."

"That was so long ago. I have heard about you too. We should have met in Boston. But Evie was arriving too soon to attend Maud's wedding then."

"She has had an incredible life. A true survivor."

"It seems so strange to me, she never came to California before this. I'm just grateful to still be alive to have seen her again. She has been my dearest friend, even though it was through letters our friendship was kept alive."

"She has suffered so much in her young life. Did she ever tell you about what happened when we went to visit my brother's grave?"

"Only that she didn't sail on the Lusitania or she would not be here now, and that one of her favorite paintings was never found. But I know something you probably don't. Peter, on one of his visits to London, purchased a painting of a yellow cottage with an orange door and a beautiful wisteria vine. The signature on the painting was not detectable, but the dealer attributed it to Maud."

"Oh, my lord. I can't believe it. That must be the painting Maud was working on when we heard the Lusitania had been torpedoed and sunk. That's almost forty years ago. God, Lillie, are we getting that old?" Priscilla said.

"Friendships are wonderful things. A good one will last forever. It seems ours has. You have been a dear friend to Maud - and there for her when she needed you. She told me how much she loved your brother."

"Yes, I'm sure she did. But she thought she loved Ted too. Andrew was wonderful. They would have had a good life together. But she and Giovanni have shared so much sorrow and horrors together, it has brought them closer, and their bond of love is strong."

"She told me yesterday, Giovanni isn't well. They have been visiting several specialists in San Francisco. But he is getting weaker and weaker. I'm just happy he has been able to see his American dream come to fruition."

"Oh, Lillie, I know he is in his seventies, but he just seems so robust to me."

"Maud tells me he puts on a good front."

"I pray he has a few more good years yet."

"Maud, my darling Caro, I have loved you so much. I hate to leave you alone. I can die peacefully knowing Peter is in your life, and your grandchildren. You won't be lonely."

"Oh Giovanni, my darling, maybe the doctors can do something more. We will talk to more doctors."

"Maud, Caro, the cancer has been spreading too quickly, and there is nothing more that can be done. The doctors have done everything possible."

"Giovanni, I can't bear life without you. You have been my heart and soul. You kept me sane through so much adversity."

"Do not grieve, my love, I have lived a long and wonderful life. We have realized a dream in America. There were days when I thought we would never get out of the war alive."

"I know." Maud was sitting at the side of their bed and holding Giovanni's hand.

"Will you bury me in our small chapel?"

"If that is what you want, my darling. We will both be buried there, my love."

A week later, Father Tim stood in the room with Maud and Giovanni. He put on his amice and anointed Giovanni.

"*Grazie*, padre. I love you, Maud." Those were his last words.

It seemed like all of St. Helena gathered in the St. Helena Catholic Church for the funeral mass. Peter and Evie with Michael and Laura, now his wife, and Penny. Dario with his wife Alba – she had taught him to speak English, and their small child. Priscilla and Kenneth even came from England. Lillie and George remained in Glendale, because Lillie was not well enough to travel.

After the burial in the small chapel on the Baronessa property, Maud asked Dario if he would help her plant a few more roses around the building, as roses were such a favorite of Giovanni's.

"It would be my honor, Maud dear. I will see it is done this week." Giovanni had made Dario second in command of the winery and vineyards. When Giovanni told him this was his new position, he asked Peter to build Dario a home on the property. Dario had become a citizen when Giovanni did, and was proud of all he had accomplished. For a man with so little schooling, he had succeeded in the American dream. Peter built a smaller Italianate house where the original old ranch house had been. La Baronessa had become a showcase winery where Maud displayed her artwork on the walls of the tasting room, as an added attraction to the fine wines now being produced at Baronessa.

Dearest Lillie,

I wanted to write you because it seemed much more fitting, since we have been writing to each other for almost sixty-five years - a lifetime. You and I both have suffered many tragedies since we missed saying goodbye at the Boston train station. You were denied your education. I was denied my child. But look at where we are today, and what we have become. You and George are pillars of your community. You have two wonderful children, and a grandchild. And at this late date, I'm able to share them all - your son-in-law, my son, and his wife my goddaughter - your daughter, and our adorable grandchild, Penny.

Life truly has blessed us, in spite of the hiccups. I'm not trivializing what occurred during the war in Italy. I have had a wonderful marriage with Giovanni. He gave me hope where I thought there was none, and led me to a rich and embracing new one I shared with him and Peter.

I want you to know all this, just because you have been the dearest and best friend in the world. I love you so much.

Maud

CHAPTER 36

"Maud?"

"Yes"

"This is Lillie."

"Oh, Lillie. It's so good to hear your voice. How are you?"

"Getting old – but I guess there is nothing we can do about it. I wanted you to know how much I appreciated your letter, and glad our lives have connected again. I wish we could turn back the clock. Then the arthritis would go away."

"Me too. I'm painting as much as I can these days. Are you still sewing and designing?"

"Yes I am. With all the other excitement, I have failed to tell anyone my news. I sold my store at a nice profit, but I still wanted to continue designing. Do you remember when I said someone should design a bathing costume that would flatter not make women look like water balloons?"

"Yes."

"Well, I designed one, and the pattern was picked up by a bathing suit company. I don't have to do anything except receive royalties from any suits sold from my idea. So I am busy designing more. The line is called 'Lillie's Swimwear'. That certainly keeps me out of trouble. I can't sew on a machine because of the arthritis in my hands, but this design business has given me a creative outlet. How about that? Your friend is still doing something artistic."

A lot of laughter could be heard through the telephone.

"Lillie, this is the best medicine you could have given me. It is like a breath of fresh air. I can't thank you enough for calling me. We will talk again soon."

"Have a happy day painting, Maud."

"I will. Goodbye for now."

Maud appeared a happy and fulfilled woman. In spite of losing Giovanni, she delighted living in the Napa Valley. Every day she busied herself painting canvas after canvas. This morning, she sat on her terrace, perched on a stool, paintbrush in hand, working on a landscape when Peter arrived asking if he could spend the day painting with her.

"I would adore it." She touched his arm.

"Maud, that's beautiful. Guess I'll have to buy that one too. You've captured all the colors in the vineyard, and the green of the valley." Peter laughed.

Maud laughed with him, making a pretend gesture to paint him with the paintbrush she was holding.

"I'll look like a tree, if you catch my shirt with that green paint."

Some weeks later, Evie was having coffee in the dining alcove of the kitchen. She saw a relaxed and tanned Peter out in the newly planted vineyard. He was deep in conversation with Dario out in the courtyard driveway. When the two of them parted, Peter began walking toward their house. Evie called to him from the kitchen doorway.

"Peter I've just made a fresh pot of coffee. Would you like a cup?"

"On my way, honey." He jogged to the back door. "Could I talk you out of a piece of that apple pie I smelled baking this morning?"

"Maybe... if you're nice to me, that is." Evie looked up at him, and kissed his craggy cheek. "I knew I could trap you with the smell of warm apples."

The two of them took their cups back to the dining alcove. Evie brought a piece of pie for Peter and set it down in front of him. Peter had his fork ready and waiting to cut into his first bite. He put it in his mouth, savoring the flavor. He then picked up his coffee to take a swallow.

"Marvelous pie, Mrs. Wells."

"I'm glad you approve, Mr. Wells."

"Look at Dario now. He has grown from being a da Neri ward into a very credible winery manager. You can see the progress of the new vineyards. Our tasting rooms are crowded every weekend, and weekdays are becoming the same way."

"I agree darling," said Evie. "Dario also is speaking beautiful English thanks to Alba. She told me she is expecting again. Isn't that wonderful?"

"Yes, it is. I certainly don't feel I need to be here every day to supervise. Wouldn't you like to go back to southern California for a while?" asked Peter. "Your mother needs to have a little celebration for the patterns she created and sold. What with Giovanni's death and funeral, and my tending the grapes, Lillie has not been given her just due."

"Oh Peter, I think that would be wonderful. I know she would be happy with a nice dinner at one of those glamorous restaurants in Los Angeles. Perino's would be perfect."

"Good idea, darling. I think Maud might like to come too and celebrate Lillie's success. Of course seeing her grandchild might be more important."

"I spoke with Mom on the phone this morning, and she said Penny can't wait for us to return. Penny wants me to take her shopping at Bullocks."

"Bullocks? Sounds like our little girl is growing up."

"Certainly knows her own mind and clothing tastes."

"It will take only a few more days to wrap up what I've been doing here, then we can make a leisurely drive back to Flintridge."

"I'll call Maud now, and see what I can do to help her pack."

CHAPTER 37

*W*hen Peter and Evie returned to Southern California, they began to focus on the Georgetown house. They wanted it to become a permanent museum housing many of Maud's paintings, and decorating the rooms with furniture Peter and Evie had left there. Evie telephoned the Smithsonian, requesting their help in finding a curator. Within nine months, the Maud Driscoll Museum of Impressionism became a reality. Now they were back in Washington DC, working with the curator to meet the opening deadline.

They began a careful walk through all the rooms of the Georgian colonial mansion Peter had remodeled and renovated at the beginning of WWII, the home he brought Evie to after they were married. When they entered the library, Peter removed a book from one of the shelves and pressed a button. One of the bookcases slid out from the wall. He opened its hidden door, and he and Evie stepped inside a small, windowless room. Peter turned on a light to reveal all the radio equipment and other pieces of government machinery still sitting there. Nothing had been touched, everything in the same condition as they left it in 1945. Only now, a ten-year accumulation of dust sat on the cloths covering the machines.

"So much of your equipment and the materials I used for decoding are still here." Evie said, as she touched a dust cloth. "It would be wonderful if the public could see this room. So much of our country's military intelligence originated in this tiny space. Don't you think people might like to see where an American spy and his wife lived and worked? The public might appreciate learning about the beginnings of the Secret Service."

"You're right, Evie. Let's see what the President will allow us to use. We'll have a few more days before the museum actually opens. We can also get rid of the dust." He laughed, as he faked a coughing spell.

"The fact Maud is your mother, and you never knew it when we lived here also adds to an already fascinating story. I know President Eisenhower will see the significance."

The two of them then proceeded upstairs to look at the rest of the house furnished with additional pieces from the 1920s.

"Maud sure did like French furniture," commented Peter. "I somehow expect Louis XV to jump out from the armoire."

"Maybe he will in your dreams. Now Peter, we really need to talk about the furniture. Mom said Andrew took her to Paris just to shop for it and the accessories she used to decorate this house. Do you like everything?"

"You did a great job with the fabrics for reupholstering. Everything blends so well."

"Why thank you, kind sir." She made a mock bow.

Evie began to inventory the number of Driscoll paintings on the wall.

"It's hard to believe how many of her paintings you collected before you ever knew of your relationship," she remarked.

"Fate plays strange tricks. We're all so lucky everything turned out the way it has," he replied. "I want your opinion on some of the paintings we can put on loan here. The museum will have much more credibility if we let the curator use one or two of our Monet's and the Sisley. I hate to part with it, but our Constable would certainly look beautiful hanging over the fireplace in the library. I want to put the large painting of Maud as a young woman over the fireplace in the living room."

"I agree, honey. The Constable will be returned to its home in our library, oops, now the museum's."

"I'm still in awe over the fact you got a curator from the Smithsonian to install not only the paintings but the furniture as well."

"She happens to be a huge Driscoll fan. I think she would have done this for no money, the way she speaks about Maud. She told me she had never seen so many Driscoll paintings in one collection."

"Guess I'd better tell her where we want the Constable, and the alleged Sargent."

Descending the wide staircase, they informed the curator they were leaving and returned to the Willard Hotel. The opening reception for the museum would be the following Saturday.

On Thursday evening before the opening, dinner would be a festive occasion. Several of the people they made friends with during their time in Washington joined them, including Harry Woodring, former Secretary of War.

"Harry, it's good to see you after so many years." Peter and Harry clasped hands in a warm handshake.

"Pete, it's my honor to be here, and I'm looking forward to Saturday."

Peter and Evie kept the conversation lively recounting tales about Maud Driscoll, and the museum opening.

"Sir Kenneth Colchester and his wife Priscilla will also be arriving in Washington for the reception," Evie told their guests.

"Kenneth was my counterpart for England, and Pete met Kenneth on assignment during the war," Harry chimed in. "I'm looking forward to seeing him. It's been several years since our paths crossed. Helluva nice guy."

"Maud and Priscilla were roommates at Wellesley," Evie said, taking a bite of her green salad.

"And Kenneth knew Eisenhower before he even received his fifth star," Harry added.

"Which reminds me," Evie said, "Maud phoned us yesterday and told me she and the Colchester's had been invited by the President and Mrs. Eisenhower for a simple family Sunday night supper while they're here. What a wonderful reunion for all of them."

"Why didn't she stay in Washington?" One of the guests asked.

"My mother loved living in the Capitol hosting constituents for Andrew Llewellyn during all his political campaigning and when he served in Congress. But the corruption of Harding's administration really sickened her," answered Peter. "Today, she lives in the Napa Valley where the topography is as close to Tuscany as she can find. She'd still be in Italy if it wasn't for what the Nazis did to Giovanni's villa and vineyards. When they came to the states after the war ended, she and Giovanni purchased land and a small winery as soon as they could."

"The winery isn't small anymore," interjected Evie. "You're drinking some of its prized cabernet."

Evie picked up her glass and lingered over her sip. "Since Giovanni's death, Maud has a young Italian man managing the winery, so she doesn't even have to think about it. She spends most of her days painting landscapes of the valley, or the flowers in her garden."

Before the museum officially opened its doors, Peter and Evie, along with Maud, Lillie and George, the Colchester's and Steven stood in the foyer toasting each other.

"I haven't been back here since I went to England after Andrew's death. So much has happened since then – it was several lifetimes." Maud closed her eyes in reminiscence.

Arrangements had been made for Steven to accompany them all back to Glendale. Then the Colchester's and Maud would return to the Napa Valley.

401

Peter led them all to the living room so they could see the newly acquired portrait.

"Oh my lord. Peter, where on earth did you find it? Priscilla," Maud called. "Look what's hanging over the fireplace. I can't believe my eyes. I'm dumbstruck."

"Peter, "said Priscilla, "Kenneth and I have my portrait hanging in Bodicea Hall---only it's signed. John went flying out our front door while Maud and I were practicing for our presentation, and he forgot to sign Maud's after making us sit for hours while he painted. Maud and I never saw him again."

"By John, you mean John Singer Sargent, don't you?" said Peter.

"Yes of course," answered Priscilla.

"Mr. Sheridan will be pleased."

"Who's that?" asked Maud.

"The man who sold me the painting. He didn't want to because it hadn't been authenticated. But I persuaded him. I paid for a Sargent. And I got a Sargent." Peter's face reflected sheer pride and pleasure.

"Evie and I will give you a quick tour of the house. Then we would like you to remain in the living room to greet all the guests."

A small commotion came from the foyer.

"Mr. President, Mr. President." It was the curator's voice.

402

Peter and Kenneth walked out of the living room to see President and Mrs. Eisenhower being ushered through the front door.

"Kenneth, it's been a long time. You've met Mamie haven't you?"

"Yes, and I believe you have met Peter Wells, Maud's son."

"You're Maud's son? I never knew she had one. Glad to meet you. There must be an interesting story in that."

"It's a long one, Mr. President. I'd be honored to tell you at another time."

"Of course, of course. Mamie and I just wanted to pay our respects to Maud and see a few of her paintings."

"We're honored to have you here, sir."

"Maud, you're still as beautiful as ever," said the President as he walked over and kissed her cheek. "We'll see you, Kenneth and Priscilla tomorrow around five, if that's agreeable. Mamie and I have a government function to attend tonight, so we must be on our way. This house makes a beautiful museum. Good luck and much success." The Eisenhower's then disappeared in a milieu of bodyguards and Secret Service.

Evie sat down in one of the overstuffed chairs. "I'm awed. I never expected the President would make a personal appearance."

"Neither did I," said Peter. "It's just about time to officially open the doors of the Maud Driscoll Museum. Maud would you like to honor us by cutting the ribbon?" he asked.

The curator had anchored a wide swath of red taffeta ribbon across the main doorway to the living room. Maud made a perfect cut and pronounced the museum open.

Evie stood next to Peter and whispered in his ear. "That was so kind of you to invite Mr. Sheridan. He'll have his provenance first hand. I'm glad we did this in her honor. Maud loved you so much, even when she didn't know you. It's a wonderful tribute to her talent, and her personally. She truly is Sargent's Lady."

Peter held Evie close. His eyes were wet. "My life was complete when I met you, darling. But I didn't know how full it would be."

Dear Penny,

My name is Lavinia Colchester. Don't you think it is about time we met? We are cousins, sort of. Your father is my uncle - if that makes sense - except his father never married his mother, your great Aunt Maud, my great Aunt Maud, and truly your grandmother.

I think it is so exciting to find one's family, and to know I have American relatives. I have enclosed my picture. I hope you will send me one of yours. Since your grandmother and my grandmother were always corresponding with each other, I thought it would be nice if you and I were to start writing each other too. I love to write letters, and it would be fun to have an American pen pal.

I'm a student at Oxford, studying literature. I have no idea what I will do with it. I understand you are a wonderful artist. Maybe your parents would let you come and visit us in England? We could do some traveling on the continent, and you could paint along the Seine. I'm 21, how old are you?

Your new friend,

Lavinia Colchester

QUESTIONS FOR BOOK CLUB DISCUSSIONS

1. What are your thoughts about the relationship between Maud and Neil? How did Maud's lack of experience and naiveté serve as the catalyst for her love affair?

2. Look at the contrasts between Maud and Lillie. Both had a love of adventure- one out of necessity to survive, and the other to live as the artist she wanted. How did Lillie manage not to feel deprived when so much sadness occurred in her life?

3. Maud and Lillie experienced their twenties in the late 1800s. Compare their lives with yours when you were in your twenties.

4. Think about the town or city where you were raised. Tell how your world changed as much as theirs: telephone, automobile, airline travel, war, escape.

5. Who do you think suffered the most, Maud or Lillie? What makes you feel more sympathetic for one over the other and why?

6. When we look at the next generation, Peter and Evie, how do you think their lives were shaped by the war?

7. Look at the education of the women or lack thereof, what do you think Lillie could have done differently to feel more educated?

8. How free were lives in the United States in the 1950s? What differences do you see today?

9. As Evie grow up, Lillie's status in life appears to change. She has become the consummate wife and mother while Maud has excitement, fame and fortune. What life would you choose, and why?

10. How do you think Sam served as a catalyst in Peter's life?

Order Copies of
Sargent's Lady
Today!

____COPIES @ $19.95 in US = _____

____COPIES @ $24.95 in CANADA _____

SUB TOTAL _____

US S&H First Book 3.50 _____

US S&H Each book thereafter $1.00 each ___

CANADIAN Postage per book $3 _____

TOTAL _____

ORDERED BY:

_____

_____

ADDRESS:

_____

_____

CITY, STATE, ZIP:

_____

_____

PHONE:

_____

_____

YOUR EMAIL ADDRESS:

_____

FOR VOLUME ORDERS EXCEEDING 10_
BOOKS, CONTACT:

AVegasPublisher.com

Make your cashier's check or money order
payable to: A. Vegas Publisher, LLC
            284 E. Lake Mead Prky #262
            Henderson, NV 89015

Made in the USA
San Bernardino, CA
22 March 2016